Workshop on the Use of Computational Methods in the Study of Endangered Languages

(ComputEL 2014)

Held at ACL 2014

Baltimore, Maryland, USA
26 June 2014

ISBN: 978-1-63439-202-0

Printed from e-media with permission by:

Curran Associates, Inc.
57 Morehouse Lane
Red Hook, NY 12571

Some format issues inherent in the e-media version may also appear in this print version.

Printed by Curran Associates, Inc. (2014)

For permission requests, please contact the Association for Computational Linguistics at the address below.

Association for Computational Linguistics
209 N. Eighth Street
Stroudsburg, Pennsylvania 18360

Phone: 1-570-476-8006
Fax: 1-570-476-0860

acl@aclweb.org

Additional copies of this publication are available from:

Curran Associates, Inc.
57 Morehouse Lane
Red Hook, NY 12571 USA
Phone: 845-758-0400
Fax: 845-758-2634
Email: curran@proceedings.com
Web: www.proceedings.com

Preface

Contemporary efforts to document the world's endangered languages—often going under the rubric of *documentary linguistics*—are dependent on the widespread availability of modern recording technologies, in particular digital audio and video recording devices and software to annotate the recordings that such devices produce. However, despite well over a decade of dedicated funding efforts aimed at the documentation of endangered languages, the technological landscape that supports the work of those involved in this research remains fragmented, and the promises of new technology remain largely unfulfilled. Moreover, the efforts of computer scientists, on the whole, are mostly disconnected from the day-to-day work of documentary linguists, making it difficult for the knowledge of each group to inform the other. On the one hand, this deprives documentary linguists of tools making use of the latest research results to speed up the time-consuming task of describing an underdocumented language. On the other hand, it severely limits the ability of computational linguists to test their methods on the full range of world's linguistic diversity.

Despite the concerns listed above, recent efforts do indicate that there is significant potential in collaboration between computational linguists (and other computer scientists) and linguists working on endangered languages. For instance, machine labeling and active learning can make the process of textual analysis for low-resource languages more efficient, and state-of-the-art tools in grammar engineering can be applied at a relatively low cost to new languages that are typologically divergent from those that primarily informed their design. Moreover, new models of data collection based on the ubiquity of low-cost, networkable devices with recording capabilities, such as smartphones, show the extent to which the barriers to collecting significant amounts of primary data have fallen in recent years, and it has similarly been found that the pairing of crowdsourcing and machine translation techniques can yield useful results for low resource languages in a short time frame. Research along these latter lines, in particular, indicates that computationally-driven advances in the documentation of the world's languages may need to rely as much on clever engineering and user interface solutions as on methods for processing language data developed within computational linguistics proper, in a manner parallel to efforts in other domains that have considered how new online services can be used to facilitate computational linguistic research.

A different set of activities within the documentary linguistics community involving the increasing use of open standards for encoding language data is also significant in this regard. For instance, in the last decade, standardized XML formats have become more widely used to encode text annotations and lexical data. This facilitates the reuse of documentary materials. Even in the absence of the use of such standards, significant results have been achieved in gathering structured data from materials placed on the web. As more data becomes available in standardized forms, there will only be increased potential for building new kinds of language resources.

The papers in these proceedings cover the full range of work at the intersection of computational and endangered language linguistics. Some contributions come from scholars primarily identifying as computer scientists who are exploring how tools developed in their areas of expertise can be applied to endangered language research. Others derive from the work of individuals primarily identifying as descriptive linguists who are reporting on the results of the application of new computational methods to traditional language work. There is also a division among contributions which have more practical orientations versus programmatic ones, with topics ranging from discussion of software under development to high-level considerations of where our research priorities should lie.

We would like to thank those who made this workshop possible: the ACL staff, 2014 annual meeting organizers, the program committee, workshop participants, and research assistant Daniel Fox. Further support came from National Science Foundation Award Nos. BCS-1404352 and IIS-1027289.

Jeff Good, Julia Hirschberg, and Owen Rambow

Organizers:

Jeff Good, University at Buffalo, USA
Julia Hirschberg, Columbia University, USA
Owen Rambow, Columbia University, USA

Program Committee:

Steven Abney, University of Michigan, USA
Helen Aristar-Dry, University of Texas at Austin, USA
Alexandre Arkhipov, Moscow State University, Russia
Timothy Baldwin, The University of Melbourne, Australia
Dorothee Beermann, Norwegian University of Science and Technology, Norway
Emily M. Bender, University of Washington, USA
Andrea Berez, University of Hawai'i, USA
Steven Bird, The University of Melbourne, Australia
Guy De Pauw, University of Antwerp, Belgium
Harald Hammarström, Max Planck Institute for Psycholinguistics, The Netherlands
Judith Klavans, University of Maryland, USA
Terry Langendoen, University of Arizona, USA
Lori Levin, Carnegie Mellon University, USA
William D. Lewis, Microsoft Research, USA
Worthy Martin, University of Virginia, USA
Mike Maxwell, Center for the Advanced Study of Language, USA
Steven Moran, University of Zurich, Switzerland
Alexander Nakhimovsky, Colgate University, USA
Alexis Palmer, Saarland University, Germany
Kevin Scannell, Saint Louis University, USA
Gary Simons, SIL International, USA
Nick Thieberger, The University of Melbourne, Australia
Paul Trilsbeek, Max Planck Institute for Psycholinguistics, The Netherlands
Doug Whalen, CUNY Graduate Center, USA
Menzo Windhouwer, Max Planck Institute for Psycholinguistics, The Netherlands
Fei Xia, University of Washington, USA

Sponsor:

US National Science Foundation (award nos. BCS-1404352 and IIS-1027289)

Table of Contents

Conference Program

Thursday, June 26, 2014

9:00–9:10 Introduction

Paper Session 1: Computational Tools for Endangered Languages Research

9:10–9:30 *Aikuma: A Mobile App for Collaborative Language Documentation*
Steven Bird, Florian R. Hanke, Oliver Adams and Haejoong Lee

9:30–9:50 *Documenting Endangered Languages with the WordsEye Linguistics Tool*
Morgan Ulinski, Anusha Balakrishnan, Daniel Bauer, Bob Coyne, Julia Hirschberg and Owen Rambow

9:50–10:10 *Small Languages, Big Data: Multilingual Computational Tools and Techniques for the Lexicography of Endangered Languages*
Martin Benjamin and Paula Radetzky

10:10–10:30 *LingSync & the Online Linguistic Database: New Models for the Collection and Management of Data for Language Communities, Linguists and Language Learners*
Joel Dunham, Gina Cook and Joshua Horner

10:30–11:00 Coffee Break

Paper Session 2: Applying Computational Methods to Endangered Languages

11:00–11:30 *Modeling the Noun Morphology of Plains Cree*
Conor Snoek, Dorothy Thunder, Kaidi Lõo, Antti Arppe, Jordan Lachler, Sjur Moshagen and Trond Trosterud

11:30–12:00 *Learning Grammar Specifications from IGT: A Case Study of Chintang*
Emily M. Bender, Joshua Crowgey, Michael Wayne Goodman and Fei Xia

12:00–12:30 *Creating Lexical Resources for Endangered Languages*
Khang Nhut Lam, Feras Al Tarouti and Jugal Kalita

12:30–14:00 Lunch

14:00–15:00 Posters and Demonstrations of Tools Presented in Paper Session 1

Estimating Native Vocabulary Size in an Endangered Language
Timofey Arkhangelskiy

Thursday, June 26, 2014 (continued)

	InterlinguaPlus Machine Translation Approach for Local Languages: Ekegusii & Swahili Edward Ombui, Peter Wagacha and Wanjiku Ng'ang'a
	Building and Evaluating Somali Language Corpora Abdillahi Nimaan
	Paper Session 3: Infrastructure and Community Development for Computational Research on Endangered Languages
15:00–15:30	*SeedLing: Building and Using a Seed corpus for the Human Language Project* Guy Emerson, Liling Tan, Susanne Fertmann, Alexis Palmer and Michaela Regneri
15:30–16:00	Coffee Break
16:00–16:20	*Short-Term Projects, Long-Term Benefits: Four Student NLP Projects for Low-Resource Languages* Alexis Palmer and Michaela Regneri
16:20–16:50	*Data Warehouse, Bronze, Gold, STEC, Software* Doug Cooper
16:50–17:20	*Time to Change the "D" in "DEL"* Stephen Beale
17:20–17:30	Concluding Remarks

Aikuma: A Mobile App for Collaborative Language Documentation

Steven Bird[1,2], **Florian R. Hanke**[1], **Oliver Adams**[1], **and Haejoong Lee**[2]
[1]Dept of Computing and Information Systems, University of Melbourne
[2]Linguistic Data Consortium, University of Pennsylvania

Abstract

Proliferating smartphones and mobile software offer linguists a scalable, networked recording device. This paper describes *Aikuma*, a mobile app that is designed to put the key language documentation tasks of recording, respeaking, and translating in the hands of a speech community. After motivating the approach we describe the system and briefly report on its use in field tests.

1 Introduction

The core of a language documentation consists of primary recordings along with transcriptions and translations (Himmelmann, 1998; Woodbury, 2003). Many members of a linguistic community may contribute to a language documentation, playing roles that depend upon their linguistic competencies. For instance, the best person to provide a text could be a monolingual elder, while the best person to translate it could be a younger bilingual speaker. Someone else again may be the best choice for performing transcription work. Whatever the workflow and degree of collaboration, there is always the need to manage files and create secondary materials, a data management problem. The problem is amplified by the usual problems that attend linguistic fieldwork: limited human resources, limited communication, and limited bandwidth.

The problem is not to collect large quantities of primary audio in the field using mobile devices (de Vries et al., 2014). Rather, the problem is to ensure the long-term interpretability of the collected recordings. At the most fundamental level, we want to know what words were spoken, and what they meant. Recordings made in the wild suffer from the expected range of problems: far-field recording, significant ambient noise, audience participation, and so forth. We address these problems via the "respeaking" task (Woodbury, 2003). Recordings made in an endangered language may not be interpretable once the language falls out of use. We address this problem via the "oral translation" task. The result is relatively clean source audio recordings with phrase-aligned translations (see Figure 1). NLP methods are applicable to such data (Dredze et al., 2010), and we can hope that ultimately, researchers working on archived bilingual audio sources will be able to automatically extract word-glossed interlinear text.

We describe *Aikuma*, an open source Android app that supports recording along with respeaking

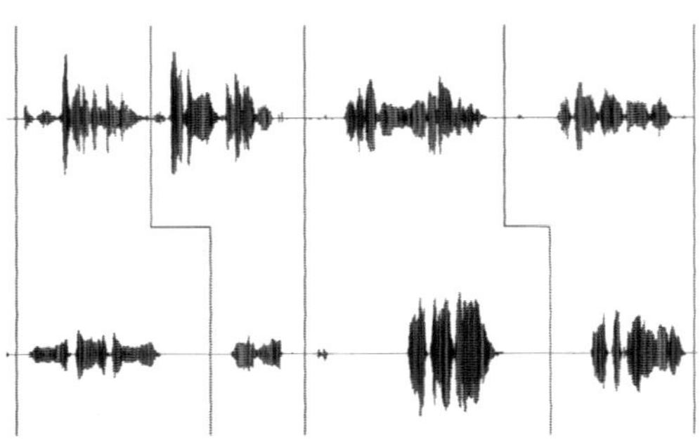

Figure 1: Phrase-aligned bilingual audio

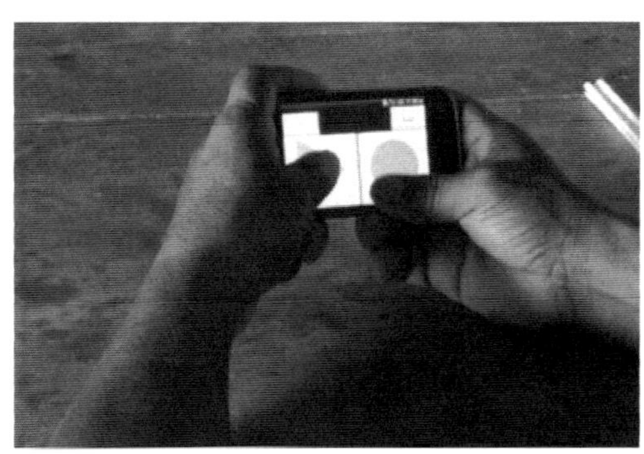

Figure 2: Adding a time-aligned translation

Proceedings of the 2014 Workshop on the Use of Computational Methods in the Study of Endangered Languages, pages 1–5,
Baltimore, Maryland, USA, 26 June 2014.

and oral translation, while capturing basic metadata. Aikuma supports local networking so that a set of mobile phones can be synchronized, and anyone can listen to and annotate the recordings made by others. Key functionality is provided via a text-less interface (Figure 2). Aikuma introduces social media and networked collaboration to village-based fieldwork, all on low-cost devices, and this is a boon for scaling up the quantity of documentary material that can be collected and processed. Field trials in Papua New Guinea, Brazil, and Nepal have demonstrated the effectiveness of the approach (Bird et al., 2014).

2 Thought Experiment: The Future Philologist

A typical language documentation project is resource-bound. So much documentation could be collected, yet the required human resources to process it all adequately are often not available. For instance, some have argued that it is not effective to collect large quantities of primary recordings because there is not the time to transcribe it.[1]

Estimates differ about the pace of language loss. Yet it is uncontroversial that – for hundreds of languages – only the oldest living speakers are well-versed in traditional folklore. While a given language may survive for several more decades, the opportunity to document significant genres may pass much sooner. Ideally, a large quantity of these nearly-extinct genres would be recorded and given sufficient further treatment in the form of respeakings and oral translations, in order to have archival value. Accordingly, we would like to determine what documentary materials would be of greatest practical value to the linguist working in the future, possibly ten to a hundred or more years in future. Given the interest of classical philology in ancient languages, we think of this researcher as the "future philologist."

Our starting point is texts, as the least processed item of the so-called "Boasian trilogy." A substantial text corpus can serve as the basis for the preparation of grammars and dictionaries even once a language is extinct, as we know from the cases of the extinct languages of the Ancient Near East.

Our primary resource is the native speaker community, both those living in the ancestral homeland and the members of the diaspora. How can we engage these communities in the tasks of recording, respeaking, and oral interpretation, in order to generate the substantial quantity of archival documentation?

Respeaking involves listening to an original recording and repeating what was heard carefully and slowly, in a quiet recording environment It gives archival value to recordings that were made "in the wild" on low-quality devices, with background noise, and by people having no training in linguistics. It provides much clearer audio content, facilitating transcription. Bettinson (2013) has shown that human transcribers, without knowledge of the language under study, can generally produce phonetic transcriptions from such recordings that are close enough to enable someone who knows the language to understand what was said, and which can be used as the basis for phonetic analysis. This means we can postpone the transcription task – by years or even decades – until such time as the required linguistic expertise is available to work with archived recordings.

By interpretation, we mean listening to a recording and producing a spoken translation of what was heard. Translation into another language obviates the need for the usual resource-intensive approaches to linguistic analysis that require syntactic treebanks along with semantic annotations, at the cost of a future decipherment effort (Xia and Lewis, 2007; Abney and Bird, 2010).

3 Design Principles

Several considerations informed the design of Aikuma. First, to facilitate use by monolingual speakers, the primary recording functions need to be text free.

Second, to facilitate collaboration and guard against loss of phones, it needs to be possible to continuously synchronise files between phones. Once any information has been captured on a phone, it is synchronized to the other phones on the local network. All content from any phone is available from any phone, and thus only a single phone needs to make it back from village-based work. After a recording is made, it needs to be possible to listen to it on the other phones on the local network. This makes it easy for people to annotate each other's recordings. This also en-

[1] E.g. Paul Newman's 2013 seminar *The Law of Unintended Consequences: How the Endangered Languages Movement Undermines Field Linguistics as a Scientific Enterprise*, `https://www.youtube.com/watch?v=xziE08ozQok`

ables users to experience the dissemination of their recordings, and to understand that a private activity of recording a narrative is tantamount to public speaking. This is useful for establishing informed consent in communities who have no previous experience of the Internet or digital archiving.

Third, to facilitate trouble-shooting and future digital archaeology, the file format of phones needs to be transparent. We have devised an easily-interpretable directory hierarchy for recordings and users, which permits direct manipulation of recordings. For instance, all the metadata and recordings that involve a particular speaker could be extracted from the hierarchy with a single filename pattern.

4 Aikuma

Thanks to proliferating smartphones, it is now relatively easy and cheap for untrained people to collect and share many sorts of recordings, for their own benefit and also for the benefit of language preservation efforts. These include oral histories, oral literature, public speaking, and discussion of popular culture. With inexpensive equipment and minimal training, a few dozen motivated people can create a hundred hours of recorded speech (approx 1M words) in a few weeks. However, adding transcription and translation by a trained linguist introduces a bottleneck: most languages will be gone before linguists will get to them.

Aikuma puts this work in the hands of language speakers. It collects recordings, respeakings, and interpretations, and organizes them for later synchronization with the cloud and archival storage. People with limited formal education and no prior experience using smartphones can readily use the app to record their stories, or listen to other people's stories to respeak or interpret them. Literate users can supply written transcriptions and translations. Items can be rated by the linguist and language workers and highly rated items are displayed more prominently, and this may be used to influence the documentary workflow. Recordings are stored alongside a wealth of metadata, including language, GPS coordinates, speaker, and offsets on time-aligned translations and comments.

4.1 Listing and saving recordings

When the app is first started, it shows a list of available recordings, indicating whether they are respeakings or translations (Figure 3(a)). These recordings could have been made on this phone, or synced to this phone from another, or downloaded from an archive. The recording functionality is accessed by pressing the red circle, and when the user is finished, s/he is prompted to add metadata to identify the person or people who were recorded (Figure 3(b)) and the language(s) of the recording (Figure 3(c)).

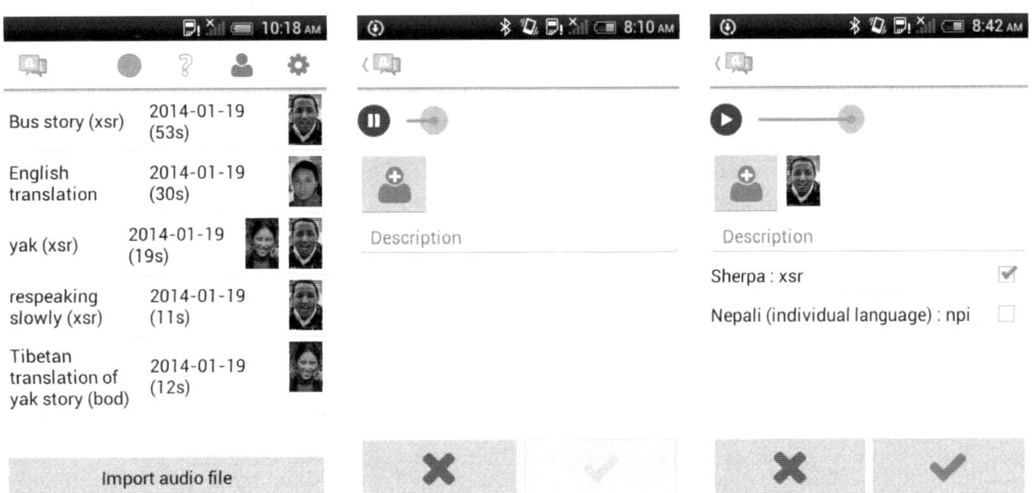

(a) Main list (b) Adding speaker metadata (c) Adding language metadata

Figure 3: Screens for listing and saving recordings

4.2 Playback and commentary

When a recording is selected, the user sees a display for the individual recording, with its name, date, duration, and images of the participants, cf. Figure 4.

Figure 4: Recording playback screen

The availability of commentaries is indicated by user images beneath the timeline. Once an original recording has commentaries, their locations are displayed within the playback slider. Playback interleaves the original recording with the spoken commentary, cf Figure 5.

Figure 5: Commentary playback screen

4.3 Gesture vs voice activation

Aikuma provides two ways to control any recording activity, using gesture or voice activation. In the gesture-activated mode, playback is started, paused, or stopped using on-screen buttons. For commentary, the user presses and holds the play button to listen to the source, and presses and holds the record button to supply a commentary, cf Figure 2. Activity is suspended when neither button is being pressed.

In the voice-activated mode, the user puts the phone to his or her ear and playback begins automatically. Playback is paused when the user lifts the phone away from the ear. When the user speaks, playback stops and the speech is recorded and aligned with the source recording.

4.4 File storage

The app supports importing of external audio files, so that existing recordings can be put through the respeaking and oral translation processes. Storage uses a hierarchical file structure and plain text metadata formats which can be easily accessed directly using command-line tools. Files are shared using FTP. Transcripts are stored using the plain text NIST HUB-4 transcription format and can be exported in Elan format.

4.5 Transcription

Aikuma incorporates a webserver and clients can connect using the phone's WiFi, Bluetooth, or USB interfaces. The app provides a browser-based transcription tool that displays the waveform for a recording along with the spoken annotations. Users listen to the source recording along with any available respeakings and oral translations, and then segment the audio and enter his or her own written transcription and translation. These are saved to the phone's storage and displayed on the phone during audio playback.

5 Deployment

We have tested Aikuma in Papua New Guinea, Brazil, and Nepal (Bird et al., 2014). We taught members of remote indigenous communities to record narratives and orally interpret them into a language of wider communication. We collected approximately 10 hours of audio, equivalent to 100k words. We found that the networking capability facilitated the contribution of multiple members of the community who have a variety of linguistic aptitudes. We demonstrated that the platform is an effective way to engage remote indigenous speech communities in the task of building phrase-aligned bilingual speech corpora. To support large scale deployment, we are adding support for workflow management, plus interfaces to the Internet Archive and to SoundCloud for long term preservation and social interaction.

Acknowledgments

We gratefully acknowledge support from the Australian Research Council, the National Science Foundation, and the Swiss National Science Foundation. We are also grateful to Isaac McAlister, Katie Gelbart, and Lauren Gawne for field-testing work. Aikuma development is hosted on GitHub.

References

Steven Abney and Steven Bird. 2010. The Human Language Project: building a universal corpus of the world's languages. In *Proceedings of the 48th Meeting of the Association for Computational Linguistics*, pages 88–97. Association for Computational Linguistics.

Mat Bettinson. 2013. The effect of respeaking on transcription accuracy. Honours Thesis, Dept of Linguistics, University of Melbourne.

Steven Bird, Isaac McAlister, Katie Gelbart, and Lauren Gawne. 2014. Collecting bilingual audio in remote indigenous villages. under review.

Nic de Vries, Marelie Davel, Jaco Badenhorst, Willem Basson, Febe de Wet, Etienne Barnard, and Alta de Waal. 2014. A smartphone-based ASR data collection tool for under-resourced languages. *Speech Communication*, 56:119–131.

Mark Dredze, Aren Jansen, Glen Coppersmith, and Ken Church. 2010. NLP on spoken documents without ASR. In *Proceedings of the 2010 Conference on Empirical Methods in Natural Language Processing*, pages 460–470. Association for Computational Linguistics.

Florian R. Hanke and Steven Bird. 2013. Large-scale text collection for unwritten languages. In *Proceedings of the 6th International Joint Conference on Natural Language Processing*, pages 1134–1138. Asian Federation of Natural Language Processing.

Nikolaus P. Himmelmann. 1998. Documentary and descriptive linguistics. *Linguistics*, 36:161–195.

Anthony C. Woodbury. 2003. Defining documentary linguistics. In Peter Austin, editor, *Language Documentation and Description*, volume 1, pages 35–51. London: SOAS.

Fei Xia and William D. Lewis. 2007. Multilingual structural projection across interlinearized text. In *Proceedings of the North American Chapter of the Association for Computational Linguistics*, pages 452–459. Association for Computational Linguistics.

Documenting Endangered Languages with the WordsEye Linguistics Tool

Morgan Ulinski*
mulinski@cs.columbia.edu

Anusha Balakrishnan*
ab3596@columbia.edu

Daniel Bauer*
bauer@cs.columbia.edu

Bob Coyne*
coyne@cs.columbia.edu

Julia Hirschberg*
julia@cs.columbia.edu

Owen Rambow†
rambow@ccls.columbia.edu

*Department of Computer Science
Columbia University
New York, NY, USA

†CCLS

Abstract

In this paper, we describe how field linguists can use the WordsEye Linguistics Tool (WELT) to study endangered languages. WELT is a tool under development for eliciting endangered language data and formally documenting a language, based on WordsEye (Coyne and Sproat, 2001), a text-to-scene generation tool that produces 3D scenes from text input. First, a linguist uses WELT to create elicitation materials and collect language data. Next, he or she uses WELT to formally document the language. Finally, the formal models are used to create a text-to-scene system that takes input in the endangered language and generates a picture representing its meaning.

1 Introduction

Although languages have appeared and disappeared throughout history, today languages are facing extinction at an unprecedented pace. Over 40% of the estimated 7,000 languages in the world are at risk of disappearing. When languages die, we lose access to an invaluable resource for studying the culture, history, and experience of people who spoke them (Alliance for Linguistic Diversity, 2013). Efforts to document languages and develop tools to support these efforts become even more important with the increasing rate of extinction. Bird (2009) emphasizes a particular need to make use of computational linguistics during fieldwork.

To address this issue, we are developing the WordsEye Linguistics Tool, WELT. In one mode of operation, we provide field linguists with tools for building elicitation sessions based on custom 3D scenes. In another, we provide a way to formally document the endangered language. Formal hypotheses can be verified using a text-to-scene system that takes input in the endangered language, analyzes it based on the formal model, and generates a picture representing the meaning.

WELT provides important advantages to field linguists for elicitation over the current practice of using a set of pre-fabricated static pictures. Using WELT the linguist can create and modify scenes in real time, based on informants' responses, creating follow-up questions and scenes to support them. Since the pictures WELT supports are 3D scenes, the viewpoint can easily be changed, allowing exploration of linguistic descriptions based on different frames of reference, as for elicitations of spatial descriptions. Finally, since scenes and objects can easily be added in the field, the linguist can customize the images used for elicitation to be maximally relevant to the current informants.

Creating a text-to-scene system for an endangered language with WELT also has advantages. First, WELT allows documentation of the semantics of a language in a formal way. Linguists can customize the focus of their studies to be as deep or shallow as they wish; however, we believe that a major advantage of documenting a language with WELT is that it enables studies that are much more precise. The fact that a text-to-scene system is created from this documentation will allow linguists to test the theories they develop with native speakers, making changes to grammars and semantics in real time. The resulting text-to-scene system can also be an important tool for language preservation, spreading interest in the language among younger generations of the community and recruiting new speakers.

In this paper, we discuss the WELT toolkit and its intended use, with examples from Arrernte and Nahuatl. In Section 2 we discuss prior work on field linguistics computational tools. In Section 3 we present an overview of the WELT system. We describe using WELT for elicitation in Section 4 and describe the tools for language documentation in Section 5. We conclude in Section 6.

Proceedings of the 2014 Workshop on the Use of Computational Methods in the Study of Endangered Languages, pages 6–14,
Baltimore, Maryland, USA, 26 June 2014.

2 Related Work

Computational tools for field linguistics fall into two categories: tools for native speakers to use directly, without substantial linguist intervention, and tools for field linguists to use. Tools intended for native speakers include the PAWS starter kit (Black and Black, 2009), which uses the answers to a series of guided questions to produce a draft of a grammar. Similarly, Bird and Chiang (2012) describe a simplified workflow and supporting MT software that lets native speakers produce useable documentation of their language on their own.

One of the most widely-used toolkits in the latter category is SIL FieldWorks (SIL FieldWorks, 2014), or specifically, FieldWorks Language Explorer (FLEx). FLEx includes tools for eliciting and recording lexical information, dictionary development, interlinearization of texts, analysis of discourse features, and morphological analysis. An important part of FLEx is its "linguist-friendly" morphological parser (Black and Simons, 2006), which uses an underlying model of morphology familiar to linguists, is fully integrated into lexicon development and interlinear text analysis, and produces a human-readable grammar sketch as well as a machine-interpretable parser. The morphological parser is constructed "stealthily" in the background, and can help a linguist by predicting glosses for interlinear texts.

Linguist's Assistant (Beale, 2011) provides a corpus of semantic representations for linguists to use as a guide for elicitation. After eliciting the language data, a linguist writes rules translating these semantic representations into surface forms. The result is a description of the language that can be used to generate text from documents that have been converted into the semantic representation. Linguists are encouraged to collect their own elicitations and naturally occurring texts and translate them into the semantic representation.

The LinGO Grammar Matrix (Bender et al., 2002) facilitates formal modeling of syntax by generating basic HPSG "starter grammars" for languages from the answers to a typological questionnaire. Extending a grammar beyond the prototype, however, does require extensive knowledge of HPSG, making this tool more feasibly used by grammar engineers and computational linguists. For semantics, the most common resource for formal documentation across languages is FrameNet (Filmore et al., 2003); FrameNets have been developed for many languages, including Spanish, Japanese, and Portuguese. However, FrameNet is also targeted toward computational linguists.

In general, we also lack tools for creating custom elicitation materials. With WELT, we hope to fill some of the gaps in the range of available field linguistics tools. WELT will enable the creation of custom elicitation material and facilitate the management sessions with an informant. WELT will also enable formal documentation of the semantics of a language without knowledge of specific computational formalisms. This is similar to the way FLEx allows linguists to create a formal model of morphology while also documenting the lexicon of a language and glossing interlinear texts.

3 Overview of WELT Workflow

In this section, we briefly describe the workflow for using WELT; a visual representation is provided in Figure 1. Since we are still in the early stages of our project, this workflow has not been tested in practice. The tools for scene creation and elicitation are currently useable, although more features will be added in the future. The tools for modeling and documentation are still in development; although some functionality has been implemented, we are still testing it with toy grammars.

First, WELT will be used to prepare a set of 3D scenes to be used to elicit targeted descriptions or narratives. An important part of this phase will be the cultural adaptation of the graphical semantics used in WordsEye, so that scenes will be relevant to the native speakers a linguist works with. We will discuss cultural adaptation in more detail in Section 4.1. Next, the linguist will work with an informant to generate language data based on prepared 3D scenes. This can be a dynamic process; as new questions come up, a linguist can easily modify existing scenes or create new ones. WELT also automatically syncs recorded audio with open scenes and provides an interface for the linguist to write notes, textual descriptions, and glosses. We will discuss creating scenes and eliciting data with WELT in Section 4.2. After the elicitation session, the linguist can use WELT to review the data collected, listen to the audio recorded for each scene, and revise notes and glosses. The linguist can then create additional scenes to elicit more data or begin the formal documentation of the language.

Creating a text-to-scene system with WELT requires formal models of the morphology, syntax,

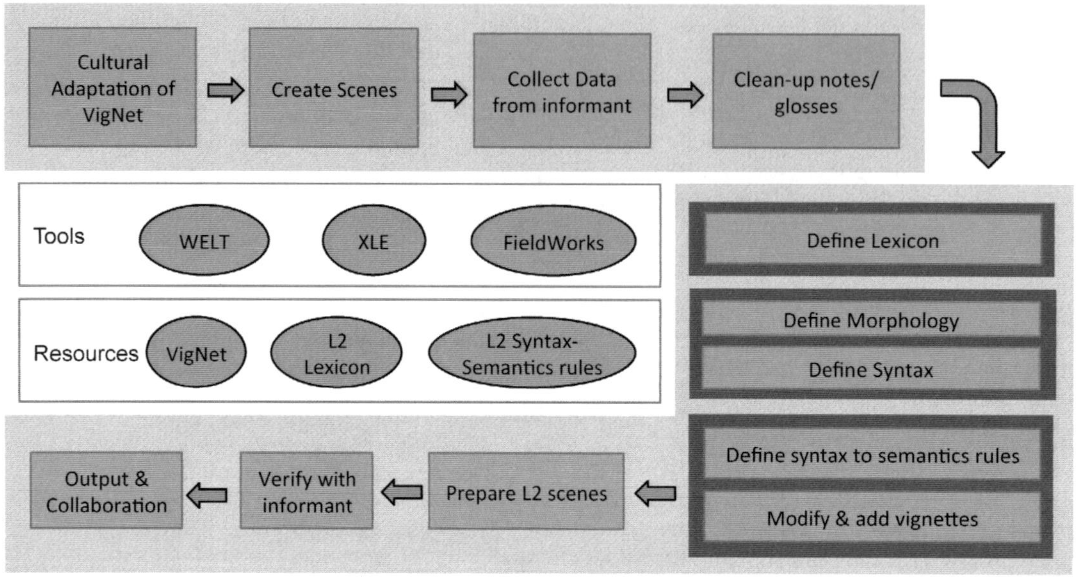

Figure 1: WELT workflow

and semantics of a language. Since the focus of WELT is on semantics, the formalisms used to model morphology and syntax may vary. We are using FieldWorks to document Nahuatl morphology, XFST (Beesley and Karttunen, 2003) to model Arrernte morphology, and XLE (Crouch et al., 2011) to model syntax in the LFG formalism (Kaplan and Bresnan, 1982). We will provide tools to export WELT descriptions and glosses into FLEx format and to export the lexicon created during documentation into FLEx and XLE. WELT will provide user interfaces for modeling the syntax-semantics interface, lexical semantics, and graphical semantics of a language. We will discuss these in more detail in Section 5.3.

Once models of morphology, syntax, and semantics are in place (note that these can be working models, and need not be complete), WELT puts the components together into a text-to-scene system that takes input in the endangered language and uses the formal models to generate pictures. This system can be used to verify theories with informants and revise grammars. As new questions arise, WELT can also continue to be used to create elicitation materials and collect linguistic data.

Finally, we will create a website for WELT so linguists can share resources such as modified versions of VigNet, 3D scenes, language data collected, and formal grammars. This will allow comparison of analyses across languages, as well as facilitate the documentation of other languages that are similar linguistically or spoken by culturally similar communities. In addition, sharing the resulting text-to-scene systems with a wider audience can generate interest in endangered languages and, if shared with endangered-language-speaking communities, encourage younger members of the community to use the language.

4 Elicitation with WELT

WELT organizes elicitation sessions around a set of 3D scenes, which are created by inputting English text into WordsEye. Scenes can be imported and exported between sessions, so that useful scenes can be reused and data compared. WELT also provides tools for recording audio (which is automatically synced with open scenes), textual descriptions, glosses, and notes during a session. Screenshots are included in Figure 2.

4.1 Cultural Adaptation of VigNet

To interpret input text, WordsEye uses VigNet (Coyne et al., 2011), a lexical resource based on FrameNet (Baker et al., 1998). As in FrameNet, lexical items are grouped in frames according to shared semantic structure. A frame contains a set of frame elements (semantic roles). FrameNet defines the mapping between syntax and semantics for a lexical item with valence patterns that map syntactic functions to frame elements.

VigNet extends FrameNet in order to capture "graphical semantics", a set of graphical constraints representing the position, orientation, size, color, texture, and poses of objects in the scene,

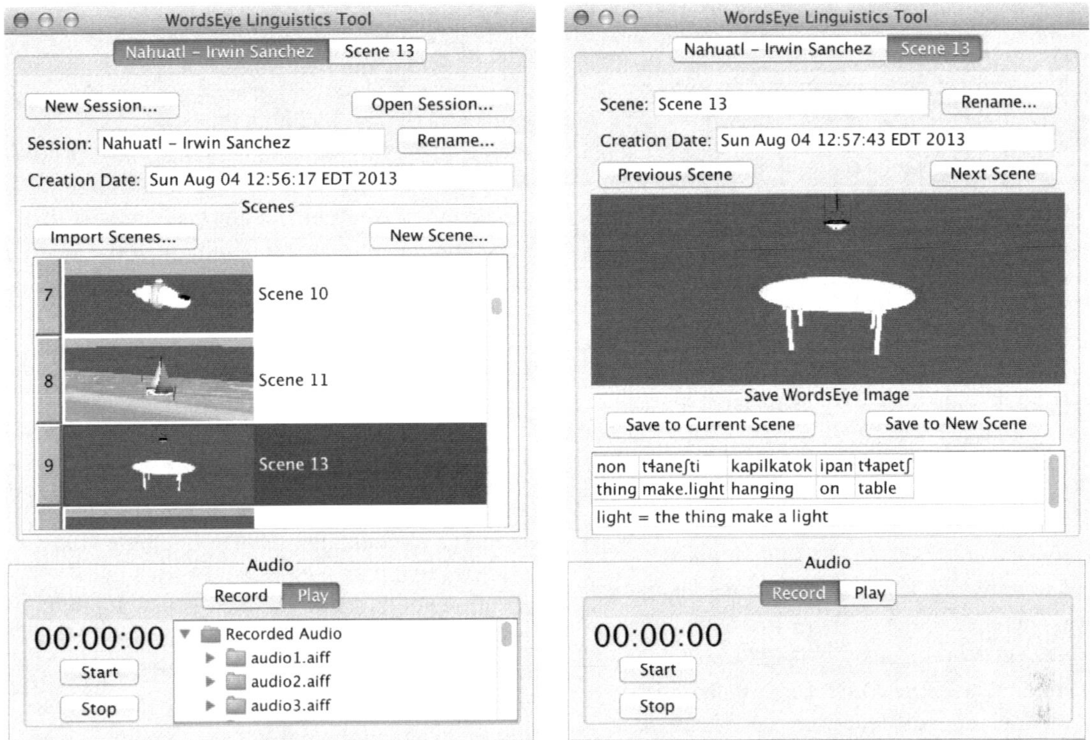

Figure 2: Screenshots of WELT elicitation interfaces

which is used to construct and render a 3D scene. Graphical semantics are added to frames by adding primitive graphical (typically, spatial) relations between frame element fillers. VigNet distinguishes between meanings of words that are distinguished graphically. For example, the specific objects (e.g., implements) and spatial relations in the graphical semantics for *cook* depend on the object being cooked and on the culture in which it is being cooked (cooking turkey in Baltimore vs. cooking an egg in Alice Springs), even though at an abstract level *cook an egg in Alice Springs* and *cook a turkey in Baltimore* are perfectly compositional semantically. Frames augmented with graphical semantics are called *vignettes*.

Vignette Tailoring: Without digressing into a discussion on linguistic relativity, we assume that large parts of VigNet are language- and culture-independent. The low-level graphical relations used to express graphical semantics are based on physics and human anatomy and do not depend on language. However, the graphical semantics for a vignette may be culture-specific, and some new vignettes will need to be added for a culture. In the U.S., for example, the sentence *The woman boiled the water* might invoke a scene with a pot of water on a stove in a kitchen. Among the Arrernte people, it would instead invoke a woman sitting on the ground in front of a kettle on a campfire. Figure 3 shows an illustration from the Eastern and Central Arrernte Picture Dictionary (Broad, 2008) of the sentence *Ipmenhe-ipmenhele kwatye urinpe-ilemele iteme*, "My grandmother is boiling the water." The lexical semantics for the English verb *boil* and the Arrente verb *urinpe-ileme* are the same, the relation APPLY-HEAT.BOIL. However, the vignettes map to different, culture-typical graphical semantics. The vignettes for our example are shown in Figure 4.

Figure 3: Illustration from Broad (2008).

To handle cultural differences like these, a linguist will use WELT to extend VigNet with new

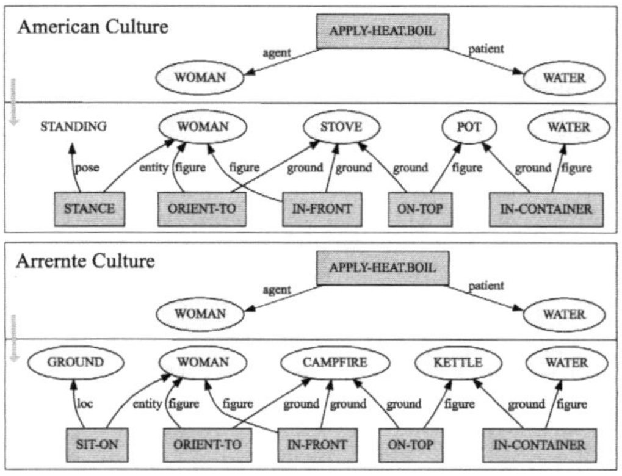

Figure 4: Vignettes for *the woman boils the water*. The high-level semantics of APPLY-HEAT.BOIL are decomposed into sets of objects and primitive graphical relations that depend on cultural context.

graphical semantics for existing vignettes that need to be modified, and new vignettes for scenarios not already covered. We will create interfaces so that VigNet can easily be adapted.

Custom WordsEye Objects: Another way to adapt WordsEye to a culture or region is to add relevant 3D objects to the database. WordsEye also supports 2D-cutout images, which is an easy way to add new material without 3D modeling. We have created a corpus of 2D and 3D models for WordsEye that are specifically relevant to aboriginal speakers of Arrernte, including native Australian plants and animals and culturally relevant objects and gestures. Many of the pictures we created are based on images from IAD Press, used with permission, which we enhanced and cropped in PhotoShop. Some scenes that use these images are included in Figure 5. Currently, each new object has to be manually incorporated into WordsEye, but we will create tools to allow WELT users to easily add pictures and objects.

New objects will also need to be incorporated into the semantic ontology. VigNet's ontology consists of semantic concepts that are linked together with ISA relations. The ontology supports multiple inheritance, allowing a given concept to be a sub-type of more than one concept. For example, a PRINCESS.N is a subtype of both FEMALE.N and ARISTOCRAT.N, and a BLACK-WIDOW.N is a subtype of SPIDER.N and POISONOUS-ENTITY.N. Concepts are often linked to corresponding lexical items. If a lexical item has more than one word sense, the different word senses would be represented by different concepts. In addition, every graphical object in VigNet is represented by a unique concept. For example, a particular 3D model of a dog would be a linked to the general DOG.N concept by the ISA relation. The semantic concepts in VigNet include the graphical objects available in WordsEye as well as concepts tied to related lexical items. While WordsEye might only have a handful of graphical objects for dogs, VigNet will have concepts representing all common types of dogs, even if there is no graphical object associated with them. We will provide interfaces both for adding new objects and for modifying the semantic concepts in VigNet to reflect the differing lexical semantics of a new language.

4.2 Preparing Scenes and Eliciting Data

The next step in the workflow is the preparation of scenes and elicitation of descriptions. To test creating elicitation materials with WELT, we built a set of scenes based on the Max Planck topological relations picture series (Bowerman and Pederson, 1992). In creating these, we used a feature of WordsEye that allows highlighting specific objects (or parts of objects) in a scene. We used these scenes to elicit descriptions from a native Nahuatl speaker; some examples are included in Figure 6.

(a) in tapametɬ tɬatsakwa se kali
the fence/wall around the house

(b) in tsopelik katsekotok tɬatsintɬa in tɬapetʃ
the candy sticking under the table

Figure 6: Nahuatl examples elicited with WELT

One topic we will explore with WELT is the relationship in Arrernte between case and semantic interpretation of a sentence. It is possible to significantly alter a sentence's meaning by changing the case on an argument. For example, the sentences in (1) from Wilkins (1989) show that adding dative

Figure 5: WordsEye scenes using custom 2D gum tree and dingo from our corpus

case to the direct object of the sentence changes the meaning from shooting and hitting the kangaroo to shooting *at* the kangaroo and *not* hitting it. Wilkins calls this the "dative of attempt."

(1) a. re aherre tyerre-ke
he kangaroo shot-pc
He shot the kangaroo.

b. re aherre-ke tyerre-ke
he kangaroo-DAT shot-pc
He shot at the kangaroo (but missed).

In order to see how this example generalizes, we will create pairs of pictures, one in which the object of the sentence is acted upon, and one in which the object fails to be acted upon. Figure 7 shows a pair of scenes contrasting an Australian football player scoring a goal with a player aiming at the goal but missing the shot. Sentences (2) and (3) are two ways of saying "score a goal" in Arrernte; we want to see if a native Arrernte speaker would use *goal-ke* in place of *goal* in this context.

(2) artwe le goal arrerne-me
man ERG goal put-NP
The man kicks a goal.

(3) artwe le goal kick-eme-ile-ke
man ERG goal kick-VF-TV-PST
The man kicked a goal.

5 Modeling a Language with WELT

WELT includes tools for documenting the semantics of the language. It also uses this documentation to automatically generate a text-to-scene system for the language. Because WELT is centered around the idea of 3D scenes, the formal documentation will tend to focus on the parts of the semantics that can be represented graphically. Note that this can include figurative concepts as well, although the visual representation of these may be culture-specific. However, linguists do not need to be limited by the graphical output; WELT can be used to document other aspects of semantics as well, but linguists will not be able to verify these theories using the text-to-scene system.

To explain the necessary documentation, we briefly describe the underlying architecture of WordsEye, and how we are adapting it to support text-to-scene systems for other languages. The WordsEye system parses each input sentence into a labeled syntactic dependency structure, then converts it into a lexical-semantic structure using lexical valence patterns and other lexical and semantic information. The resulting set of semantic relations is converted to a "graphical semantics", the knowledge needed to generate graphical scenes from language.

To produce a text-to-scene system for a new language, WELT must replace the English linguistic processing modules with models for the new language. The WELT processing pipeline is illustrated in Figure 8, with stages of the pipeline on top and required resources below. In this section, we will discuss creating the lexicon, morphological and syntactic parsers, and syntax-to-semantics rules. The vignettes and 3D objects will largely have been done during cultural adaptation of VigNet; additional modifications needed to handle the semantics can be defined using the same tools.

5.1 The Lexicon

The lexicon in WELT is a list of word forms mapped to semantic concepts. The process of building the lexicon begins during elicitation. WELT's elicitation interface includes an option to display each object in the scene individually before progressing to the full scene. When an object is labeled and glossed in this way, the word and the semantic concept represented by the 3D object are immediately added to the lexicon. Word forms glossed in scene descriptions will also be added to the lexicon, but will need to be mapped to semantic concepts later. WELT will provide

Figure 7: WordsEye scenes to elicit the "dative of attempt."

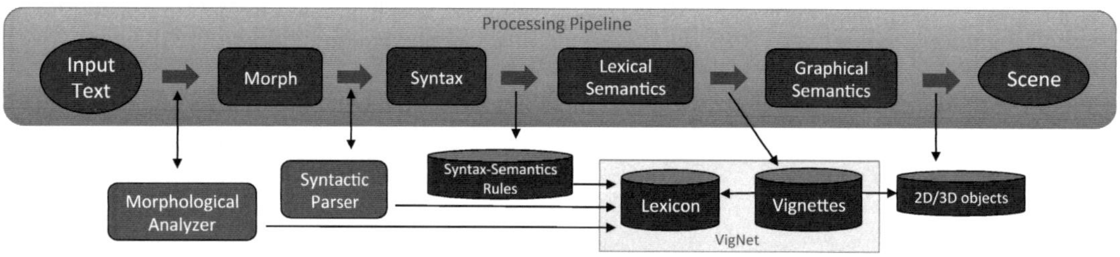

Figure 8: WELT architecture

tools for completing the lexicon by modifying the automatically-added items, adding new lexical items, and mapping each lexical item to a semantic concept in VigNet. Figure 9(a) shows a partial mapping of the nouns in our Arrernte lexicon.

WELT includes a visual interface for searching VigNet's ontology for semantic concepts and browsing through the hierarchy to select a particular category. Figure 9(b) shows a portion of the ontology that results from searching for *cup*. Here, we have decided to map *panikane* to CUP.N. Semantic categories are displayed one level at a time, so initially only the concepts directly above and below the search term are shown. From there, it is simple to click on relevant concepts and navigate the graph to find an appropriate semantic category. To facilitate the modeling of morphology and syntax, WELT will also export the lexicon into formats compatible with FieldWorks and XLE, so the list of word forms can be used as a starting point.

Lexical Item	VigNet Concept
artwe	PERSON.N
panikane	CUP.N
angepe	CROW.N
akngwelye	DOG.N
tipwele	TABLE.N

(a)

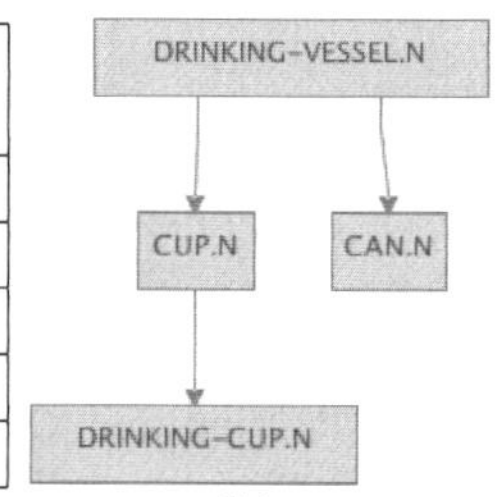

(b)

Figure 9: (a) Arrernte lexical items mapped to VigNet concepts; (b) part of the VigNet ontology

5.2 Morphology and Syntax

As mentioned earlier, the focus of our work on WELT is on modeling the interface between syntax, lexical semantics, and graphical semantics. Therefore, although WELT requires models of morphology and syntax to generate a text-to-scene system, we are relying on third-party tools to build those models. For morphology, a very good tool already exists in FLEx, which allows the creation of a morphological parser without knowledge of any particular grammatical formalism. For syntax, we are using XLE for our own work while researching other options that would be more accessible to non-computational linguists. It is important to note, though, that the modeling done in WELT does not require a perfect syntactic parser. In fact, one can vastly over-generate syntax and still accurately model semantics. Therefore, the syntactic grammars provided as models do not need to be complex. However, the question of syntax is still an open area of research in our project.

5.3 Semantics

To use the WordsEye architecture, the system needs to be able to map between the formal syntax of the endangered language and a representation of semantics compatible with VigNet. To accomplish

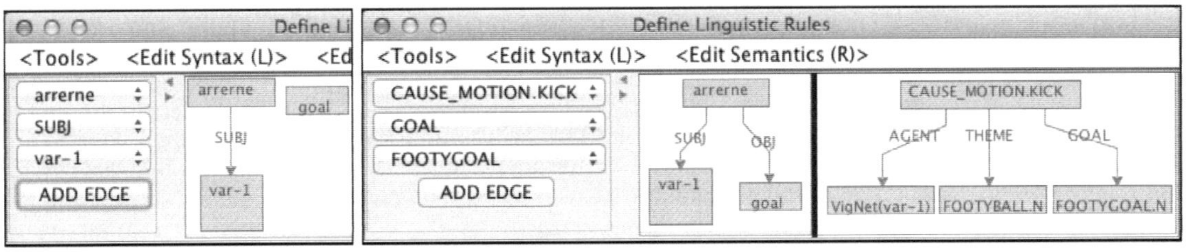

Figure 10: Creating syntax-semantics rules in WELT

this, WELT includes an interface for the linguist to specify a set of rules that map from syntax to (lexical) semantics. Since we are modeling Arrernte syntax with LFG, the rules currently take syntactic f-structures as input, but the system could easily be modified to accommodate other formalisms. The left-hand side of a rule consists of a set of conditions on the f-structure elements and the right-hand side is the desired semantic structure. Rules are specified by defining a tree structure for the left-hand (syntax) side and a DAG for the right-hand (semantics) side.

As an example, we will construct a rule to process sentence (2) from Section 4.2, *artwe le goal arrerneme*. For this sentence, our Arrernte grammar produces the f-structure in Figure 11. We create a rule that selects for predicate *arrerne* with object *goal* and any subject. Figure 10 shows the construction of this rule in WELT. Note that `var-1` on the left-hand side becomes VIGNET(`var-1`) on the right-hand side; this indicates that the lexical item found in the input is mapped into a semantic concept using the lexicon.

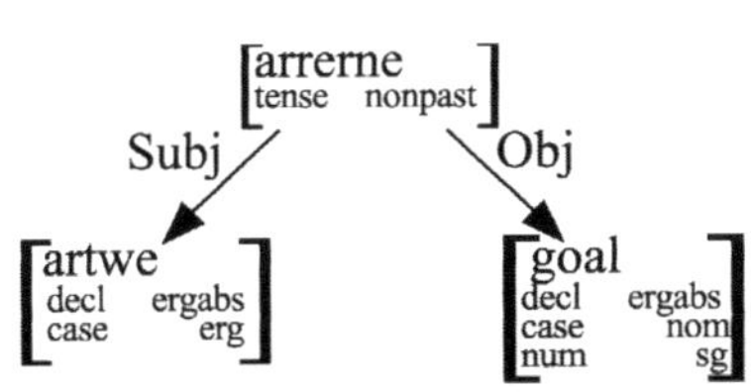

Figure 11: F-structure for sentence 2, Section 4.2.

The rule shown in Figure 10 is a very simple example. Nodes on the left-hand side of the rule can also contain boolean logic, if we wanted to allow the subject to be [(*artwe* 'man' OR *arhele* 'woman') AND NOT *ampe* 'child']. Rules need not specify lexical items directly but may refer to more general semantic categories. For example, our rule could require a particular semantic category for VIGNET(`var-1`), such as ANIMATE-BEING.N. These categories are chosen through the same ontology browser used to create the lexicon. Finally, to ensure that our sentence can be converted into graphics, we need to make sure that a vignette definition exists for CAUSE_MOTION.KICK so that the lexical semantics on the right-hand side of our rule can be augmented with graphical semantics; the vignette definition is given in Figure 12. The WordsEye system will use the graphical constraints in the vignette to build a scene and render it in 3D.

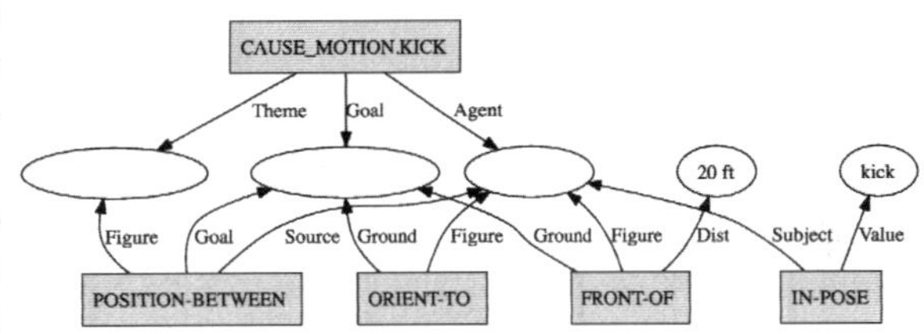

Figure 12: Vignette definition for CAUSE_MOTION.KICK

6 Summary

We have described a novel tool under development for linguists working with endangered languages. It will provide a new way to elicit data from informants, an interface for formally documenting the lexical semantics of a language, and allow the creation of a text-to-scene system for any language. In this paper, we have focused specifically on the workflow that a linguist would follow while studying an endangered language with WELT. WELT will provide useful tools for field linguistics and language documentation, from creating elicitation materials, to eliciting data, to formally documenting a language. In addition, the text-to-scene system that results from documenting an endangered language with WELT will be valuable for language preservation, generating interest in the wider world, as well as encouraging younger members of endangered language communities to use the language.

Acknowledgments

This material is based upon work supported by the National Science Foundation under Grant No. 1160700.

References

Alliance for Linguistic Diversity. 2013. The Endangered Languages Project. http://www.endangeredlanguages.com.

C. Baker, J. Fillmore, and J. Lowe. 1998. The Berkeley FrameNet project. In *36th Meeting of the Association for Computational Linguistics and 17th International Conference on Computational Linguistics (COLING-ACL'98)*, pages 86–90, Montréal.

Stephen Beale. 2011. Using Linguist's Assistant for Language Description and Translation. In *IJCNLP 2011 System Demonstrations*, pages 5–8.

Kenneth R. Beesley and Lauri Karttunen. 2003. Finite-State Morphology Homepage. http://www.fsmbook.com.

E. Bender, D. Flickinger, and S. Oepen. 2002. The Grammar Matrix. In J. Carroll, N. Oostdijk, and R. Sutcliffe, editors, *Workshop on Grammar Engineering and Evaluation at the 19th International Conference on Computational Linguistics*, pages 8–14, Taipei, Taiwan.

S. Bird and D. Chiang. 2012. Machine translation for language preservation. In *COLING 2012: Posters*, pages 125–134, Mumbai, December.

S. Bird. 2009. Natural language processing and linguistic fieldwork. *Computational Linguistics*, 35(3):469–474.

Cheryl A Black and H Andrew Black. 2009. PAWS: Parser and Writer for Syntax. In *SIL Forum for Language Fieldwork 2009-002*.

H.A. Black and G.F. Simons. 2006. The SIL FieldWorks Language Explorer approach to morphological parsing. In *Computational Linguistics for Less-studied Languages: Texas Linguistics Society 10*, Austin, TX, November.

M. Bowerman and E. Pederson. 1992. Topological relations picture series. In S. Levinson, editor, *Space stimuli kit 1.2*, page 51, Nijmegen. Max Planck Institute for Psycholinguistics.

N. Broad. 2008. *Eastern and Central Arrernte Picture Dictionary*. IAD Press.

B. Coyne and R. Sproat. 2001. WordsEye: An automatic text-to-scene conversion system. In *SIGGRAPH*.

B. Coyne, D. Bauer, and O. Rambow. 2011. Vignet: Grounding language in graphics using frame semantics. In *ACL Workshop on Relational Models of Semantics (RELMS)*, Portland, OR.

D. Crouch, M. Dalrymple, R. Kaplan, T. King, J. Maxwell, and P. Newman. 2011. XLE Documentation. http://www2.parc.com/isl/groups/nltt/xle/doc/xle_toc.html.

C. Filmore, C. Johnson, and M. Petruck. 2003. Background to FrameNet. In *International Journal of Lexicography*, pages 235–250.

R.M. Kaplan and J.W. Bresnan. 1982. Lexical-functional grammar: A formal system for grammatical representation. In J.W. Bresnan, editor, *The Mental Representation of Grammatical Relations*. MIT Press, Cambridge, Mass., December.

SIL FieldWorks. 2014. SIL FieldWorks. http://fieldworks.sil.org.

D. Wilkins. 1989. *Mparntwe Arrernte (Aranda): Studies in the structure and semantics of grammar.* Ph.D. thesis, Australian National University.

Small Languages, Big Data: Multilingual Computational Tools and Techniques for the Lexicography of Endangered Languages

Martin Benjamin
École Polytechnique Fédérale de Lausanne
Lausanne, Switzerland
martin.benjamin@epfl.ch

Paula Radetzky
Kamusi Project International
Geneva, Switzerland
paula@kamusi.org

Abstract

The Kamusi Project, a multilingual online dictionary website, has as one of its goals to document the lexicons of endangered and less-resourced languages (LRLs). Kamusi.org provides a unified platform and repository for this kind of data that is both simple to use and free to researchers and the public. Since Kamusi has a separate entry for each homophone or polyseme, it can be used to produce sophisticated multilingual dictionaries. We have recently been confronting issues inherent in contact language-based lexicography, especially the elicitation of culturally-specific semantic terms, which cannot be obtained through fieldwork purely reliant on a contact language. To address this, we have designed a system of "balloons." Based on a variety of factors, balloons raise the likelihood of revealing terms and fields that have particular relevance within a culture, rather than perpetuating linguistic bias toward the concerns and artifacts of more powerful groups. Kamusi has also developed a smartphone application which can be used for crowdsourcing contributions and validation. It will also be invaluable in gathering oral data from speakers of endangered languages for the production of monolingual talking dictionaries. The first of these projects is planned for the Arrernte language in central Australia.

1 Introduction

The Kamusi Project is a multilingual online dictionary and language-resource website at www.kamusi.org, whose primary purpose is to provide a unified platform designed for documenting the lexicons of the world's languages. The main goal of this effort is a set of monolingual written and audio dictionaries for both large languages and less-resourced ones (LRLs), connected together at the concept level to produce viable bilingual dictionaries between each language in the system, as well as bedrock linguistic data that can be used in advanced machine applications. Linguistic data is contributed by individual researchers and also via crowdsourcing. As a massively multilingual dictionary project, Kamusi has been wrestling with the conceptual challenge of how to elicit terms in a way that minimizes cultural bias but results in lexicons that can be linked between languages. At the same time, we have been developing tools that will enable citizen lexicography without necessarily involving a field researcher. Such tools need to be highly systematic in order to yield usable and trustworthy dictionaries.

In this paper, we first provide an overview of Kamusi (§2); describe "balloons," our system for overcoming the problems of using a contact language to elicit endangered language lexicons (§3); introduce our smartphone application, designed to gather oral data from non-literate speakers and both oral and written data from literate speakers (§4); and, finally, discuss our efforts to produce monolingual talking dictionaries,

Proceedings of the 2014 Workshop on the Use of Computational Methods in the Study of Endangered Languages, pages 15–23,
Baltimore, Maryland, USA, 26 June 2014. ©2014 Association for Computational Linguistics

the first of which involves the Arrernte language (Pama-Nyungan; central Australia) (§5).[1]

2 Kamusi as a Platform for Endangered Language Lexicography

Several technological resources provide good data-gathering solutions for individual lexicographic projects, including Max Planck's LEXUS;[2] TLex;[3] WeSay;[4] and SIL's triad of Lexique Pro, Toolbox, and FLEx.[5] Yet each of these solutions leaves gaps for the individual projects making use of them, and none is suitable for development of sophisticated multilingual dictionaries as envisioned by Kamusi. The learning curve can be steep, particularly the initial effort to set up an effective structure for a language. Each project must reinvent the entire process of bilingual translation, choosing which contact language terms to treat, working out anew how to reference different senses, and coping with or ignoring non-equivalence between languages. The comparison between two languages in different projects is impractical or impossible, even if the two dictionaries share one of their languages. For example, using Lexique Pro to find terms in Bakwé and cross-border Bambara (both Niger-Congo; Côte d'Ivoire) that correspond to English *light* 'illumination' is a Herculean research task. One must visit the multiple entries glossed as 'light' in each dictionary, then compare the Bakwé with Bambara words to try to discern which definition or term matches with which.[6] The dissemination of data becomes an exercise in reinventing multiple wheels: creating a website and finding hosting or using the limited services of Lexique Pro, publicizing the data's availability, finding a publisher who is interested in a language without a market. More extensive ambitions, such as mobile applications or ongoing expansion of the lexicon, are unlikely to be addressed for underfunded LRLs.

The Kamusi Project speaks to each of these gaps. Anyone who is able to purchase an airline ticket online has the technical skills to use the editing system, although some concepts (such as the difference between a definition, a translation, and a definition translation) must be mastered with the aid of tutorials.[7] Setting up a language involves a few hours of back-and-forth with Kamusi staff to configure the parts of speech and the fields for inflections and attributes that vary from language to language. The editing system handles all of the data fields that have been identified for the thirty-odd languages currently configured for the system, with the possibility of adding more data categories if necessary. Lexicon development can proceed via elicitation from an English priority list (§3 below), or directly from deeper lexical research. There is little ambiguity about translation senses; each English sense of *light* (homophones and polysemes) is its own entry with a clear definition, as is each German *Licht*, each Mandarin or Urdu homophone and polyseme, and so on. Equivalence between languages is shown by labeling translations as either parallel, similar, or an explanation in language B of a term in language A (or vice versa). When a concept in language A is linked to a term in language B, the links from language B to other languages are carefully tracked, along with the degree of separation; in this way, were a Bambara term and a Bakwé term both linked to a particular English sense of *light*, they would inherently be shown as second degree links to each other, with the possibility to validate or reject the computer pairing. Each piece of data is published immediately upon validation, so there is no need for the lexicographer to spend time setting up a website, find hosting and pay for it indefinitely, update files, manage a server, attempt search engine optimization, etc. Each language will share access to new tools and resources as they are rolled out on Kamusi.org, such as custom printing, integration with social media, and mobile apps and other improved methods for collecting linguistic data from community members (§3-§5 below).

3 Balloons: Addressing Problems of Contact Language-Based Elicitation

It is a trope in the field-linguistics world that LRLs, especially those that are spoken by small-

[1] Our app, described in §4, will be demonstrated at the present meeting, the ComputEL Workshop of the Association for Computational Linguistics, June 2014.

[2] http://tla.mpi.nl/tools/tla-tools/lexus/release-notes/

[3] http://tshwanedje.com/tshwanelex/

[4] http://wesay.palaso.org

[5] http://www-01.sil.org/computing/catalog/show_software_catalog.asp?by=cat&name=Data+Management

[6] http://www.bambara.org/lexique/index-english/main.htm; http://bakwe.org/e107_files/LexiquePro/bakwe_lexicon/index-english/main.htm

[7] Rather than suffer through a dry description of the editing process, registered users are invited to click "Edit this entry" on any entry where they see opportunities for improvement at http://kamusi.org, or add new terms or senses through the form at http://kamusi.org/node/add/dictionary-term.

er linguistic minorities, pose special challenges for efforts at documentation. These include scarcity of speakers and researchers, remoteness of field sites, lack of funding, and academic evaluation systems in the humanities and social sciences which reward only certain kinds of investigation—to the exclusion of, notably, lexicographic research, linguistic resource- and website-building, and any sort of research product that is the result of a significant number of participants or community-based input.[8]

Due to the scarcity of speakers and researchers (and especially native-speaker researchers) of endangered languages, the process of lexicographic documentation for such languages almost always begins with elicitation of terms from a major contact language—English, Spanish, Thai, Swahili, etc.—with or without a tool such as a word list.[9] Definitions or, more often, translation equivalents are then recorded in the major contact language as well. It is rare to find dictionaries with own-language definitions for endangered or small minority languages.[10]

There are, however, several problems that are inherent in using a major contact language as the starting point for eliciting LRL lexical items. One problem is that it inhibits the discovery of terms and entire semantic fields which exist in the field language but not in the contact language. In a sense, this is akin to an archaeologist using a metal detector—the technology will reveal iron objects, but ceramic artifacts will remain hidden. Another issue is the cultural imperialism of an approach that privileges the concepts and categories that are important to politically-, religiously-, and economically-dominant sociolinguistic groups. (For a discussion of these and other issues relating to contact language-based elicitation, see Calvet (1974), Raison-Jourde (1977), Fabian (1983), Geeraerts et al. (1994), Errington (2001), Anderson (2003), Enfield (2003), Bowern (2010), Mosel (2011), and Clynes (2012), among others.) Below, we describe how Kamusi is using a device we call "balloons," so that contributors can avoid these pitfalls and expedite the production of a dictionary with terms derived as much as possible from the local lexicon.

Our springboard into lexicographic elicitation is a prioritized list of English concepts that combines corpus results together with other term sets with particular foci, such as the Comparative African Word List[11] and the basic Special English vocabulary list of the Voice of America.[12] Our master list has some drawbacks, however (Benjamin, 2013). As a starting point for endangered languages, many highly-ranked terms are indisputably useful: *wind, bird, dry*. Other terms, however, do not exist in these languages, nor do their speakers have much need of referencing them: *baseball, subway, century*. The advantages of a cross-cutting, English-biased concept list certainly outweigh a haphazard butterfly-collection approach, but rigid adherence to such a list would foist irrelevant terms on a language documentation team while simultaneously causing them to miss many concepts of local importance.

To rectify the weaknesses of the English-centric approach, we have designed a system of "balloons" to prioritize terms more relevant to a particular language. The simplest balloons attach to the overall number of languages in which a particular concept has been submitted.[13] In addition, balloons provide lift in one language for terms deemed important by contributors in other languages related in some manner—for instance, balloons can attach based on geography, language tree proximity, shared cultural spheres, or other aspects of affinity. When contributors are fed a list of lexical items to elicit, balloons levitate certain terms to higher positions on the list, based on a variety of factors selected by the language moderator or individual contributor. A team working on a river language of Cameroon, for example, could set balloons to raise terms that have been treated by other Cameroonian

[8] Although the hard sciences (including computer science) value collaborative resource-building, the traditional role of the lone-wolf researcher persists as a powerful image among linguists (see Crippen and Robinson (2013) and also the rest of the ink spilled against this ideal in the journal *Language Documentation and Conservation*).

[9] An exception to the wordlist method is the Dictionary Development Process (DDP, http://www-01.sil.org/computing/ddp/) developed by Ron Moe at SIL, which steps away from wordlists to focus on semantic domains.

[10] Some exceptions are monolingual dictionaries of K'ichee' [Quiché] (Mayan; Guatemala) (Ajpacajá Túm, 2001) and Yiddish (Joffe & Marq, 1961-1980). The latter was abandoned after the publication of four volumes, all devoted to the letter *alef*.

[11] https://www.eva.mpg.de/lingua/tools-at-lingboard/pdf/Snider_silewp2006-005.pdf

[12] http://www.manythings.org/voa/words.htm

[13] Features are under development at the time of writing that are expected to be completed for showcasing at ComputEL in June 2014. However, software delivery schedules are notoriously slippery, particularly in a non-profit environment, so features such as balloons for related cultural characteristics may remain temporarily promissory.

languages, by related Bantu languages, or by other groups with a fishing economy.

Central to the mechanism of balloons is that contributors always have the option of skipping on the priority list terms that they do not know or do not deem important. For example, they could provide a term equivalent to English *plant* as a living organism but skip the homophonous *plant* referring to an industrial processing facility. The vegetal sense of *plant* would then float upward as more languages validate its importance, while the industrial sense would linger in the depths.

Languages do not enter Kamusi only when a contributor adds terms by working through a priority list; terms from other languages can become incorporated via the merging of existing lexical data sets. A team from one language could use balloons to find concepts that exist in related languages already in Kamusi, such as terms glossed with explanatory translations. For example, if the Bakwé data set is merged into Kamusi, *-srüpö* 'rolled up dead leaves or cloth, used to cushion the carrying of loads on the head or shoulder' would become available to Bambara and other languages of the region, and the concept would rise in importance as participants around Africa recognized the item and provided their equivalent term. Kamusi's system of balloons, then, ensures that the concept base available to a given language will include many items and semantic fields that would not otherwise come to light.

While development of the balloons system will still be a work in progress at the time of the workshop for which this paper is a contribution, and the task of choosing categories for balloons and the amount of lift they provide will involve ongoing adjustments in response to testing with field lexicographers, we nevertheless want to highlight it as a method for overcoming certain aspects of bias in the selection of vocabulary in a multilingual dictionary. In particular, it is proposed that this method will tend to float concepts that are most universal, while also encouraging the development of vocabularies that have special cultural relevance. We acknowledge, however, that this approach will not elicit concepts that are unique to a culture and are therefore not represented in either the English priority list or the lists that we incorporate from other sources; for a fine-grained investigation of local concepts, there can be no replacement for researcher-directed field study. Kamusi.org has other established tools for adding such indigenous terms, as many as lexicographers can catch in their nets.[14] One of these tools is our smartphone application, discussed in the following section.

4 The Smartphone App: Rapid Elicitation and Validation from the Crowd

The Kamusi Project began as an online bilingual dictionary between English and Swahili. The experience of building a resource for Swahili led to an expansion of the system to other languages, with the technical capacity to document the full lexical scope of any language. One of Kamusi's objectives is to move beyond lists of translations between languages by creating monolingual dictionaries with own-language written and/or spoken definitions for each lexical item. In conjunction with this, we have developed a range of tools designed to support online collection of sophisticated data.[15]

The Big Data ambitions of this project rely on numerous inputs of very small data, most of which must come directly from a language's speakers (including through fieldwork), rather than from digitized data sets.[16] For reasons discussed in Benjamin and Radetzky (2014), relying only on experts using Kamusi's advanced online tools will not be a successful strategy for the expedited production of lexicons for many LRLs. Instead, much data collection will occur through crowdsourcing, using validation procedures to

[14] The only caveat is that a translation link must be provided to English or another contact language in order for the new term to be understandable by people who do not speak the source language, which may necessitate the additional task of creating a new entry on the contact language side.

[15] There do exist online projects for baseline documentation, but not actual lexicography, of the vocabularies of endangered languages, such as LEGO (http://lego.linguistlist.org) and PanLex (http://panlex.org), with whom we work collaboratively. To date, these are involved in linking wordlists and are rarely involved in collecting new or rich data. In their disclaimer at http://lego.linguistlist.org/disclaimer, LEGO states, "[W]e are primarily interested in allowing existing lexical data to be included in our datanet and promoting standards to allow others to construct comparable datanets.... [W]e have converted a number of legacy resources..., but we have not engaged in collecting new lexical data...." Regarding PanLex, Kamholz et al. (2014) write: "[P]rojects that are designed to be panlingual tend to have specific and limited objectives... PanLex, with its objective of documenting only the lemmatic forms of lexemes, is no exception."

[16] Each entry is a container for dozens of fine-grained data elements, ranging from inflections to geo-tagged pronunciations to videos, multiplied by tens of thousands of terms in thousands of languages, with complex translational, semantic, and ontological interconnections for every concept.

ensure that the data is reliable prior to its being integrated into the system.

In order to collect millions of pieces of linguistic microdata, we have created a mobile smartphone application, the Kamusi Fidget Widget, that asks users specific, targeted questions about their language.[17] This app gathers data for integration into the project's online multilingual resources, and it is designed for participants who access networks through handheld devices—a major mode of connectivity for many oases of endangered languages.

The Fidget Widget pilots a new approach to eliciting terms and definitions that accelerates data collection for LRLs and advances talking dictionaries into monolingually-useful reference resources, while also using Kamusi's ballooning to address issues of cultural bias within lexicographic data collection. Version 1.0 of the app loops through a circumscribed set of question types, beginning with questions geared toward the collection of individual terms. First, we present terms and their definitions from the balloon-modified English priority list (e.g., *light* 'being low in weight') and ask, "What word would you use in [your language]?" (Figure 1).

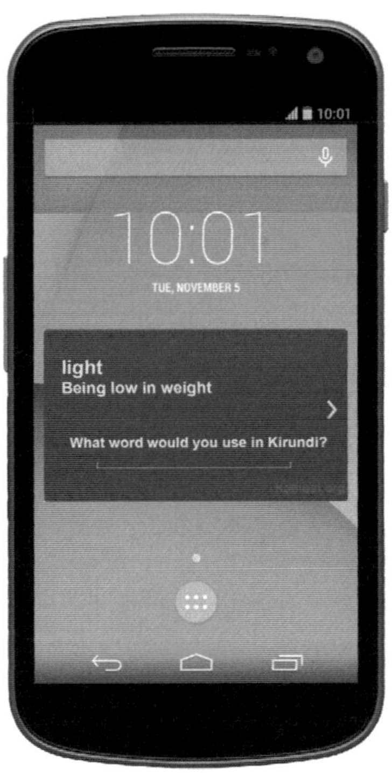

Figure 1. Initial request for translation.

[17] All programming features discussed in this section are anticipated to be functional by June 2014.

If the system is set to field-collection mode, the term will be accepted as is, without passing through crowd validation procedures; in this way, a field researcher can use the tool with one or more consultants to rapidly generate an initial term list. If the system is set to crowd mode, some participants will then be asked to rate the validity of terms submitted by other contributors (Figure 2).

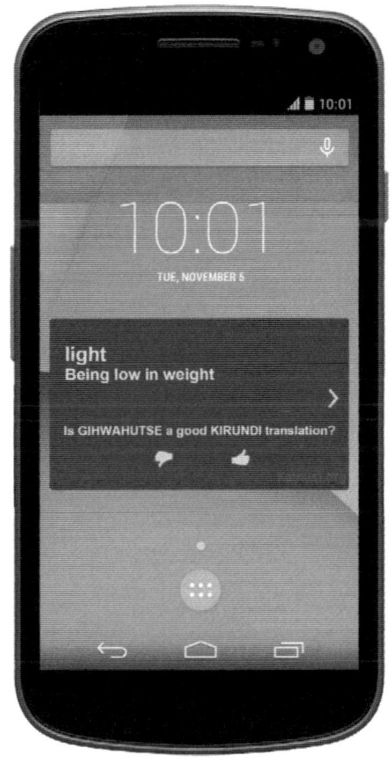

Figure 2. Rating of submitted term.

Once a translation has passed the validation threshold, further contributors will be asked to provide an own-language definition (Figure 3, localized to Kirundi) or to rate definitions submitted by others.

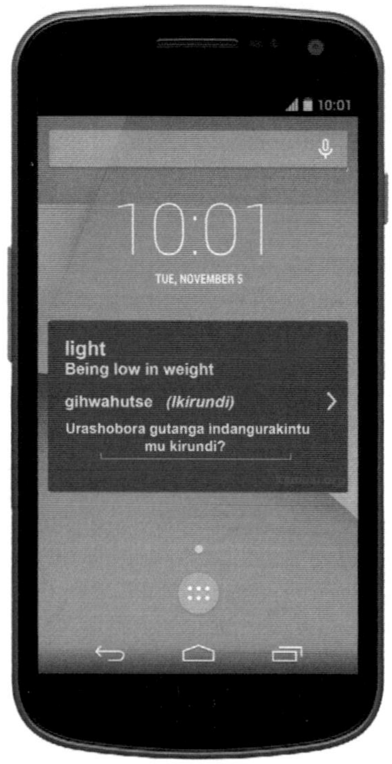

Figure 3. Localized request for own-language definition.

This system is well-tailored for researcher-driven fieldwork or written languages with numerous speakers who have persistent smartphone network access.

In many cases, the people involved in preserving a language speak it but do not write it. The app's 2.0 version is intended to extend the mobile technology to languages that are not commonly written or do not have a critical mass of participants, or both.[18] Although network access is currently necessary to use the system, an offline version is anticipated when synchronization and funding issues are resolved. The principal new feature of version 2.0 will be the collection of structured audio data, including pronunciations, own-language definitions, and possible retellings of the definitions in a contact language. This is discussed in the following section.

5 Monolingual Talking Dictionaries

Talking (or audio) dictionaries are an important technology for preserving the sounds of particular languages and dialects. Traditionally, for LRLs, the sound files simply appear in association with contact-language descriptions or translations of the terms.[19] Other language preservation projects endeavor to record stories as told by speakers of endangered languages, with italk library (italklibrary.com) providing an excellent example for Australia. The Fidget Widget's version 2 approach to talking dictionaries combines the idea of codifying the sounds of a language and the practice of preserving narratives about what a culture's concepts represent.

The new version will proceed as follows. After finishing version 1's set of questions focused on the gathering of lexical terms, the app will request that each term be pronounced. The smartphone will provide a visual countdown and a beep. This process will yield data on a par with most (if not all) talking dictionaries for endangered languages: as mentioned above, this consists of the written lexical item, the contact-language gloss, and a sound file of the term being pronounced in the indigenous language. The third step will ask the user to explain the concept in their language, with a timer to encourage brevity. It will be necessary to tinker with the timing system to find a sweet spot that allows answers of good quality, minimizes stress, and does not cut speakers off mid-stride but still discourages rambling. The fourth step will ask the user for a similarly pithy explanation of the concept in a contact language that they know. In the Australian case, where almost all participants also speak English, the contributors will also be asked to provide an English resume of their own-language definition, providing a gateway for people who are not already familiar with the language—including many of their own youth. With these simple procedures that integrate the basic capacities of smartphones with the data design of Kamusi, talking dictionaries will become valuable internal reference sources for their own communities, as well as repositories that enable

[18] The existence of some sort of functional Unicode-supported orthography and the involvement of at least one person who can bridge writing and orality are minimum conditions for participating in the system. Where orthographies are still in contention, Kamusi's internal structure is programmed to support multiple writing systems.

[19] See, for example, the Koasati Digital Dictionary (Koasati and English) (http://koasati.wm.edu); the Nganasan Multimedia Dictionary (Nganasan and Russian) (http://www.speech.nw.ru/Nganasan/); and the Talking Dictionary of Ainu (Ainu and Japanese, with further translations of the Japanese glosses into English) (http://lah.soas.ac.uk/projects/ainu/).

interested others to support the language's continued existence and revitalization.

Working with italk library, Kamusi's design of the app's version 2.0 is being developed for the Arrernte community as first users; a field trial with the initial one hundred terms from the Kamusi priority list is scheduled to be completed before late June 2014. The Arrernte are interested in preserving the specific terms of their language as well as the way they are expressed in context, and they also want to revitalize the tongue's use among its younger generations. The stories that italk library has been recording have proven enjoyable, but they do not provide a structure for accessing content in a way focused on reference or language learning. The mobile app will be used to term by term elicit pointillistic accounts and working definitions, keyed to each term's dictionary data container, that together paint a full picture of the language and culture. For example, Kamusi's English definition of the adjective *yellow* is 'being of the color of sunflowers or ripe lemons, between green and orange in the visible light spectrum'.[20] A contributor from the Australian group might say (in Arrernte or in English), "Yellow is, like, it's the color that we see, it's the color of the sun when it's going down, before it turns orange like a cooling fire," and such an unedited vignette would serve as the talking definition.

In addition to own-language definitions, recorded English definitions will make it possible to transcribe the meanings of each term with the aid of a wider crowd (who do not necessarily speak the endangered language); as text, transcriptions can be indexed and searched to provide access to the dictionary data through technological tools. Transcription of the own-language definitions is not planned in the near term, but it remains a desirable possibility with time and resources, especially as a community activity. In the first iteration, terms will be elicited via the mobile app from the English list (since little "ballooning" will be in effect for the first language from the Australian continent to enter the Kamusi system), but it will also be possible to upload native concepts to the system and then use the app for gathering audio.

Monolingual dictionaries have not generally been conceived of as practical for endangered languages, and sophisticated multilingual dictionaries have long been deemed impossible (Zgusta, 1971: 210; Haensch, 1991; Landau, 2001: 11). The tools and methods discussed in this article, however, make it possible to document endangered languages effectively, both by (a) generating term lists rapidly and in association with concepts from related languages, and (b) incorporating spoken definitions that encapsulate the essence of each idea. As mentioned above, the result will be a useful resource for the community, something that can be understood by the segment that does not read the contact language and used by younger generations interested in revitalization. Additionally, the system produces bridges to many other languages, allowing local knowledge to endure beyond the boundaries of shrinking linguistic communities.

6 New Directions

Kamusi.org has a long task list, with a goal of providing a full range of lexical resources for both people and machines. Some of these objectives, such as detection of malicious users and validation procedures for crowdsourced data, are informatics challenges. Many other objectives are technical, and will apply across all languages—enhancements to the data model for bridging concepts that are expressed with different parts of speech in different languages (e.g., where colors act as verbs), and a host of improvements to the editing system based on lessons learned during the multilingual pilot phase. A few are noteworthy in this concluding section because of their specific interest to endangered languages.

Determining the boundary between a language and a dialect is frequently problematic. In the case of two tongues (Kinyarwanda and Kirundi) that are often considered dialects separated by a political border, Kamusi discovered in the process of creating separate dictionaries that there are substantial differences between the two which had not previously been documented. However, it would be impractical to create full dictionaries of every dialect of a language when a large portion of their vocabularies are shared. We will therefore produce a system to geo-tag entries based on where a term is known to be in use. As the map becomes populated with zones of use, it will be possible to visualize where one dialect fades into the next, and where one language territory ends and the next begins. Similarly, programming is planned for geo-tagging the specific location where a participating speaker in a talking dictionary acquired their language (in-

[20] http://kamusi.org/define?headword=yellow&to_language=366.

cluding people contributing pronunciations for well-resourced languages). This will build an audio portrait of dialect, sociolinguistic, gender, and other variation. These mapping features, combined with expanded data collection, will enhance the possibilities for linguists to study language contact, spread, and historical change. Other improvements and new features, such as an app to upload photos of cultural items directly to a dictionary entry, or the expansion of audio features to the existing open-ended cultural notes field, will allow contributors to flesh out dictionary entries with relevant ethnographic information that contextualizes a language within the lives of the people who speak it.

In terms of innovations to the system itself, we see as a priority the development of offline input systems, both for contributors who want to use an interface like the one at www.kamusi.org, as well as those who wish to use the smartphone app when not connected to the internet. In fact, we did release offline software for the bilingual dictionary between English and Swahili, but the multilingual model added so many complexities that the program must be completely rewritten. Synchronization and the management of large data sets on small devices are major technical challenges, which can only be tackled with solid funding. Similarly, money permitting, we aim to code the system architecture to include a privacy system for linguistic groups who wish to document but also restrict access to certain lexical items (e.g., taboo words) or even their entire language. In addition, as we discussed in Benjamin and Radetzky (2014), we are committed to incorporating gamification, or games with a purpose, into both mobile and web platforms (Castellote et al., 2013; Paraschakis, 2013; Hamari et al., 2014). This will propel the accumulation of data and its validation by the crowd, pushing the project along the path toward obtaining as much open data for as many languages as possible.

Market forces will never support the creation of widely-available print dictionaries for most LRLs, and scholarly interest and available funding for online dictionaries will remain hit-or-miss, even as languages fade away. The tools presented in this paper are offered as methods for rapidly and reliably developing lexicographic resources for the world's endangered languages.

References

Pedro Florentino Ajpacajá Túm. 2001. *K'ichee' Choltziij.* Cholsamaj, Ciudad Guatemala, Guatemala.

Earl Anderson. 2003. *Folk-Taxonomies in Early English.* Fairleigh Dickinson University Press, Madison, New Jersey.

Martin Benjamin. 2013. http://kamusi.org/priority-list

Martin Benjamin and Paula Radetzky. 2014. Multilingual Lexicography with a Focus on Less-Resourced Languages: Data Mining, Expert Input, Crowdsourcing, and Gamification. In *Proceedings of the International Conference on Language Resources (LREC '14),* Reykjavik.

Claire Bowern. 2010. Fieldwork in contact situations. In Raymond Hickey, editor, *The Handbook of Language Contact.* Wiley-Blackwell, London, pages 340-357.

Louis-Jean Calvet. 1974. *Linguistique et Colonialisme: Petit Traité de Glottophagie.* Payot, Paris.

Jesús Castellote, Joaquín Huerta, Javier Pescador, and Michael Brown. 2013. Towns conquer: A gamified application to collect geographical names (vernacular names/toponyms). In *Proceedings of the 15th AGILE International Conference on Geographic Information Science,* Leuven. http://www.agile-online.org/index.php/conference/proceedings/proceedings-2013.

Adrian Clynes. 2012. Dominant language transfer in minority language documentation projects: Some examples from Brunei. *Language Documentation and Conservation,* 6:253-267.

James Crippen and Laura Robinson. 2013. In defense of the lone wolf: Collaboration in language documentation. *Language Documentation and Conservation,* 7:123-135.

Nick Enfield. 2003. *Linguistic Epidemiology: Semantics and Grammar of Language Contact in Mainland Southeast Asia.* RoutledgeCurzon, Oxon, UK.

Joseph Errington. 2001. Colonial linguistics. *Annual Review of Anthropology,* 30:19-39.

Dirk Geeraerts et al. 1994. *The Structure of Lexical Variation: Meaning, Naming, and Context.* Mouton de Gruyter, Berlin.

Johanne Fabian. 1983. Missions and the colonization of African languages: Developments in the former Belgian Congo. *Canadian Journal of African Studies/La Revue Canadienne des Études Africaines,* 17:165-187.

Günther Haensch. 1991. Die Mehrsprachigen Wörterbücher und ihre Probleme. In Franz Joseph Hausmann et al., editors, *Wörterbücher: Ein internationales Handbuch zur Lexikographie,* vol. 3. Walter de Gruyter, Berlin, pages 2909-2937.

Juho Hamari, Jonna Koivisto, and Harri Sarsa. 2014. Does gamification work? – A literature review of empirical studies on gamification. In *Proceedings of the 47th Annual Hawaii International Confer-*

ence on System Sciences, pages 3025-3034, Waikoloa.

Juda Joffe and Judl Marq, eds. 1961, 1966, 1971, 1980. *Groyser Verterbukh fun der Yidisher Shprakh,* vols. 1-4. Yiddish Dictionary Committee, New York.

David Kamholz, Jonathan Pool, and Susan Colowick. 2014. PanLex: Building a resource for panlingual lexical translation. In *Proceedings of the International Conference on Language Resources (LREC '14),* Reykjavik.

Sidney Landau. 2001. *Dictionaries: The Art and Craft of Lexicography,* 2nd ed. Cambridge University Press, Cambridge.

Ulrike Mosel. 2011. Lexicography in endangered language communities. In Peter Austin and Julia Sallabank, editors, *The Cambridge Handbook of Endangered Languages.* Cambridge University Press, Cambridge, pages 337-353.

Dimitris Paraschakis. 2013. Crowdsourcing cultural heritage metadata through social media gaming. Master's thesis, Malmo University.

Françoise Raison-Jourde. 1977. L'échange inégal de la langue: La pénétration des techniques linguistiques dans une civilisation de l'oral (Imerina, début du XIXe siècle). *Annales: Économies, Sociétés, Civilisations,* 32:639-669.

Ladislav Zgusta. 1971. *Manual of Lexicography.* Mouton, The Hague.

LingSync & the Online Linguistic Database: New models for the collection and management of data for language communities, linguists and language learners

Joel Dunham
University of British Columbia,
Department of Linguistics
jrwdunham@gmail.com

Gina Cook
iLanguage Lab
Montréal
gina.c.cook@gmail.com

Joshua Horner
Amilia
Montréal
josh.horner@gmail.com

Abstract

LingSync and the Online Linguistic Database (OLD) are new models for the collection and management of data in endangered language settings. The LingSync and OLD projects seek to close a feedback loop between field linguists, language communities, software developers, and computational linguists by creating web services and user interfaces (UIs) which facilitate collaborative and inclusive language documentation. This paper presents the architectures of these tools and the resources generated thus far. We also briefly discuss some of the features of the systems which are particularly helpful to endangered languages fieldwork and which should also be of interest to computational linguists, these being a service that automates the identification of utterances within audio/video, another that automates the alignment of audio recordings and transcriptions, and a number of services that automate the morphological parsing task. The paper discusses the requirements of software used for endangered language documentation, and presents novel data which demonstrates that users are actively seeking alternatives despite existing software.

1 Introduction

In this paper we argue that the LingSync/OLD project is a sustainable new model for data management which facilitates a feedback loop between fieldworkers, language communities, computational linguists, and software developers, thereby improving the effectiveness of language documentation efforts for low-resource language communities. In §2.1 we present five requirements for endangered languages fieldwork software which are currently not met by existing tools, as discussed in §2.2. Architectural considerations[1] under LingSync and the OLD which address these requirements are briefly outlined in §3. The ability of LingSync/OLD to integrate with existing software libraries commonly used in language documentation projects is demonstrated in §5. Finally, §6 demonstrates how the LingSync/OLD project is already seeing some closure of the feedback loop both in creating language learning apps for heritage speakers and in training Kartuli speakers to build speech recognition systems built on LingSync/OLD data.

2 Endangered languages fieldwork

Endangered languages are valuable culturally and scientifically, to their communities of origin (Ironstrack, 2012) and to humanity as a whole (Harrison, 2007). Efforts must be made to document these languages while there is still time (Good, 2012a; Thieberger, 2012). In cases where there are no longer any native speakers, a community may embark upon a language reclamation project that is wholly dependent upon the the products of past language documentation efforts (Leonard, 2012; Costa, 2012). Alongside such documentation and revitalization/reclamation projects is research-driven linguistic fieldwork. These diversely motivated yet interconnected strands within endangered languages fieldwork conspire to produce a particular set of requirements for effective software in this domain.

2.1 Software requirements

The following five requirements are essential, we claim, to effective language documentation soft-

[1] For further discussion of actual user interaction, screenshots and how LingSync/OLD data can be exported/published in existing online linguistics repositories such as EOPAS http://www.eopas.org/ and OLAC http://www.language-archives.org/ see Cathcart et al. (2012).

Proceedings of the 2014 Workshop on the Use of Computational Methods in the Study of Endangered Languages, pages 24–33,
Baltimore, Maryland, USA, 26 June 2014.

ware: *integration of primary data*, *curation of data*, *inclusion of stakeholders*, *openable data*, and *user productivity*.

Requirement 1 *Integration of primary data*

While language reclamation projects founded solely on textual data can achieve some degree of success (Ironstrack, 2012), primary audio/video data *in the form of engaging content* is crucial to fostering native-like proficiency. Primary audio has formed part of language documentation efforts since the days of phonographs, yet only rarely have such audio products been made accessible. Securely and efficiently supporting the integration of primary audio/video data with text artifacts (e.g., dictionaries, grammars, collections of narratives) is part of the requirements of any modern language documentation effort (Schroeter and Thieberger, 2006; Good, 2012b).[2]

Requirement 2 *Curation of data*

While most language documentation literature places emphasis on the creation of publishable artifacts, our experience has shown that a significant percentage of language documentation hours are actually dedicated to the curation and filtering of the data in preparation for publication.[3] Even "a funding body like the ELDP cannot get all of its grantees [only 110 out of 216] to deposit in an archive in a timely fashion (or at all)" (Thieberger, 2012). We argue that facilitating the collaborative curation of data is, in fact, a core requirement of any data management or content management software, one which is largely overlooked by existing software (cf. §2.2).

Requirement 3 *Inclusion of stakeholders*

A sustainable language documentation effort involves crucially the creation of a positive feedback loop where the outputs of certain activities fuel the advancement of others. However, realizing this feedback loop requires tools that facilitate the inclusion of the various stakeholders involved in the process of language documentation *while* a project is underway, not *post hoc* when the data is "polished," which in 50% of projects never happens (Thieberger, 2012). This inclusivity requirement means that data and data processes must be available in formats that are usable to both humans—i.e., via graphical user interfaces (GUIs)—and machines—i.e., via software libraries and application programming interfaces (APIs).

Requirement 4 *Openable data*

One of the unique challenges associated with endangered languages fieldwork is the possibility that speakers or language communities may require that all or aspects of the raw data be kept confidential for a certain period of time.[4] Labs looking to reuse the data collected by field teams may, in particular, be unaware of the post-colonial context in which many fieldwork situations are embedded.

In the field it often happens that a speaker will speak quite candidly or receive a phone call during a recorded elicitation session and may want to restrict access to all or parts of that recording for personal reasons.[5] In some cases the living speakers of the language are so few that even anonymizing the data does not conceal the identity of the speaker from other speakers in the community. It also happens that particular stories or descriptions of rituals and cultural practices may need to be restricted to just the language community or even to sub-groups within the community.[6]

In order to provide access to all team members and stakeholders (including stakeholders who are distrustful of the project) language documentation software must support a non-trivial permissions system while also facilitating transparency

[2]For a more detailed discussion of the technical limitations which are no longer blocking the implementation of these requirements see Cathcart et al. (2012).

[3]Such artifacts might include engaging content to be reused in revitalization efforts, or citable/traceable data sets used to support research claims.

[4]Outside of language documentation contexts there are numerous valid reasons for facilitating data privacy. As with social websites (Facebook, YouTube), user data is generally considered private and not accessible to data scientists. Many content curation sites (Google Docs, WordPress) allow for content that is private indefinitely or during a pre-publication stage.

[5]Of course, as one reviewer points out, basing claims on private data runs contrary to a core tenet of the scientific method, namely that claims must be able to be assessed with transparent access to the methods and data used to support them. However, in these contexts field linguists generally protect the privacy of their language consultants by eliciting novel sentences which have similar grammatical features for publication, rather than using the original narrative. In the contexts of open data, such highly personal sections of transcripts must be "blacked out" so that the majority of the data can be made open.

[6]It is highly preferable for language communities to produce their own content using YouTube and other content sites, permitting the community to manage censorship of sensitive topics and personal narratives while creating more public data.

and encouraging open collaboration. Even language documentation projects using ad hoc content creation solutions (discussed in §2.2) cannot be fully inclusive for fear that when speakers of different dialects disagree they will "correct" each other's data if neither social pressure nor the permissions system prevents it. In fact, disagreements about data judgments remain an untapped indirect source of grammaticality information for linguistics researchers as there are no language documentation systems which permit inclusion of all stakeholders via traceable user activity, non-trivial permissions systems, and confidentiality of attributes on data. While not all teams will resort to data encryption or private data, implementing these features permits more stakeholders to have direct conditional access to data and removes barriers to adoption by language communities who may be initially distrustful of language documentation projects.

Requirement 5 *User productivity*

Users are accustomed to professionally crafted software built by teams of hundreds of software engineers, software designers, and user experience experts (e.g., Facebook, Gmail, Google Docs, YouTube, Evernote, Dropbox). They can read their email on all devices, download and sync photos and videos automatically, and have offline and mobile data there seamlessly when they need it. Yet research software is often built by computer science students with no experience in software engineering and human computer interaction. Overwhelmingly, users attribute their use of generic data curation software such as Microsoft Excel or Google Spreadsheets, rather than software specifically designed for language documentation, to the productivity of the user experience itself (Cathcart et al., 2012). In some cases users are so productive using Google Spreadsheets that the actual data entry of a project can be completed before an existing language documentation tool can be evaluated and/or customized (Troy and Strack, 2014).

2.2 Existing software

Fieldwork teams typically have the choice between using general-purpose content curation software (Google Spreadsheets, Evernote, Dropbox, MediaWikis, WordPress, etc.), creating/customizing their own tools, or using specialized field linguistics desktop applications such as those developed by SIL International: FieldWorks Language Explorer (FLEx),[7] Toolbox/Shoebox,[8] and/or WeSay.[9]

The SIL tools[10] require a not inconsiderable level of training in order to be used productively. However, many research teams are unable to impose lengthy training upon all team members and require tools that are easy to learn and re-learn months or years later when they return to their data. In addition, the SIL tools are tailored towards the collection of texts and the production of dictionaries and descriptive grammars based on such. However, this focus does not always accord with the needs of research-oriented fieldworkers, many of whom deal primarily in sentences elicited in isolation and grammaticality judgments.

Existing language documentation software tools, with the exception of WeSay (a collaborative dictionary tool), have only ad hoc support for collaboration (Req. 4) and inclusive language documentation (Req. 3) while the project is active, generally using a shared network drive or email with no concurrent editing. FLEx and many private tools in the language technology industry are able to support concurrent editing in most data entry situations via a Mercurial/SVN/CVS/Git repository (SIL International, 2013). However, as no permissions are built into Mercurial/SVN/CVS/Git, users with read only access must use a manual review process to offer their modifications to the project. The FLEx Send/Receive collaboration module also limits the integration of audio/video primary data; it unfortunately does not support formats used by field linguists including .ogg, .avi, .mp4, and .mov, and limits the maximum file size to 1MB (SIL International, 2013), despite the fact that most elicitation sessions or long utterances can range between 10MB and 200MB. While these scenarios may seem like rare edge cases, they can, in fact, result in teams opting not to use software designed for language documentation.

Over the past decade or so, a number of language-specific collaborative websites have arisen, examples of which are the Yurok Documentation Project (Garrett et al., 2001), the Washo

[7] http://fieldworks.sil.org/flex

[8] Toolbox is the community-supported continuation of Shoebox http://www-01.sil.org/computing/toolbox/information.htm

[9] http://www.sil.org/resources/software_fonts/wesay

[10] For reviews of FLEx and Toolbox, see Butler and van Volkinburg (2007), Rogers (2010), and Robinson et al. (2007).

Project (Yu et al., 2005; Cihlar, 2008), the Washo Mobile Lexicon (Yu et al., 2008), Karuk Dictionary and Texts (Garrett et al., 2009), and the Ilaatawaakani project (Troy and Strack, 2014). More recently, collaborative tools have arisen that, like FLEx and Toolbox, are not specific to any one language, but unlike FLEx and Toolbox, run on all devices in a web browser. In this family belong TypeCraft (Beermann and Mihaylov, 2012), the OLD (Dunham, 2014), and LingSync (Cathcart et al., 2012).

TypeCraft uses a MediaWiki UI combined with additional functionality written in Java for managing collaboration permissions and sharing. TypeCraft falls into the category of field databases designed by corpus linguists. As such it imposes upon users closed lists of categories for languages and parts of speech (Farrar, 2010), an imposition which is unacceptable to field linguists who are dealing with evolving fine-grained analyses of data categories. In addition, TypeCraft is online only, a limitation which, as Farrar (2010) correctly points out, is "not inconsiderable, especially for fieldworkers who may not have Internet access."

None of the software projects discussed in this section meet the software requirements for endangered languages fieldwork outlined in §2.1. We argue that this mismatch in requirements is nontrivial and is the reason why so much fragmentation and introduction of novel language documentation tools and software has occurred.[11]

3 New models for data collection and management

3.1 LingSync

LingSync is composed of existing and novel open source software modules (rich client-side web components and task-specific web services) which allow all stakeholders of a language documentation effort to collaboratively create corpora of primary analyzed and unanalyzed language data (Cathcart et al., 2012).

To meet the user productivity requirement (Req. 5), LingSync uses a quasi-blackboard system architecture similar to Android;[12] that is, modules can be registered to perform certain tasks, and users can discover and choose between registered modules. Similar to Praat,[13] all events in the system provide an audit trail which can be used by users,[14] but also serve as data for automated reasoning engines, should labs choose to make use of the audit data to assist in data cleaning and data quality assurance.

Based on the LingSync team's collective prior experience as field linguists, research assistants, professional lexicographers, and linguists in the language technologies industry, we hypothesize that perhaps 50% of data curation/cleaning tasks are monotonous, repetitive and consistent and thus are candidates for data manipulation best done by machines or crowdsourcing rather than by one individual human for extended periods of time. The automation of tasks in field linguistic research is rarely done, and for good reason. Unlike corpus linguistics, field linguistics seeks fine-grained analysis of novel data on under-documented languages, and data curators must be sensitive to the slightest "off" feeling of analysis which could easily be flattened by over-generalizing cleaning scripts. Automated modifications must be fully traceable so as to detect side effects of cleaning long after it has occurred. They must also be easily undoable so as not to introduce consistency or systematicity which in fact does not exist in the data.

The potential time-saving features of LingSync's system design will not bear usable data without the explicit and overarching goal of providing a user-friendly experience for both expert and novice users with differing data description vocabularies and interests (Troy and Strack, 2014). Notable user-facing features include complete UI customization, powerful searches and mapping over data sets, encryption at a field level, flexible enforcement of data consistency, social collaborative software features, an inclusive permissions system, pluggable semi-automatic glossers, numerous task-oriented web services which wrap existing libraries and scripts for audio, video, image and text analysis, two native Android GUIs

[11] We would like to point out that there are numerous other projects that have started and failed in the past 10 years which we have not had space to mention. The only stable long-term fieldwork software projects have been those which have been undertaken by the Summer Institute of Linguistics (SIL). The SIL development team is also on GitHub (https://github.com/sillsdev), a social tool for open source project management; this will likely yield technical crossover with research teams and more use of HTML5 to facilitate meeting the requirements delineated in §2.1 in future SIL software.

[12] http://developer.android.com

[13] http://praat.org

[14] In the case of Praat users are able to generate automation scripts by clicking to create a repeatable sequence of events.

which function offline (Learn X and the Elicitation Session Recorder), and five browser-based GUIs (the Prototype, Spreadsheet, Activity Feeds, Corpus Pages, Lexicon Browser), one of which functions offline and provides flexible import and export functionality. Nearly all logic is performed on the client-side which permits users to go offline and consume low bandwidth when there is limited connectivity through 3G or dial-up connections. For up-to-date examples of GUI interaction, readers are encouraged to search for LingSync on YouTube. As of April 2014 there are over 40 videos made by users demonstrating diverse features in the systems.

3.2 OLD

The OLD is software for creating web services that facilitate collaborative linguistic fieldwork. A language-specific OLD web service exposes a consistent API,[15] meaning that it can easily be used as the backend to multiple user-facing applications or as a component in a larger suite of tools. An OLD web service and the current OLD GUI together provide a number of features that respond to the requirements given in §2.1.

A language-specific OLD application allows for multiple contributors to simultaneously create, modify, browse, and search language data. This data consists of linguistic forms (i.e., morphemes, words, or phrases) that can be used to build corpora and texts. The OLD supports the integration of primary audio/video data by allowing for individual forms to be associated to any number of audio or video files (or even to subintervals of such files) and by generating representations wherein textual and audio/video data are simultaneously accessible. Data is presented in interlinear glossed text (IGT) format and individual forms, collections of forms, and texts can be exported as (Xe)LaTeX, tab-separated values (TSV), or plain text. The system provides powerful search functionality including filters over system-generated serializations of morphological analyses and, via integration with TGrep2,[16] the matching of structural patterns within treebank corpora.

Features promoting consistency include configurable orthography converters, inventory-based input validation, and the provision of visual feedback on the extent to which user-generated morphological analyses match existing lexical entries in the database. That last feature means that when a user creates a morphologically complex entry, the IGT representation indicates, via colour-coded internal links, whether the morpheme shapes and glosses match current lexical entries. It has proved to be quite useful in helping groups of fieldworkers to generate consistent morphological analyses.

3.3 LingSync/OLD

While LingSync and the OLD arose independently and consequently use different technology stacks, the teams behind the tools have largely complementary interests and are collaborating on future developments in order to combine strengths and reduce fragmentation of efforts. In the coming years, if resources permit, we hope to bring OLD's glossing UIs, logic for connecting documents to utterances as well as structural search and morphological parsing (§5.2) into the LingSync plugin architecture, with OLD UIs being used by field linguists and LingSync UIs being used by language community members and computational linguists. When referring collectively to both tools, we will henceforth use the term LingSync/OLD.

4 User adoption

In the year and a half LingSync's launch, over 300 unique users have registered; this despite the availability of a sample user (username: LingLlama, password: phoneme). We argue this demonstrates a general interest in novel, even unheard-of, language documentation software, despite the existing solutions discussed in §2.2.

Table 1 provides an overview of the corpora being edited using the system. Currently there are about 13,400 active records, 38 active users, 15 active corpora, and 1GB of primary audio/image/text data. We expect that the low ratio of active vs. registered users (12%) is due to both the multitask nature of language documentation projects and early launch of LingSync while it was still in the alpha testing and the requirements gathering phase. There are currently no published mea-

[15] The OLD API is RESTful and JavaScript Object Notation (JSON) is used as the medium of exchange throughout. This means that OLD resources (e.g., linguistic data points such as sentences) can be created, retrieved, updated, deleted, and searched using standard combinations of Hypertext Transfer Protocol (HTTP) methods and uniform resource locator (URL) patterns. The system is written in Python using the Pylons web framework (http://www.pylonsproject.org/projects/pylons-framework/about) and the relational database software MySQL.

[16] http://tedlab.mit.edu/~dr/Tgrep2/.

sures of user attrition in language documentation projects, however social websites/mobile apps developers report 30% retention rate is acceptable.[17] We will know more about rates for different stakeholders in language documentation projects as the retention rate changes over time in correlation to the release of new modules.

	Active	Investigating	In-active	Total
Public Corpora	2	1	2	5
Private Corpora	15	37	321	373
Users	38	43	220	301
Documents	13,408	2,763	4,541	23,487
Disk Size	1GB	.9GB	5.3GB	7.2GB

Table 1: Data in LingSync corpora (Feb 14, 2014). Active corpora: >300 activities; Investigating corpora: 300-10 activities; Active users: >100 activities; Investigating users: 100-10 activities.

There are currently nine language-specific OLD applications in use. In total, there are about 19,000 records (primarily sentences), 300 texts, and 20 GB of audio files. There are 180 registered users across all applications, of which 98 have entered and 87 have elicited at least one record. The applications for Blackfoot, Nata, Gitksan, Okanagan, and Tlingit are seeing the most use. The exact figures are summarized in Table 2.[18]

language	*forms*	texts	audio	GB	speakers
Blackfoot (*bla*)	8,847	171	2,057	3.8	3,350
Nata (*ntk*)	3,219	32	0	0	36,000
Gitksan (*git*)	2,174	6	36	3.5	930
Okanagan (*oka*)	1,798	39	87	0.3	770
Tlingit (*tli*)	1,521	32	107	12	630
Plains Cree (*crk*)	686	10	0	0	260
Ktunaxa (*kut*)	467	33	112	0.2	106
Coeur d'Alene (*crd*)	377	0	199	0.0	2
Kwak'wala (*kwk*)	98	1	1	0.0	585
TOTAL	19,187	324	2,599	19.8	

Table 2: Data in OLD applications (Feb 14, 2014)

The data in Table 1 and Table 2 indicate that the systems are in fact being used by language documentation teams.

[17]There are no official published statistics; however, in answers on StackOverflow developers report averages to be 30%, cf. http://stackoverflow.com/questions/6969191/what-is-a-good-active-installs-rate-for-a-free-android-app.

[18]Note that the values in the speakers column are taken from Ethnologue (http://www.ethnologue.com) and are provided only to give a rough indication of the speaker populations of the languages. Also, the three-character codes in the first column are the ISO 639-3 (http://www-01.sil.org/iso639-3) identifiers of the languages.

5 Reusing existing tools and libraries

Both the LingSync and the OLD projects were founded with the goal of making it easier to integrate existing software libraries to better automate data curation (Req. 2) and improve data quality (Req. 4) while doing fieldwork. There have been numerous plugins in both systems to this end; however in this paper we will discuss only those which may be of most interest to computational linguists working on low-resource languages: morphological parsers in §5.1, §5.2 and §5.3 (precursors for Information Retrieval and Machine Translation tasks) and phone-level alignment of audio and text in §5.4 (a precursor for acoustic model training in Speech Recognition systems).

5.1 Existing morphological parsers

For one LingSync team working on Inuktitut, a web service was written which wraps an existing morphological analyzer for Inuktitut built in Java (Farley, 2012). This source code can be used to wrap other existing language-specific morphological analyzers.[19]

5.2 Novel morphological parsers

An OLD web service provides functionality that allows users to create any number of morphological parsers. The phonological mappings of these parsers are declared explicitly, using a formalism—context-sensitive (CS) phonological rewrite rules (Chomsky and Halle, 1968)—that is well understood by linguists. The lexicon, morphotactic rules, and parse candidate disambiguator components are automatically induced from corpora specified by the user. The fact that this implementation requires a good deal of explicit specification by the user should not be considered a demerit. By granting linguist fieldworkers control over the specification of phonological, lexical, and morphotactic generalizations, the parser functionality allows for the automatic testing of these generalizations against large data sets. This assists in the discovery of counterexamples to generalizations, thereby expediting the improvement of models and advancing linguistic research. The OLD morphological parser implementation can, of course, co-exist with and complement less

[19]All modules discussed in this paper are available by searching the GitHub organization page https://github.com/opensourcefieldlinguistics

expert-dependent Machine Learning approaches to creating morphological parsers.

The core component of an OLD morphological parser is a morphophonology that is modelled as a finite-state transducer (FST)[20] and which maps transcriptions to morphological analyses, i.e., morpheme segmentations, glosses, and categories. The morphophonology FST is the composition of a phonology FST that is created explicitly by the user (using CS phonological rewrite rules) and a morphology (i.e., lexicon and morphotactic rules) that is induced from corpora constructed by the user, cf. Beesley and Karttunen (2003) and Hulden (2012). When the morphophonology returns multiple parse candidates, the system employs an N-gram language model (LM)[21] (estimated from a corpus specified by the parser's creator) to determine the most probable parse.

Preliminary tests of the OLD morphological parser implementation have been performed using data from the Blackfoot OLD[22] and the standard grammar (Frantz, 1991) and dictionary (Frantz and Russell, 1995) of the language. An initial parser implemented the phonology specified in Frantz (1991) and defined a morphology with lexical items extracted from Frantz and Russell (1995) and morphotactic rules induced from words analyzed by contributors to the system. Analysis of the performance of this parser (f-score: 0.21) confirms what researchers (Weber, 2013) have already observed, namely that the phonological and morphological generalizations of Frantz (1991) cannot account for the location of morphologically conditioned prominence (i.e., pitch accent) in Blackfoot words.

An improved Blackfoot parser, i.e., one which can predict prominence location based on the generalizations of Weber (2013), is currently under development. The phonology of this parser makes use of a novel and useful feature, viz. the ability to specify phonological transformations that are aware of categorial context. This allows the phonology to capture the distinct nominal and verbal prominence location generalizations of Blackfoot.

Since OLD morphological parsers can be created and parses retrieved entirely by issuing RESTful requests, other applications can easily make use of them. In addition, OLD morphological parser objects can be exported as .zip archives that contain all of the requisite binaries (i.e., compiled foma and MITLM files) and a Python module and executable which together allow for the parser to be used locally via the command line or from within a Python program.

5.3 Semi-supervised morphological parsers

LingSync's glosser uses a MapReduce function which efficiently indexes and transforms data to create a current "mental lexicon" of the corpus. The mental lexicon is modelled as a connected graph of morphemes, including precedence relations which are used to seed finite-state automata (Cook, 2009)[23] which represent morphological templates in the corpus. In this way the glosser is "trained" on the user's existing segmentation and glossing, and automatically "learns" as the user adds more data and the glossing/segmentation evolves over the course of data collection and analysis. LingSync has a lexicon browser component which permits users to browse the corpus via learned relations between morphemes, clean the data for consistency, enter novel data, and explicitly document generalizations on lexical nodes which might not be immediately evident in the primary data. Unlike FLEx (Black and Simons, 2006), the OLD, and WeSay, LingSync does not provide a way to explicit add rules/relations or morphemes which are not gleaned from the data. To add a morpheme or a relation users must add an example sentence to the corpus. This grounding of morphemes and rules/relations provides arguably better learning tools as collocation dictionaries and lexicon creators are always able to provide headwords and grammatical rules in context and researchers working on relations between morphemes are able to extract lists of relevant data.

5.4 Audio-transcription alignment

There are currently three audio web services. The first executes Sphinx speech recognition routines for languages with known language models. The second, illustrated in Figure 2a, uses

[20] FSTs are constructed using the open source finite-state compiler and C library foma: http://code.google.com/p/foma

[21] OLD N-gram LMs are estimated using MITLM: https://code.google.com/p/mitlm/.

[22] http://bla.onlinelinguisticdatabase.org/

[23] One reviewer requests more details which have not yet been published: in the interim please consult the code which is entirely open source and commented: https://github.com/OpenSourceFieldlinguistics/FieldDBGlosser

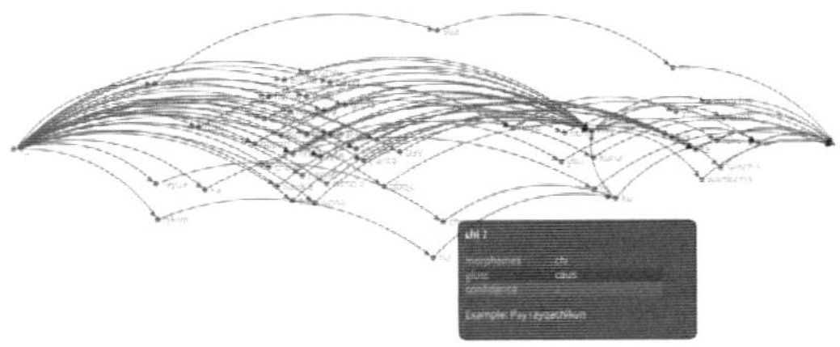

Figure 1: Screenshot of the Lexicon Browser, a web widget which lets users browse relations between morphemes in their corpus, clean and add declarative knowledge not found in the lexicon training process.

the Prosodylab-Aligner[24] tool (developed at the McGill Prosody Lab) to significantly automate the association of transcriptions to relevant audio clips and therefore help to provide a class of data that will prove valuable in applications such as talking dictionaries and language learning tools. The third, illustrated in Figure 2b, is a service that wraps FFmpeg[25] and Praat[26] to convert any video or audio format to .mp3 and automatically generate syllable timings and suggested utterance boundaries (De Jong and Wempe, 2009) for automatic chunking of data.

```
a) $ curl --cookie my-cookies.txt\
   --request POST\
   -F files[]=@omi_imitaa.mov\
   -F files[]=@omi_imitaa.lab\
   https://api.lingsync.org/v2/corpora/public-curldemo/
   utterances?process=align

b) $ curl --cookie my-cookies.txt\
   --request POST\
   -F files[]=@omi_imitaa.mov\
   https://api.lingsync.org/v2/corpora/public-curldemo/
   utterances?process=detect

c) $ curl --cookie my-cookies.txt\
   --request GET\
   https://api.lingsync.org/v2/corpora/public-curldemo/
   files/omi_imitaa.mp3

d) $ curl --cookie my-cookies.txt\
   --request GET\
   https://api.lingsync.org/v2/corpora/public-curldemo/
   files/omi_imitaa.TextGrid
```

Figure 2: Audio/video and text alignment via Prosodylab-Aligner web service (a), detecting utterances and syllable timing from audio/video files (b), retrieving web playable audio (c), and TextGrid results (d).

[24]https://github.com/kylebgorman/Prosodylab-Aligner
[25]http://www.ffmpeg.org/
[26]http://www.praat.org/

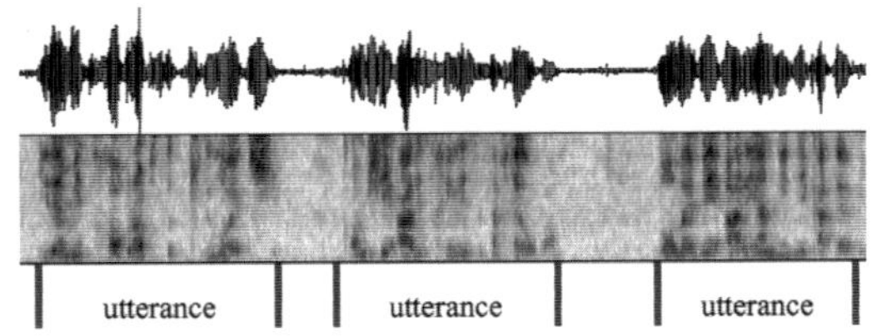

Figure 3: Screenshot of the utterance extraction process which converts any audio/video into utterance intervals encoded either as JSON or TextGrid using the PraatTextGridJS library.

6 Using LingSync/OLD

Current notable results of the LingSync/OLD project include Kartuli Glasses for Facebook (a transliterator from the Latin alphabet to the Kartuli alphabet),[27] Georgian Together for Android (a language learning app),[28] and Kartuli Speech Recognizer for Android.[29] These apps were developed in collaboration with Kartuli speakers and Kartuli software developers in Batumi, Georgia during the Spring 2014 semester.

Field linguists interested in a more detailed feature breakdown of LingSync and the OLD are encouraged to consult Cathcart et al. (2012) and Dunham (2014), respectively. Additional details on LingSync—which may be useful to those interested in developing tools with language communities or to computational linguists interested in contributing to the project—can be found in the LingSync WhitePaper (LingSync, 2012).

7 Conclusion

In this paper we hope to have illuminated some of the complexity involved in building software for endangered language documentation which has resulted in software fragmentation. We have presented LingSync/OLD, an open-ended plugin architecture which puts Software Engineering best practices and our collective experience in the language technology industry to use to address this fragmentation. The LingSync/OLD project has worked in an iterative fashion, beginning with UIs

[27]Chrome Store https://chrome.google.com/webstore/detail/kartuli-glasses/ccmledaklimnhjchkcgideafpglhejja
[28]Android Store https://play.google.com/store/apps/details?id=com.github.opensourcefieldlinguistics.fielddb.lessons.georgian
[29]Android Store https://play.google.com/store/apps/details?id=com.github.opensourcefieldlinguistics.fielddb.speech.kartuli

for field linguists in 2012-2013 and UIs for community members, and software libraries and training for software developers in 2013-2014. User studies and the dissemination of potentially novel language documentation and/or computational linguistics contributions are expected in 2014-2015 and in the future as the project continues to iterate. For technical updates, interested readers may view the project's completed milestones;[30] for user-facing updates, readers may visit LingSync.org and OnlineLinguisticDatabase.org.

Acknowledgements

We would like to express our deep thanks to Tobin Skinner, Elise McClay, Louisa Bielig, MaryEllen Cathcart, Theresa Deering, Yuliya Manyakina, Gretchen McCulloch, Hisako Noguchi, Brian Doherty, Gay Hazan, Oriana Kilbourn, Kim Dan Nguyen, Rakshit Majithiya, Mietta Lennes, Nivja de Jong, Ton Wempe, Kyle Gorman, Curtis Mesher, Beso Beridze, Tornike Lasuridze, Zviadi Beradze, Rezo Turmanidze, Jason Smith, Martin Gausby, Pablo Duboue, Xianli Sun, James Crippen, Patrick Littell, Michael McAuliffe as well as countless other linguistics students, computer science students and open source software developers who directly or indirectly helped build LingSync/OLD to what it is today and will be in the future. We would like to thank the ComputEL workshop reviewers, LingSync/OLD users and would-be users for providing feedback, suggestions, asking tough questions, and sending bug reports, all of which have been instrumental to the project's success and helped drive the its development. We would like to thank Faryal Abbassi, Farah Abbasi, Tamilla Paghava, Esma Chkhikvadze, Nina Gatenadze, and Mari Mgeladze for their friendship, patience and for sharing their language with us. Finally, we would like to thank Jessica Coon, Alan Bale and Michael Wagner for their guidance and challenging us to keep the user interfaces simple and yet flexible, as well as SSHRC Connection Grant (#611-2012-0001) and SSHRC Standard Research Grant (#410-2011-2401) which advocates open source approaches to knowledge mobilization and partially funded the students who have doubled as fieldwork research assistants and interns on the project. All errors and oversights are naturally our own.

[30]https://github.com/OpenSourceFieldlinguistics/FieldDB/issues/milestones?state=closed

References

Dorothee Beermann and Pavel Mihaylov. 2012. TypeCraft collaborative databasing and resource sharing for linguists. *Language Resources and Evaluation*, pages 1–23.

Kenneth R Beesley and Lauri Karttunen. 2003. Finite-state morphology: Xerox tools and techniques. *CSLI, Stanford.*

H. Andrew Black and Gary F. Simons. 2006. The SIL FieldWorks Language Explorer approach to morphological parsing. In *Computational Linguistics for Less-studied Languages: Proceedings of Texas Linguistics Society, Austin, TX.*

Lynnika Butler and Heather van Volkinburg. 2007. Review of FieldWorks Language Explorer (FLEx). *Language Documentation & Conservation*, 1(1):100–106.

MaryEllen Cathcart, Gina Cook, Theresa Deering, Yuliya Manyakina, Gretchen McCulloch, and Hisako Noguchi. 2012. LingSync: A free tool for creating and maintaining a shared database for communities, linguists and language learners. In Robert Henderson and Pablo Pablo, editors, *Proceedings of FAMLi II: workshop on Corpus Approaches to Mayan Linguistics 2012*, pages 247–250.

N. Chomsky and M. Halle. 1968. *The Sound Pattern of English.* Harper & Row, New York.

Jonathon E. Cihlar. 2008. Database development for language documentation: A case study in the Washo language. Master's thesis, University of Chicago.

Gina Cook. 2009. Morphological parsing of Inuktitut. Ms, Concordia University, Faculty of Engineering and Computer Science.

David Costa. 2012. Surveying the sources on the Myaamia language. In *Proceedings of the 2012 Myaamiaki Conference.*

N.H. De Jong and T Wempe. 2009. Praat script to detect syllable nuclei and measure speech rate automatically. *Behavior research methods*, 41(2):385–390.

Joel Dunham. 2014. Online Linguistic Database documentation. http://online-linguistic-database.readthedocs.org, March.

Benoit Farley. 2012. The Uqailaut project. http://www.inuktitutcomputing.ca, January.

Scott Farrar. 2010. Review of TypeCraft. *Language Documentation & Conservation*, 4:60–65.

Donald G. Frantz and Norma Jean Russell. 1995. *Blackfoot Dictionary of Stems, Roots, and Affixes.* Toronto: University of Toronto Press.

Donald G. Frantz. 1991. *Blackfoot Grammar.* Toronto: University of Toronto Press.

Andrew Garrett, Juliette Blevins, Lisa Conathan, Anna Jurgensen, Herman Leung, Adrienne Mamin, Rachel Maxson, Yoram Meroz, Mary Paster, Alysoun Quinby, William Richard, Ruth Rouvier, Kevin Ryan, and Tess Woo. 2001. The Yurok language project. http://linguistics.berkeley.edu/~yurok/index.php, January.

Andrew Garrett, Susan Gehr, Line Mikkelsen, Nicholas Baier, Kayla Carpenter, Erin Donnelly, Matthew Faytak, Kelsey Neely, Melanie Redeye, Clare Sandy, Tammy Stark, Shane Bilowitz, Anna Currey, Kouros Falati, Nina Gliozzo, Morgan Jacobs, Erik Maier, Karie Moorman, Olga Pipko, Jeff Spingeld, and Whitney White. 2009. Karuk dictionary and texts. http://linguistics.berkeley.edu/~karuk/links.php, January.

Jeff Good. 2012a. 'Community' collaboration in Africa: Experiences from northwest Cameroon. *Language Documentation and Description*, 11(1):28–58.

Jeff Good. 2012b. Valuing technology: Finding the linguist's place in a new technological universe. In Louanna Furbee and Lenore Grenoble, editors, *Language documentation: Practice and values*, pages 111–131. Benjamins, Amsterdam.

K David Harrison. 2007. *When Languages Die: The Extinction of the World's Languages and the Erosion of Human Knowledge*. Oxford University Press.

M. Hulden. 2012. foma: finite state compiler and C library (documentation). https://code.google.com/p/foma/w/list.

George Ironstrack. 2012. Miloniteeheetaawi eehinki pimihkanaweeyankwi: Let's reflect on how far we have traveled. In *Proceedings of the 2012 Myaamiaki Conference*.

Wesley Leonard. 2012. Your language isn't extinct: the role of Myaamia in Language Reclamation. In *Proceedings of the 2012 Myaamiaki Conference*.

LingSync. 2012. WhitePaper. http://OpenSourceFieldlinguistics.github.io/FieldDB/, January.

Stuart Robinson, Greg Aumann, and Steven Bird. 2007. Managing fieldwork data with ToolBox and the Natural Language Toolkit. *Language Documentation & Conservation*, 1(1):44–57.

Chris Rogers. 2010. Review of FieldWorks Language Explorer (FLEx) 3.0. *Language Documentationation & Conservation*, 4:78–84.

R. Schroeter and N. Thieberger. 2006. EOPAS, the EthnoER online representation of interlinear text. In Sebastian Nordoff, editor, *Sustainable Data from Digital Fieldwork*. University of Sydney, Sydney.

SIL International. 2013. *Technical Notes on FieldWorks Send/Receive*. http://fieldworks.sil.org/wp-content/TechnicalDocs/, November.

Nick Thieberger. 2012. Using language documentation data in a broader context. In Frank Seifart, Geoffrey Haig, Nikolaus P. Himmelmann, Dagmar Jung, Anna Margetts, and Paul Trilsbeek, editors, *Potentials of Language Documentation: Methods, Analyses, and Utilization*. University of Hawai'i Press, Honolulu.

Doug Troy and Andrew J. Strack. 2014. Metimankwiki kimehšoominaanaki - we follow our ancestors trail: Sharing historical Myaamia language documents across myaamionki. In *Proceedings of the 2014 Myaamiaki Conference*.

N. Weber. 2013. Accent and prosody in Blackfoot verbs. http://www.academia.edu/4250143/Accent_and_prosody_in_Blackfoot_verbs.

Alan Yu, Ryan Bochnak, Katie Franich, Özge Sarigul, Peter Snyder, Christina Weaver, Juan Bueno-Holle, Matt Faytak, Eric Morley, and Alice Rhomieux. 2005. The Washo project. http://washo.uchicago.edu/dictionary/dictionary.php, January.

Alan Yu, Ryan Bochnak, Katie Franich, Özge Sarigul, Peter Snyder, Christina Weaver, Juan Bueno-Holle, Matt Faytak, Eric Morley, and Alice Rhomieux. 2008. The Washo mobile lexicon. http://washo.uchicago.edu/mobile/, January.

Modeling the Noun Morphology of Plains Cree

Conor Snoek[1], **Dorothy Thunder**[1], **Kaidi Lõo**[1], **Antti Arppe**[1],
Jordan Lachler[1], **Sjur Moshagen**[2], **Trond Trosterud**[2]
[1] University of Alberta, Canada
[2] University of Tromsø, Norway
snoek@ualberta.ca, dthunder@ualberta.ca, kloo@ualberta.ca,
arppe@ualberta.ca, lachler@ualberta.ca,
sjur.n.moshagen@uit.no, trond.trosterud@uit.no

Abstract

This paper presents aspects of a computational model of the morphology of Plains Cree based on the technology of finite state transducers (FST). The paper focuses in particular on the modeling of nominal morphology. Plains Cree is a polysynthetic language whose nominal morphology relies on prefixes, suffixes and circumfixes. The model of Plains Cree morphology is capable of handling these complex affixation patterns and the morphophonological alternations that they engender. Plains Cree is an endangered Algonquian language spoken in numerous communities across Canada. The language has no agreed upon standard orthography, and exhibits widespread variation. We describe problems encountered and solutions found, while contextualizing the endeavor in the description, documentation and revitalization of First Nations Languages in Canada.

1 Introduction

The Department of Linguistics at the University of Alberta has a long tradition of working with First Nations communities in Alberta and beyond. Recently a collaboration has begun with Giellatekno, a research institute at the University of Tromsø, which has specialized in creating language technologies, particularly for the indigenous Saami languages of Scandinavia, but also for other languages that have received less attention from the computational linguistic mainstream. This collaboration is currently focusing on developing computational tools for promoting and supporting literacy, language learning and language teaching. Plains Cree is a morphologically complex language, especially with regard to nouns and verbs. While we are working to develop a complete finite-state model of Plains Cree morphology, we focus on nominal morphology in this paper.

In the first section we briefly describe Plains Cree nominal morphology and give some background on the language. This is followed by details on the model and its implementation. Finally, we discuss the particular situation of developing tools for a language that lacks a formal, agreed-upon standard and the challenges that this presents. We conclude with some comments on the benefits of this technology to language revitalization efforts.

2 Background

2.1 Plains Cree

Plains Cree or *nêhiyawêwin* is an Algonquian language spoken across the Prairie Provinces in what today is Canada. It forms part of the Cree-Montagnais-Naskapi dialect continuum that stretches from Labrador to British Columbia. Estimates as to the number of speakers of Plains Cree vary a lot and the exact number is not known, from a high of just over 83,000 (Statistics Canada 2011, for Cree without differentiating for Cree dialects) to as low as 160 (Ethnologue 2013). Wolfart (1973) estimated there to be about 20,000 native speakers, but some recent figures are more conservative.

Regardless of the exact number of speakers, there is general agreement that the language is under threat of extinction. In many, if not most, communities where Cree is spoken, children are learning English as a first language, and encounter Cree only in the language classroom. However, vigorous revitalization efforts are underway and Cree is regarded as one of the Canadian First Nations languages with the best chances to prosper (Cook and Flynn, 2008).

As a polysynthetic language (Wolvengrey,

Proceedings of the 2014 Workshop on the Use of Computational Methods in the Study of Endangered Languages, pages 34–42,
Baltimore, Maryland, USA, 26 June 2014.

2011, 35), Plains Cree exhibits substantial morphological complexity. Nouns come in two gender classes: animate and inanimate. Each of these classes is associated with distinct morphological patterns. Both animate and inanimate nouns carry inflectional morphology expressing the grammatical categories of number and locativity. The number suffixes for animate and inanimate nouns are different, the plural being marked by *-ak* in animates and *-a* in inanimates. Locativity is marked by a suffix taking the form *-ihk* (with a number of allomorphs). The locative suffix cannot co-occur with suffixes marking number or obviation, but does occur in conjunction with possessive affixes. Obviation is a grammatical category marked on animate nouns that indicates relative position on the animacy hierarchy, when there are two third person participants in the same clause. Obviation is expressed through the suffix *-a*, which forms a mutually exclusive paradigmatic structure with the locative and number prefixes.

The possessor of a noun in Plains Cree is expressed through affixes attached to the noun stem. These affixes mark person and number of the possessor by means of a paradigmatic inflectional pattern that includes both prefixes and suffixes. Since matching prefixes and suffixes need to co-occur with the noun when it is possessed, it is possible to treat such prefix-suffix pairings as circumfixes expressing a single person-number meaning. The noun *maskisin* in (1) below[1] is marked for third person plural possessors as well as being plural itself. The inanimate gender class is recognizable in the plural suffix *-a*, which would be *-ak* in the case of an animate noun.

(1)
omaskisiniwâwa
o-maskisin-iwâw-a
3PL.POSS-shoe-3PL.POSS-PL.IN
'their shoes'

Nouns also occur with derivational morphology in the form of diminutive and augmentative suffixes. The diminutive suffix is productive and forms taking the diminutive suffix can occur with all the inflectional morphology described above.

[1]The following abbreviations are used POSS = possessive prefix/suffix; LOC = locative suffix; OBV = obviative suffix; DIM = diminutive suffix; NUM = number marking suffix; IN = inanimate; PL = plural.

(2)
omaskisinisiwâwa
o-maskisin-is-iwâw-a
3PL.POSS-shoe-DIM-3PL.POSS-PL.IN
'their little shoes'

The particular form of the diminutive, however, varies considerably. For example, the most common form of the suffix is *-is*.

The suffix triggers morphophonemic changes in the stem. For example, the '*t*' in *oskâtâskw-* 'carrot' changes to 'c' (the alveolar affricate [ts]) when the diminutive suffix is present resulting in the form *oskâcâskos*. Since the form *oskâtâskw-* is a -*w* final form a further phonological change occurs, namely the initial vowel in the suffix changes from *i* > *o*.

To sum up, Plains Cree nominal morphology allows the following productive pattern types:

(3)
stem+NUM
stem+OBV
stem+LOC
stem+DIM+NUM
stem+DIM+OBV
stem+DIM+LOC
POSS+*stem*+POSS+NUM
POSS+*stem*+DIM+POSS+NUM
POSS+*stem*+DIM+POSS+OBV
POSS+*stem*+POSS+LOC
POSS+*stem*+DIM+POSS+LOC

Plains Cree can be written both with the Roman alphabet and with a Syllabary. Theoretically there is a one-to-one match between the two. However, a number of factors complicate this relationship. Differing punctuation conventions, such as capitalization, and the treatment of loanwords make conversion from one writing system to another anything but a trivial matter. Orthography presents a general problem for the development of computer-based tools, because unlike nationally standardized languages, orthographic conventions can vary considerably from community to community, even from one user to another. Certain authors have argued for the adoption of orthographic standards for Plains Cree (Okimâsis and Wolvengrey, 2008), but there simply is no centralized institution to enforce orthographic or other standardization. This means that the wealth of varying forms and dialectal diversity of the language are apparent in each individual community. This situation poses specific challenges to the project of developing language tools that are more seldom encountered when making spell-checkers and language learning tools for more standardized languages.

Similar situations have been encountered in work on the Saami languages of Scandinavia (Johnson, 2013). Following their work, we include dialectal variants in the model, but mark them with specific tags. This permits a tool such as a spell-checker to be configured to accept and output a subset of the total possible forms in the morphological model. An example here is the distribution of the locative suffix described in more detail in section 4. There is a disparity between communities regarding the acceptability of the occurrence of the suffix with certain nouns. The suffix can be marked with a tag in the FST-model. This tag can then be used to block the acceptance or generation of this particular form. The key notion here is that language learning and teaching tools are built on the basis of the general FST model. For Plains Cree there is one inclusive model, encompassing as much dialectal variation as possible. From this, individual tools are created, e.g. spell-checkers, that selects an appropriate subset of the dialectally marked forms. A community can therefore have their own spell-checker, specific to their own preferences. It is also possible to allow for "spelling relaxations" (Johnson, 2013, 67) at the level of user input, meaning that variant forms will be recognized, but constraining the output to a selection of forms deemed appropriate for a given community. Hence, the spell-checker used in one particular community could accept certain noun-locative combinations. At the same time, other tools, such as paradigm learning applications, could block this particular noun-locative combination from being generated: certain forms are understood, but not taught by the model. In general, the variation is not difficult to deal with in terms of the model itself, rather it represents a difficulty in the availability of accurate descriptions, since their specifics must be known and understood to be successfully included in the model.

This method could, in principle, be used to extend the Plains Cree FST-model to closely related Algonquian languages. However, rather than creating a proliferation of dialectal tags, it is easier to reproduce the architecture of the model and use it to create a new model for the related language. This allows the preservation of formal structures that follow essentially the same pattern, such as possessive inflection for example, while replacing the actual surface forms with those of the target language.

2.2 Previous computational modeling of Algonquian languages

Previous work on Algonquian languages that has taken a computational approach is not extensive. Hewson (1993) compiled a dictionary of Proto-Algonquian terms generated through an algorithm. His data were drawn from fieldwork carried out by Leonard Bloomfield. Kondrak (2002) applied algorithms for cognate identification to Algonquian data with considerable success. Wolfart and Pardo (1973) worked on a sizable corpus of Cree data and developed tools for data management and analysis in PL/I. Junker and Stewart (2008) have written on the difficulties of creating search engine tools for East Cree and describe challenges similar to the ones we have encountered with regard to dialectal variation and the absence of agreed on standard orthographies and other widespread conventions.

In general, computational approaches to Algonquian, and other Indigenous North American languages, have been hampered by the fact that in many cases large bodies of data to develop and test methods on are just not available. Even for Plains Cree, which is relatively widely spoken, and relatively well documented, the available descriptions are still lacking in many places. As a result, fieldwork must be undertaken in order to establish patterns that can be modeled in the formalism necessary for the finite state transducer (FST) to work, a point that will be expanded on below.

3 Modeling Plains Cree morphology

The finite state transducer technology that forms the backbone of our morphological model, and consequently of all the language applications we are currently developing, is based historically on work on computational modeling of natural languages known as two-level morphology (TWOL) by Koskenniemi (1983). His ideas were further developed by Beesley and Karttunen (2003).

Their framework offers two basic formalisms with which to encode linguistic data, *lexc* and *twolc*. The Lexicon Compiler, or *lexc*, is "a high-level declarative language and associated compiler" (Beesley and Karttunen, 2003, 203) used for encoding stem forms and basic concatenative morphology. The source files are structured in terms of a sequence of continuation lexica. Beginning with an inventory of stems the continuation lexica form states along a path, adding surface morphological forms and underlying analytic structure at each stage. A colon (:) separates underlying and surface forms. Example (4) demonstrates paths through just three continuation lexica for the animate nouns *apiscacihkos* 'antelope' and *apisimôsos* 'deer'. By convention, the names of continuation lexica are given in upper case. Stems and affixes represent actual word forms, and are thus given in lower case. The '+' sign indicates a morphological tag.

(4)

```
LEXICON ANSTEMLIST
apiscacihkos ANDECL ;
apisimôsos ANDECL ;
LEXICON ANDECL
< +N:0 +AN:0 +Sg:0 @U.noun.abs@ # > ;
< +N:0 +AN:0 @U.noun.abs@ OBVIATIVE > ;
LEXICON OBVIATIVE
< +Obv:a # > ;
```

Both forms are directed to the continuation lexicon here named ANDECL which provides some morphological tagging in the form of +N to mark the word as a noun and +AN to denote the gender class 'animate'. Each of the two nouns has the possibility of passing through the continuation lexicon ANDECL as an 'absolutive' noun – as indicated by the tag `@U.noun.abs@` (a *flag diacritic*, as will be explained below). The colons in the code indicate a distinction between upper and lower levels of the transducer. The upper form to the left of the colon is a string containing the the lemma as well as a number of tags that contain information about grammatical properties. For the word form *apiscacihkos*, the analysis once it has passed through the ANDECL continuation lexicon is `apiscacihkos+N+AN+Sg`.

The surface forms *apiscacihkos* and *apisimôsos* are well-formed strings of Plains Cree, following the Standard Roman Orthography. Hence, the path can terminate here as indicated by the hash mark. The other path, also open to both forms since they pass through the same continuation lexicon, leads to a further continuation lexicon named OBVIATIVE. This rather small lexicon adds a final *-a* suffix and the tag `+Obv` indicating that the form is inflected for the grammatical category of obviation. Since no number suffixes can occur in this form the path does not add a `+Sg` or `+Pl` tag to the underlying form.

(5)
`apiscacihkos+N+AN+Obv`
apiscacihkosa
'antelope'

These circumfixes were modeled using Flag Diacritics, which are an "extension of the finite state implementation, providing feature-setting and feature-unification operations" (Beesley and Karttunen, 2003, 339). Flag diacritics make it possible for the transducer to *remember* earlier states. The transducer may travel all paths through the prefixes via thousands of stems to all the suffixes, but the flag diacritics ensure that only strings with prefixes and suffixes belonging to the same person-number value are generated. In our solution for nouns, the continuation lexica allow all combinations of possession suffixes and prefixes, but the flag diacritics serve to filter out all undesired combinations. For example, in the noun *omaskisiniwâwa* from (1) above, the third person prefix *o-* and the suffix marking both person and number *-iwâw* are annotated in the *lexc* file with identical flag diacritics, so that they will always occur together.

Plains Cree has some very regular and predictable morphophonological alternations that can be modeled successfully in the finite state transducer framework. The formalism used here is not *lexc* as in the listing of stems and the concatenative morphology, but an additional formalism called the two-level compiler or *twolc* that is well suited to this task. The *twolc* formalism was developed by Lauri Karttunen, Todd Yampol, Kenneth R. Beesley and Ronald M. Kaplan based on ideas set forth in Koskenniemi (1983).

(6)
acâwewikamikosis
atâwewikamikw-isis
store-DIM
'little store'

In (6) above, *atâwewikamikw-* 'store' is modified by the derivational suffix *-isis* marking the diminutive form. This derivation is highly productive in Plains Cree. The underlying form of the suffix is *-isis* but in conjunction with a stem-final *-w*, the initial vowel of the suffix changes to *-o*. This morphophonemic alternation can be written in *twolc* much like a phonological rule:

(7)
```
i:o <=> w: %>:0 _s: +Dim ;
```

The sign %> is used to mark a suffix boundary, which, along with the +Dim tag, ensures that it is the first vowel of the suffix that undergoes substitution. Thus the context is given by the occurrence of a *-w* before the suffix boundary, i.e. stem finally. An additional complication here is that the presence of the diminutive suffix in a form again triggers a phonological change in the stem by which all *t*'s change to *c*'s (phonetically [ts]). In *twolc* the rules dictating morphophonological alternations apply in parallel, avoiding possible problems caused by sequential rule interactions. The noun completes the path through the continuation lexica and is passed to *twolc* as `atâwewikamikwisis`. There it undergoes two morphophonological changes giving the correct surface form *acâwewikamikosis*.

Twolc is a powerful mechanism for dealing with regular alternations. Reliance on *twolc* can reduce the number of continuation lexica and hence complexity of the morphology modeling carried out in *lexc*. The downside of using large numbers of *twolc* rules is the increasing complexity of rule interactions. We have found that decisions about which strategy to pursue in the modeling of a particular morphological pattern must frequently be made on a case by case basis. For example, in modeling the interesting case of the form *atimw-* 'dog' several strategies needed to be employed. The form triggers a vowel change *i* > *o* in conjunction with the diminutive suffix *-isis* resulting in *-osis*, a change falling under a rule described in (8) above. A further change here is that the *t* in *atimw-* 'dog' changes to *c* when the diminutive suffix is present resulting in the surface form *acimosis*. Both these forms can be handled by *twolc* rules such as the one exemplified in (8) above. However, *atimw-* also undergoes changes in the stem vowel when the noun is marked for a possessor so that *a* > *i* and *i* > *ê*. In the first person, the possessive prefix takes the form *ni-* leading to a sequence of two vowels arising from the prefix final *-i-* and stem initial *-i-*, which is not permitted in Plains Cree. This situation is handled by a general rule deleting the first vowel in preference for the latter. However, a set of *twolc* rules would be required to change the stem vowels – a set that would be specific to this particular word only. The full set of two level rules are accessible online[2].

Since the addition of further rules poses the risk of rule conflicts in an increasingly complex *twolc* code, the stem vowel changes are handled in *lexc* instead. There are currently over 40 continuation lexica in the model of nominal morphology alone.

(8)
```
LEXICON IRREGULARANIMATESTEMS
atim IRREGULARINFLECTION-1 ;
atim:têm IRREGULARINFLECTION-2 ;
```

The continuation lexicon contains two versions of the form *atim* with two different paths leading to further inflectional suffixes. In the second instance of *atim*, writing the base form to the left of the colon and the suppletive stem to the right ensures both that the form *-têm* surfaces correctly. In the analysis the base form *atim* can still be recovered. The forms are sent to differing continuation lexica, since only the suppletive forms occurs within the paradigm of possessive prefixes. The word meaning 'my little dog' is given as an example in (10) below.

(9)
nicêmisis
ni-atimw-isis
1SG.POSS-dog-DIM
'my little dog'

The suppletive form also does not carry an underlying *-w* and hence no longer triggers the vowel change in the diminutive suffix. With this

[2] `https://victorio.uit.no/langtech/trunk/langs/crk/src/phonology/crk-phon.twolc`

solution we can handle the regular and more straightforward morphophonological alternations in *twolc*, while avoiding undue complexity by modeling the suppletive forms in *lexc*.

Finally, we have adopted a system of using special tags to denote dialectal variants that are not equally acceptable in different communities. The seemingly high level of variation found in Plains Cree can be related to several reasons described in more detail in the next section. The variation is dealt with in the morphological model with a tagging strategy that marks dialectal forms. This tagging allows for the systems based on the morphological model to behave in accordance with the wishes of the user or community of users. In the setting of a particular teaching institution, for instance, only a certain subset of the variants encoded in the morphological model might be deemed acceptable. Our model permits this community to adjust the applications they are employing, e.g. a spell-checker, so that their community-specific forms are accepted as correct.

The stems are accessible online[3], and may be analysed and generated at the webpage for Plains Cree grammar tools[4].

4 The necessity for fieldwork in modeling Plains Cree

We began working on the morphological model of Plains Cree by examining published sources, such as *Plains Cree: A grammatical study* (Wolfart, 1973) and *Cree: Language of the Plains* (Okimâsis, 2004). Okimâsis' work is clearly structured and contains a wealth of information. Nevertheless, the level of explicitness required to capture the nature of a language in enough detail for applications such as, for example, spell-checkers is beyond the scope of her work. This is to say that in formalizing Okimâsis' description we needed to generalize grammatical patterns that were not always explicitly spelled out in her work in every detail. It should be apparent here that a number of factors come in to play here that make working on Plains Cree quite a different undertaking from working on a European language with a long history of research in the Western academic tradition. While official national European languages such as German, Finnish or Estonian can look on scholarly work dating back some centuries, and are supported by work from a community of specialists numbering hundreds of people, work on Plains Cree (and other languages in similar situations) is being carried out by what is at best a handful of people. While Cree language specialists form a professional body of researchers with a proud tradition, they are faced with the enormous task of documenting a language spoken in many small communities spread over a huge geographical area. In addition, many of those specialists are also involved with language revitalization and language teaching, with the result that less time can be devoted to language description, scholarship and the pursuit of larger projects such as the development of corpora. While such projects are under development in many areas, the demands placed on individual researchers and activists has resulted in an overall scarcity of resources. While compared to other Indigenous languages spoken in Canada, Plains Cree is relatively well documented, many of the resources that would be desirable assets for the development of a finite state model are not available. As a result, we have carried out fieldwork to further make explicit the full inflectional paradigm of nouns in Plains Cree.

There is considerable variation among speakers and specialists regarding the acceptability of certain inflectional possibilities. For example, in the case of one animate noun *atim* 'dog' it seems formally reasonable to allow its combination with the locative suffix *-ohk* rendering *atimohk*. This combination of stem and affix was considered impossible or at least implausible by some of our native speaker consultants. However, the form itself does occur, albeit in the guise of a place name for a lake island in northern Saskatchewan named *atim* 'dog'. Therefore the form *atimohk* 'on the dog' with locative suffix attached can occur in this very specific and geographically bounded context[5]. The way of coping with this is to lexicalize *atimohk* as locative of the island *Atim*, and to keep the noun *atim* outside the set of nouns getting regular locatives.

Further inquiry into this matter revealed that some speakers see the locative suffix as potentially occurring quite widely, while others are more restrictive (Arok Wolvengrey – p.c.). Here again there is a problem of scale: individual speakers of

[3] `https://victorio.uit.no/langtech/trunk/langs/crk/src/morphology/stems/`

[4] `http://giellatekno.uit.no/cgi/index.crk.eng.html`

[5] Thanks to Jan Van Eijk for pointing this out.

any language have only a partial experience of the possible extent of the language. In the modeling of the morphology for the purposes of such technologies as spell-checkers, for example, the experience of any potential speaker must be taken into account. While the information that this particular form is rare or semantically not well-formed is valuable, retaining the form is important, if the model is to cover the range of potential usage patterns of all Plains Cree speakers. Ideally, if the written use of the language is supported by the tools that can be developed based on our morphological model, that would lead to a gradually increasing electronic corpus of texts, providing frequency information on both the stems and morphological forms.

We have developed a workflow in which we construct the maximal paradigms that are theoretically possible and then submit them to intense native speaker scrutiny. Only once native speakers and specialists have approved the forms do they become part of the actual model. The paradigms are chosen so as to provide the coverage of the entire span of morphologically possible forms as well as all morphophonemic alternations. As such they present a maximal testbed for the patterns encoded in the formalism. Each paradigm consists of about sixty inflected forms.

Overall, a careful balance must be struck between directly explicit speaker/specialist input and theoretically possible forms. We aim to achieve this balance by taking a threefold approach: First, by careful consultation with speakers and specialists; second, by building a corpus[6] which can serve as a testing ground for the morphological analyzer and as a source of data, and third by working closely with communities willing to test the model and provide feedback.

5 Applications in language teaching and revitalization

The development of an explicit model of the morphology of Plains Cree as outlined above is of benefit not just to researchers but also those involved in teaching and revitalizing the language within their home communities. Using the general technological infrastructure developed by the researchers at Giellatekno, we are able to take the FST model of Plains Cree morphology and use it to create in one go a variety of language tools including a spellchecker, a morphological analyzer and a paradigm generator, which can be integrated as modules within general software applications such as a word-processor, an electronic dictionary or a intelligent computer-aided language learning (ICALL) application. Each of these tools can assist fluent speakers, as well as new learners, in their use of Plains Cree as a written language.

The spellchecking functionality within a word-processor will be a valuable tool for the small-but-growing number of Plains Cree language professionals who are engaged in the development of teaching and literary resources for the language. It will allow for greater accuracy and consistency in spelling, as well as faster production of materials. Because dialectal variation is being encoded directly into the FST model, the spellchecker can be configured so that writers from all communities and dialects can use this tool, without worry that the technology is covertly imposing particular orthographic standards which the communities have not all agreed upon.

The morphological analysis functionality built from the FST model and integrated within e.g. a web-based electronic dictionary will allow readers to highlight Plains Cree text in a document or webpage to perform a lookup of words in any inflected form, and not only with the citation (base) form. This will enable readers to more easily read Plains Cree documents with unfamiliar words without needing to stop to repeatedly consult paper dictionaries and grammars. While this does not obviate the need for printed resources in learning and teaching of the language, such added functionality can greatly increase the pace at which texts are read through by language learners. This is not inconsequential as it can slow down considerably the onset of weariness brought on by needing to interrupt the reading process to consult reference materials, and hence maintain the motivation for language learning.

The paradigm generation functionality within e.g. an electronic dictionary allows users to select a word and receive the full, or alternatively a smaller but representative, inflected paradigm of that word. This will be of direct benefit to instructors developing materials to teach the complex morphology of the Plains Cree, as well as their students.

[6] As noted above, a tool like a spell-checker promotes literacy and hence contributes naturally to the increase in textual materials. Until that begins to happen, however, we are collecting texts through recording and transcription.

We are working in collaboration with Plains Cree communities in the development and piloting of these tools, to ensure their accuracy and their usefulness for teachers, developers, learners and other community members. The full range of uses that these tools will be put to will only become apparent over time, but we expect that they will have a positive impact for community language maintenance by supporting the continued development Plains Cree literacy.

6 Conclusion

We have found the technology of Finite State Transducers so useful in developing language applications for Plains Cree because it permits us to integrate native speaker competence and specialized linguistic understanding of grammatical structures into the model directly.

At present the analyzer contains 72 nominal lexemes, carefully chosen to cover all morphological and morphophonological aspects of the Plains Cree nominal system. Once the morphological modeling of this core set of nouns has been finalized, scaling up the lexicon will be a trivial task, as all lexicographic resources classify their stem in the same way as is done in the morphological transducer.

We have described our method of working with native speaker specialists and how their insights are reflected in the design of the model. This interaction also allows enough possibilities for interactions with language teachers, learners and activists so that we make our work truly useful to the effort of preserving and revitalizing the precious cultural heritage that is Plains Cree. We are aware of the limits of tools that relate primarily to the written forms for languages that have rich oral histories and cultures, but feel that writing and reading Plains Cree will play an ever growing role in the future of this language.

This work makes practical contributions to linguistic research on Plains Cree. On the one hand, creating the model required the formalization of many aspects of Plains Cree morphology which had not previously been spelled out in full detail, i.e. it makes explicit what is known, or not known, about Plains Cree morphology, and thus allows us to extend the description of Plains Cree morphology accordingly. On the other, the morphological analyses can aid in future linguistic discovery especially when used in conjunction with corpora.

In the future, we will continue to expand the morphological model both in its grammatical coverage and in the size of the lexical resources which go into it. In regard to the latter, we are working with Cree-speaking communities in Alberta to expand on existing dictionaries and develop collections of recordings. The development of this morphological model has led us to carry out fieldwork on Plains Cree and to actively engage with Cree-speaking communities. We have worked hard to bridge the unfortunate gap that sometimes forms between the linguistic work being carried within academia and the needs of communities that are active in language documentation and revitalization. We look forward to further fruitful cooperation between activists, educators and researchers.

Acknowledgments

Building a computational model of Plains Cree morphology is a task that relies on the knowledge, time and goodwill of many people. We thank the University of Alberta's Killam Research Fund Cornerstones Grant for supporting this project. We would like to acknowledge in particular the crucial advice, attention and effort of Jean Okimâsis and Arok Wolvengrey, and thank them for the resources they have contributed. We wish also to thank Jeff Muehlbauer for his time and materials, as well as the attendees of the first Prairies Workshop on Language and Linguistics for their insights and expertise. Further, it is important to acknowledge the helpfulness of Earle Waugh who at the very start of our project made his dictionary available to us, and who has been very supportive. Arden Ogg has worked tirelessly to build connections among researchers working on Cree, which has greatly promoted and facilitated our work. Ahmad Jawad and Intellimedia, Inc. who have for some time provided the technological platform to make available a number of Plains Cree dictionaries through a web-based interface, have given us invaluable assistance in terms of resources and introductions. We would also especially like to thank the staff at Miyo Wahkohtowin Education for their wonderful enthusiasm, and for welcoming us into their community. Last but by no means least, we are indebted to innumerable Elders and native speakers of Plains Cree whose contributions have made possible all the dictionaries and text collections we are fortunate to have today.

References

Kenneth R. Beesley and Lauri Karttunen. 2003. *Finite State Morphology*. CSLI Publications, Stanford (CA).

Eung-Do Cook and Darin Flynn. 2008. Aboriginal languages of Canada. In: O'Grady, William and John Archibald (eds.) *Contemporary Linguistic Analysis*. Pearson, Toronto (ON).

John Hewson. 1993. *A computer-generated dictionary of Proto-Algonquian*, Canadian Museum of Civilization and Canadian Ethnology Service, Ottawa (ON).

Ryan Johnson, Lene Antonsen and Trond Trosterud. 2013. Using Finite State Transducers for Making Efficient Reading Comprehension Dictionaries. In Stephan Oepen & Kristin Hagen & Janne Bondi Johannessen (eds.), *Proceedings of the 19th Nordic Conference of Computational Linguistics (NODALIDA 2013)*, 378-411. Linköping Electronic Conference Proceedings No. 85.

Marie-Odile Junker and Terry Stewart. 2008. Building Search Engines for Algonquian Languages. In Karl S. Hele & Regna Darnell (eds.), *Papers of the 39th Algonquian Conference*, 59-71. University of Western Ontario Press, London (ON).

Grzegorz Kondrak. 2002. *Algorithms for Language Reconstruction*, Department of Computer Science, University of Toronto.

Kimmo Koskenniemi. 1983. *Two-level Morphology: A General Computational Model for Word-Form Recognition and Production*, Publication No. 11. Department of General Linguistics, University of Helsinki.

Jean Okimâsis. 2004. *Cree: Language of the Plains*, Volume 13 of University of Regina publications. University of Regina Press, Regina (SK).

Jean Okimâsis and Arok Wolvengrey. 2008. *How to Spell it in Cree*. miywâsin ink, Regina (SK).

H. Christoph Wolfart. 1973. Plains Cree: A grammatical study, *Transactions of the American Philosophical Society No. 5*.

H. Christoph Wolfart and Francis Pardo 1973. *Computer-assisted linguistic analysis*, University of Manitoba Anthropology Papers No. 6. Department of Anthropology, University of Manitoba.

Arok E. Wolvengrey. 2011. *Semantic and pragmatic functions in Plains Cree syntax*, LOT, Utrecht (NL).

Learning Grammar Specifications from IGT: A Case Study of Chintang

Emily M. Bender **Joshua Crowgey** **Michael Wayne Goodman** **Fei Xia**
Department of Linguistics
University of Washington
Seattle, WA 98195-4340 USA
{ebender, jcrowgey, goodmami, fxia}@uw.edu

Abstract

We present a case study of the methodology of using information extracted from interlinear glossed text (IGT) to create of actual working HPSG grammar fragments using the Grammar Matrix focusing on one language: Chintang. Though the results are barely measurable in terms of coverage over running text, they nonetheless provide a proof of concept. Our experience report reflects on the ways in which this task is non-trivial and on mismatches between the assumptions of the methodology and the realities of IGT as produced in a large-scale field project.

1 Introduction

We explore the possibility of learning precision grammar fragments from existing products of documentary linguistic work. A *precision grammar* is a grammar which encodes a sharp notion of grammaticality and furthermore relates strings to elaborate semantic representations. Such objects are of interest in the context of documentary linguistics because: (1) they are valuable tools in the exploration of linguistic hypotheses (especially regarding the interaction of various phenomena); (2) they facilitate the search for examples in corpora which are not yet understood; and (3) they can support the development of treebanks (see Bender et al., 2012a). However, they are expensive to build. The present work is carried out in the context of the AGGREGATION project,[1] which is exploring whether such grammars can be learned on the basis of data already collected and enriched through the work of descriptive linguists, specifically, collections of IGT (interlinear glossed text).

The grammars themselves are not likely targets for machine learning, especially in the absence of treebanks, which are not generally available for languages that are the focus of descriptive and documentary linguistics. Instead, we take advantage of the LinGO Grammar Matrix customization system (Bender et al., 2002; Bender et al., 2010) which maps from collections of statements of linguistic properties (encoded in *choices files*) to HPSG (Pollard and Sag, 1994) grammar fragments which in turn can be used to parse strings into semantic representations in the format of Minimal Recursion Semantics (MRS; Copestake et al., 2005) and conversely, to generate strings from MRS representations. The choices files are a much simpler representation than the grammars derived from them and therefore a more approachable learning target. Furthermore, using the Grammar Matrix customization system to produce the grammars results in much less noise in the automatically derived grammar code than would arise in a system learning grammars directly.

Here, we focus on a case study of Chintang, a Kiranti language of Nepal, described by the Chintang Language Research Project (CLRP) (Bickel et al., 2009). Where Lewis and Xia (2008) and Bender et al. (2013) apply similar methodologies to extract large scale properties for many languages, we focus on a case study of a single language, looking at both the large scale properties and the lexical details. This is important for two reasons: First, it gives us a chance to look in-depth at the possible sources of difficulty in extracting the large scale properties. Second, while large-scale properties are undoubtedly important, the bulk of the information specified in a precision grammar is far more fine-grained. In this case study we apply the methodology of Bender et al. (2013) to extract general word order and case properties and examine the sources of error affecting those results. We also explore extensions of those methodologies and that of Wax (2014) to extract lexical entries and specifications for morpho-

[1] http://depts.washington.edu/uwcl/aggregation/

Proceedings of the 2014 Workshop on the Use of Computational Methods in the Study of Endangered Languages, pages 43–53,
Baltimore, Maryland, USA, 26 June 2014.

logical rules. Together with a few default specifications, this information is enough to allow us to define grammars through the Grammar Matrix customization system and thus evaluate the results in terms of parsing coverage, accuracy and ambiguity over running text. Chintang is particularly well-suited for this case study because it is an actual endangered language subject to active descriptive research, making the evaluation of our techniques realistic. Furthermore, the descriptive research on Chintang is fairly advanced, having produced both large corpora of high-quality IGT and sophisticated linguistic descriptions, making the evaluation and error analysis possible.

```
word-order=v-final
has-dets=yes
noun-det-order=det-noun
...
case-marking=erg-abs
erg-abs-erg-case-name=erg
erg-abs-abs-case-name=abs
...
verb4_valence=erg-abs
  verb4_stem1_orth=sams-i-ne
  verb4_stem1_pred=_sams-i-ne_v_re
...
verb-pc3_inputs=verb-pc2
  verb-pc3_lrt1_name=2nd-person-subj
    verb-pc3_lrt1_feat1_name=pernum
    verb-pc3_lrt1_feat1_value=2nd
    verb-pc3_lrt1_feat1_head=subj
    verb-pc3_lrt1_lri1_inflecting=yes
    verb-pc3_lrt1_lri1_orth=a-
```

Figure 1: Excerpts from a choices file

2 Related Work

This work can be understood as a task related to both grammar induction and grammar extraction, though it is distinct from both. It also connects with and extends previous work using interlinear glossed text to extract grammatical properties.

Grammar induction (Clark, 2001; Klein and Manning, 2002; Klein and Manning, 2004; Haghighi and Klein, 2006; Smith and Eisner, 2006; Snyder et al., 2009, inter alios) involves the learning of grammars from unlabeled sentences. Here, *unlabeled* means that the sentences are often POS tagged, but no syntactic structures for the sentences are available. Most of those studies choose probabilistic context-free grammars (PCFGs) or dependency grammars as the grammar framework, and estimate the probability of the context-free rules or dependency arcs from the data. These studies improve parsing performance significantly over some baselines such as the EM algorithm, but the induced grammars are very different from precision grammars with respect to content, quality, and grammar framework.

Grammar extraction, on the other hand, learns grammars (sets of rules) from treebanks. Here the idea is to use heuristics to convert the syntactic structures in a treebank into derivation trees conforming to a particular framework, and then extract grammars from those trees. This has been done in a wide range of grammar frameworks, including PCFG (e.g. Krotov et al., 1998), LTAG (e.g. Xia, 1999; Chen and Vijay-Shanker, 2000), LFG (e.g. Cahill et al., 2004), CCG (e.g. Hockenmaier and Steedman, 2002, 2007), and HPSG (e.g. Miyao et al., 2004; Cramer and Zhang, 2009). However, this approach is not applicable to work on endangered language documentation, as treebanks are not available for such languages.

A third line of research attempts to bootstrap NLP tools for resource-poor languages by taking advantage of IGT data and resources for resource-rich languages. The canonical form of an IGT instance includes a language line, a word-to-word or morpheme-to-morpheme gloss line, and a translation line (typically in a resource-rich language). The bootstrapping process starts with word alignment of the language line and translation line with the help of the gloss line. Then the translation line is parsed and the parse tree is projected to the language line using the alignments (Xia and Lewis, 2007). The projected trees can be used to answer linguistic questions such as word order (Lewis and Xia, 2008) or bootstrap parsers (Georgi et al., 2013). Our work extends this methodology to the construction of precision grammars.

3 Methodology

Our goal in this work is to automatically create *choices files* on the basis of IGT data. The choices files encode both general properties about the language we are trying to model as well as more specific information including lexical classes, lexical items within lexical classes and definitions of lexical rules. Lexical rule definitions can include both morphotactic information (ordering of affixes) as well as morphosyntactic information, though here our focus is on the former. Sample excerpts from a choices file are given in Fig 1. These choices files are then input into the Grammar Matrix customization system[2] which produces HPSG gram-

[2]SVN revision (for reproducibility): 27678.

mar fragments that meet the specifications in the choices files. The Grammar Matrix customization system provides analyses of a range of linguistic phenomena. Here, we focus on a few that we consider the most basic: major constituent word order, the general case system, case frames for specific verbs, case marking on nouns, and morphotactics for verbs. In §3.1 we describe the dataset we are working with. §3.2 describes the different approaches we take to building choices files on the basis of this dataset. §3.3 explains the metrics we will use to evaluate the resulting grammars in §4.

3.1 The Chintang Dataset

Chintang (ISO639-3: ctn) is a language spoken by about 5000 people in Nepal and believed to belong to the Eastern subgroup of the Kiranti languages, which in turn are argued to belong to the larger Tibeto-Burman family (Bickel et al., 2007; Schikowski et al., in press). Here we briefly summarize properties of the language that relate to the information we are attempting to automatically detect in the IGT, and in many cases make the problem interestingly difficult.

Schikowski et al. (in press) describe Chintang as exhibiting information-structurally constrained word order: All permutations of the major sentential constituents are expected to be valid, with the different orders subject to different felicity conditions. They state, however, that no detailed analysis of word order has yet been carried out, and so this description should be taken as preliminary.

In contrast, much detailed work has been done on the marking of arguments, both via agreement on the verb and via case marking of dependents (Bickel et al., 2010; Stoll and Bickel, 2012; Schikowski et al., in press). The case marking system can be understood as following an ergative-absolutive pattern, but with several variations from that theme. In an ergative-absolutive pattern, the sole argument of an intransitive verb (here called S) is marked the same as the most patient-like argument of a transitive verb (here called O) and differentiated from the most agent-like argument of a transitive verb (here called A). Most A arguments are marked with an overt case marker called ergative, while S and O arguments appear without a case marker. In most writing about the language, this unmarked case is called nominative; here we will use the term absolutive. Similarly, verbs agree with up to two arguments, and the agreement markers for S and O are generally shared and distinguished from those for A.

Divergences from the ergative-absolutive pattern include variable marking of ergative case on first and second person pronouns as well as valence alternations such as one that licenses occurrences of transitive verbs with two absolutive arguments (and S-style agreement with the A argument) when the O argument is of an indefinite quantity (Schikowski et al., in press). Furthermore, the language allows dropping of arguments (A, S, and O). Finally, there are of course valences beyond simple intransitive and transitive, as well as case frames even for two-argument verbs other than { ERG, ABS }. As a result of the combination of these facts, the actual occurrence of ergative-case-marked arguments in speech is relatively low: Examining a corpus of speech spoken to and around children, Stoll and Bickel (2012) find that only 11% of (semantically) transitive verb tokens have an overt, ergative-marked NP A argument. As discussed below, these properties make it difficult for automated methods to detect both the overall case system of the language and accurate information regarding the case frames of individual verbs.

The dataset we are using contains 9793 (8863 train, 930 test) IGT instances which come from the corpus of narratives and other speech collected, transcribed, translated and glossed by the CLRP.[3] An example is shown in Fig. 2. As can be seen in Fig. 2, the glossing in this dataset is extremely thorough. It is also supported by a detailed Toolbox lexicon that encodes not only alternative forms for each lemma as well as glosses in English and Nepali, but also valence frames for most verb entries which list the expected case marking on the arguments. Finally, note that morphosyntactic properties without a morphological reflex are systematically unglossed in the data, so that ABS never appears (nor does SG for singular nouns, etc.).

In our experiments, we abstract away from the problem of morphophonological analysis in order to focus on morphosyntax and lexical acquisition. Accordingly, our grammars target the second line of the IGT, which represents each form as a sequence of phonologically regularized morphemes.

3.2 Grammars

In this section, we describe the different means we use for extracting the different kinds of informa-

[3] http://www.spw.uzh.ch/clrp

unisaŋa	khatte	mo	kosi	moba
u-nisa-ŋa	khatt-e	mo	kosi-i	mo-pe
3sPOSS-younger.brother-ERG.A	take-IND.PST	DEM.DOWN	river-LOC	DEM.DOWN-LOC

'The younger brother took it to the river.' [ctn] (Bickel et al., 2013c)

Figure 2: Sample IGT

tion required to build the choices files (see Fig 1 above). We first describe our points of comparison (oracle, §3.2.1 and baseline, §3.2.2), and then consider different ways of detecting the large-scale properties (word order, §3.2.3; overall case system, §3.2.4). Next we turn to different ways of extracting two kinds of lexical information: the constraints on case (i.e. case frames of verbs and the case marking on nouns, §3.2.5) and verbal morphotactics (§3.2.6). Finally, we describe a small set of hand-coded 'choices' which are added to all choices files (except the oracle one) in order to create working grammars (§3.2.7).

The alternative approaches to extracting the various kinds of information can be cross-classified with each other, giving the set of choices files described in Table 1. The first column gives identifiers for the choices files. The second specifies how the lexicon was created, the third how the value for major constituent word order was determined, and the fourth how the values for case were determined, including the overall case system, the case frames, and the case values for nouns. These options are all described in more detail below.

3.2.1 Oracle choices file

As an upper-bound, we use the choices file developed in Bender et al., 2012b. This file includes hand-specified definitions of lexical rules for nouns and verbs as well as lexical entries created by importing lexical entries from the Toolbox lexicon developed by the CLRP. This lexicon, as noted above, lists valence frames for most verbal entries. As the Grammar Matrix customization system currently only provides for simple transitive and intransitive verbs, only two verb classes were defined: intransitives with the case frame { ABS } and transitives with the case frame { ERG, ABS }. In addition, there is one class of nouns. Finally, the choices file includes hand-coded lexical entries for pronouns. As an upper-bound, this choices file can be expected to represent high precision and moderate recall: verbs that don't fit the two classes defined aren't imported.

Note that the Grammar Matrix customization system does not currently support the definition of adjectives, adverbs, or other parts of speech outside of verb, noun, determiner, (certain) adpositions, conjunctions and auxiliaries. Thus while we expect each grammar to be able to parse at least some sentences in the corpus, to the extent that sentences tend to include words outside the classes noun, verb and determiner, we expect relatively low coverage, even from our upper-bound.

3.2.2 Baseline choices file

Our baseline choices file is designed to create a working grammar, without particular high-level information about Chintang, that focuses on coverage at the expense of precision. We hand-specified the (counter-factual) assertion that there is no case marking in Chintang, and in addition that Chintang allows free word order (on the grounds that this is the least constrained word order possibility). It also defines bare-bones classes of nouns, determiners and transitive verbs, and then populates the lexicon by using a variant of the methodology in Xia and Lewis 2007. In particular, we parse the translation line using the Charniak parser (Charniak, 1997) and then use the correspondences inherent in IGT to create a projected tree structure for the language line, following Xia and Lewis. An example of the result for Chintang is shown in Fig 3. The projected trees include part of speech tags for each word that can be aligned. For each such word tagged as noun, verb, or determiner, we create an instance in the corresponding lexical type. In this baseline grammar, all verbs are assumed to be transitive, but since all arguments can (optionally) be dropped, the grammar is expected to be able to cover intransitive sentences, even if the semantic representation is wrong.

Since this baseline choices file models Chintang as if it had no case marking, we expect it the resulting grammar to have relatively high recall in terms of the combination of nominal and verbal constituents. On the other hand, since it is building a full-form lexicon and Chintang is a morphologically complex language, we expect it to have relatively low lexical coverage on held-out data.

Choices file	Lexicon	Word order	Case
ORACLE	Manual	Manual	Manual
BASELINE	Fullform	Default	None
FF-AUTO-NONE	Fullform	Auto	None
FF-DEFAULT-GRAM	Fullform	Default	Auto (GRAM)
FF-AUTO-GRAM	Fullform	Auto	Auto (GRAM)
FF-DEFAULT-SAO*	Fullform	Default	Auto (SAO)
FF-AUTO-SAO*	Fullform	Auto	Auto (SAO)
MOM-DEFAULT-NONE	MOM	Default	None
MOM-AUTO-NONE	MOM	Auto	None
MOM-DEFAULT-GRAM*	MOM	Default	Auto (GRAM)
MOM-AUTO-GRAM*	MOM	Auto	Auto (GRAM)
MOM-DEFAULT-SAO*	MOM	Default	Auto (SAO)
MOM-AUTO-SAO*	MOM	Auto	Auto (SAO)

Table 1: Choices files generated

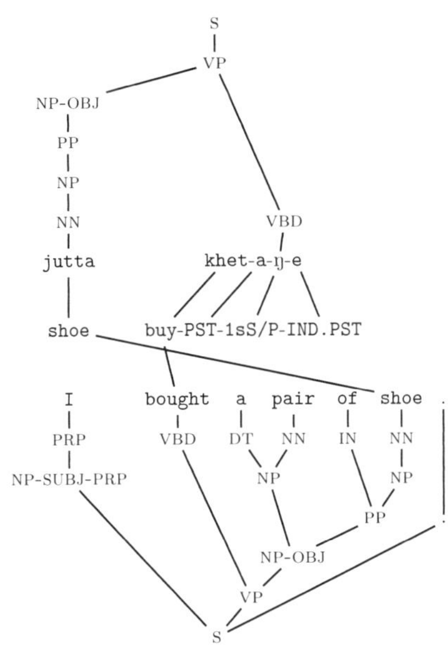

Figure 3: Projected tree structure (ex. from (Bickel et al., 2013d))

3.2.3 Word order

We applied the methodology of Bender et al. (2013) for determining major constituent order. For our dataset, the algorithm chose 'v-final', which matches what is in the ORACLE choices file, but is not necessarily correct. We created two versions of each of the other choices files, one with the default (baseline) answer of 'free word order' and one with this automatically supplied answer.

3.2.4 Case system

Similarly, we applied extended versions of the two methods for automatically discovering case systems from Bender et al. 2013: GRAM which looks for known case grams in glosses (not using projected trees) and SAO which extends the structure-projection methodology of Xia and Lewis (2007) to detect S, A and O arguments and then looks for the most frequent gram associated with each of these.[4] The GRAM method determines the case system of Chintang to be ergative-absolutive, while the SAO method indicates 'none' (no case). Specifying a case system in a choices file has no effect on the coverage or precision of the resulting grammar if the lexical items don't constrain case. Thus the case system choices only make sense in combination with the case frames choices (§3.2.5).

3.2.5 Case frames and case values

The HPSG analysis of case involves a feature CASE which is constrained by both verbs and nouns: Nouns constrain their own CASE value, while verbs constrain the CASE value of the arguments they select for.[5] In order to constrain verbs and nouns appropriately, we first need a range of possible case values. For choices files built based on the GRAM system, we consider case markers to be any of those included in the set of grams defined by the Leipzig Glossing Rules (Bickel et al., 2008): ABL, ABS, ACC, ALL, COM, DAT, ERG, GEN, INS, LOC, and OBL. For choices files built based on the SAO system, we consider as case markers only those grams (automatically) identified as marking S, A, or O. In the present study, that should only be ergative; as there is no marked case for absolutive, all other nouns were treated as absolutive (regardless of their actual case marking, since the SAO system has no way to detect other case grams).

[4]Our extensions involved making the system able to handle the situation where one or more of S, A and O are morphologically unmarked and therefore unreflected in the glosses.

[5]For the details of the analyses of case systems provided by the Grammar Matrix, see Drellishak 2009.

In choices files which specify case systems, we constrain the case value for nouns by creating one noun class for every case value, and then assigning the lexical entries for nouns to those lexical classes based on the grams in the gloss of the noun.[6]

Similarly, we create lexical classes for each case frame identified for transitive and intransitive verbs: We look for case grams on each argument of the verb, as determined by the function tags in the projected tree (e.g. NP-SUBJ-PRP in Fig 3).[7] For each case frame we identify, we create a lexical class, and we create lexical entries for verbs based on the case frames we extract for them. When the system identifies both an overt subject and an overt object, it considers the verb to be transitive and constrains the case of its two arguments based on the observed case values. If either argument is overt but not marked for case, the verb is constrained to select for the default case on that argument, according to the detected case marking system (i.e. ergative for transitive subjects and absolutive for transitive objects, in this instance). When there is an overt subject but no overt object, the verb is treated as intransitive and is constrained to select for a subject of the observed case (or the default case, here absolutive, if the overt subject bears no case marker). When there is an overt object but no subject, the verb is assumed to be transitive and the object's case assigned as with other transitives but the subject's case is constrained to the default (i.e. ergative, in this instance). Verbs with no overt arguments are not matched.

3.2.6 MOM choices file: Automatically extracted lemmas and lexical rules

The final refinement we try on our baseline is to apply the 'Matrix-ODIN Morphology' (MOM) methodology of Wax 2014. This methodology attempts to automatically identify affixes and create appropriate descriptions of lexical rules in a choices file to model those affixes. As a result, it also identifies stems. Thus we use the same basic choices as in the baseline choices file, but now populate the lexicon with stems rather than full-forms. Compared to BASELINE, this one should result in a grammar with better lexical coverage on held-out data, to the extent that the MOM system is able to correctly extract both stems and inflectional rules. We note that while the MOM system uses the same conceptual approach to alignment as that in the BASELINE, GRAM and SAO approaches, the implementation is separate, and so does not find exactly the same set of verbs.

3.2.7 Shared choices

The ORACLE choices file ran as-is. For the remaining choices files, we also needed to answer the questions about determiners (whether there are any, position with respect to the noun). Based on initial experiments, we chose 'yes' for the presence of determiners and 'det-noun' order. In an attempt to boost coverage generally, we also coded the choices that allow any argument to be dropped. While the determiner-related choices are specific to Chintang, the latter set of choices could be expected to boost coverage (at the cost of some precision) for any language.

3.2.8 Summary

Table 1 shows the 10 logical possibilities that arise from combining the methods discussed in this section, in addition to the ORACLE grammar and the BASELINE grammar. However, we test only a subset of these possibilities for the following reasons:[8] The SAO system chose no case as the case system for Chintang. As a result, this makes FF-DEFAULT-SAO and FF-AUTO-SAO the same as BASELINE and FF-AUTO-NONE, respectively. In future work, we aim to improve the SAO system but until it is effective enough to pick some case system for Chintang, these options do not require further testing. Secondly, while it is possible in principle to combine the output of the MOM system (which classifies verbs based on their morphological combinatoric potential) with the output of the system behind the GRAM choices files (which classifies verbs based on their case frames), doing so is non-trivial because these classifications are orthogonal, yet each verb must inherit from each dimension. We thus leave the exploration of MOM-DEFAULT-GRAM and MOM-AUTO-GRAM (and likewise MOM-DEFAULT-SAO and MOM-AUTO-SAO) for future work.

3.3 Evaluation

We evaluate the grammars generated by the choices files over both the data used to develop them ('training'; 8863 items) as well as data not included in the development process (held-out

[6] In future work, we plan to extend the MOM approach (§3.2.6) from verbs to nouns, but for now, the nouns are treated as full-form lexical entries across all choices files.

[7] While the GRAM method doesn't require the projected trees to determine the overall case system, we do need them here to find case frames for particular verbs.

[8] Untested choices files are marked with an * in the table.

'test' data; 930 items). We run both of these evaluations because we are actually testing two separate questions. The first is whether the grammars generated in this way can provide useful analytical tools to linguists. In this primary use-case, we expect a linguist to provide the system with all of their IGT and then use the generated grammars in order to gain insights into that same data. This does not amount to a case of testing on the training data because the annotations provided to the system (IGT) are not the same as those produced by the system (full parses, including semantic representations). However, we are still interested in also testing on held-out data in order to answer the second question: whether grammars generated in this way can also generalize to further texts.

We evaluate the grammars generated by the choices files we create in terms of *lexical coverage*, *parse coverage*, *parse accuracy* and *ambiguity*. Lexical coverage measures how many items consist only of word forms recognized by the grammar. Any item with unknown lexical items won't parse.[9] Parse coverage is the number of items that receive any analysis at all, where ambiguity is the number of different analyses each item receives. To measure parse accuracy, we examined the items that parse and determined which parses had semantic representations whose predicate-argument structures plausibly matched what was indicated in the gloss.

4 Results

Table 2 compares the lexical information encoded in each of the choices files in a quantitative fashion. The first thing to note is that the grammars vary widely in the size of their lexicons. The BASELINE/FF lexicons are expected to be larger than the others because they take each fully inflected form encountered as a separate lexical entry. On the other hand, the ORACLE choices file was built on the basis of the Toolbox lexicon (dictionary) from the CLRP and thus is effectively created on the basis of a much larger dataset. The GRAM choices files only contain verbs for which a case frame could be identified. If the projected tree was not interpretable by our extraction heuristics or if the example had no overt arguments, then the verb will not be extracted. The MOM choices files, on the other hand, only need to identify verbs in the string to be able to extract them, and should be able to generalize across different inflected forms of the same verb. This gives a number of verb entries intermediate between that for BASELINE/FF and the GRAM files. For nouns, there is less variation: the MOM files use the same data as the BASELINE, while the GRAM method faces as simpler problem than for verbs: it only needs to identify the case gram (if any) in a noun's gloss. The slightly larger numbers of nouns in the GRAM files v. the others can be explained by the same form being glossed in two different ways in the training data.

The remaining differences can be briefly explained as follows: The ORACLE choices file does not contain any entries for determiners. The others all contain the same 240 entries; one for any word aligned by the algorithm to a determiner in the English translation. Only the ORACLE and MOM choices files attempt to handle morphology, and so far MOM only does verbal morphology.

Table 3 presents the results of parsing training and test data with the various grammars, in absolute numbers and in percentages of the entire data set. The 'lexical coverage' columns indicate for how many items the grammars were able to recognize each constituent word form. The 'items parsed' columns show the number of items that received any analysis at all, while 'items correct' show the number of items that were judged (by one of the authors) to have a predicate-argument structure that plausibly reflects the gloss given in the IGT. The final column shows the average number of distinct analyses the grammars find for the items they parse at all.

The results are in fact barely measurable with these metrics (especially on the test data), but nonetheless speak to the differences between the grammars. Regarding lexical coverage, the ORACLE grammar does best on the test data set. This is because it is the only choices file not derived from the training data. Not surprisingly, the BASELINE grammar has the highest number of readings per item parsed, followed closely by FF-AUTO-NONE which adds only a minor constraint on word order.[10] On the other hand, comparing the number of items parsed to the number judged correct, except for the MOM choices files, the 'survival rate' was over 50% for all other tests.[11] This suggests

[9] There are methods for handling unknown lexical items (e.g. Adolphs et al., 2008) in more mature grammars of this type, but these are not applicable at this stage.

[10] It is in this relative lack of constraint that BASELINE mostly clearly forms a baseline to improve upon.

[11] The vast majority of the incorrect parses for the MOM

Choices file	# verb entries	# noun entries	# det entries	# verb affixes	# noun affixes
ORACLE	900	4751	0	160	24
BASELINE	3005	1719	240	0	0
FF-AUTO-NONE	3005	1719	240	0	0
FF-DEFAULT-GRAM	739	1724	240	0	0
FF-AUTO-GRAM	739	1724	240	0	0
MOM-DEFAULT-NONE	1177	1719	240	262	0
MOM-AUTO-NONE	1177	1719	240	262	0

Table 2: Amount of lexical information in each choices file

	Training Data (N = 8863)				Test Data (N = 930)			
choices file	lexical coverage (%)	items parsed (%)	items correct (%)	average readings	lexical coverage (%)	items parsed (%)	items correct (%)	average readings
ORACLE	1165 (13)	174 (3.5)	132 (1.5)	2.17	116 (12.5)	20 (2.2)	10 (1.1)	1.35
BASELINE	1276 (14)	398 (7.9)	216 (2.4)	8.30	41 (4.4)	15 (1.6)	8 (0.9)	28.87
FF-AUTO-NONE	1276 (14)	354 (4.0)	196 (2.2)	7.12	41 (4.4)	13 (1.4)	7 (0.8)	13.92
FF-DEFAULT-GRAM	911 (10)	126 (1.4)	84 (0.9)	4.08	18 (1.9)	4 (0.4)	2 (0.2)	5.00
FF-AUTO-GRAM	911 (10)	120 (1.4)	82 (0.9)	3.84	18 (1.9)	4 (0.4)	2 (0.2)	5.00
MOM-DEFAULT-NONE	1102 (12)	814 (9.2)	52 (0.6)	6.04	39 (4.2)	16 (1.7)	3 (0.3)	10.81
MOM-AUTO-NONE	1102 (12)	753 (8.5)	49 (0.6)	4.20	39 (4.2)	10 (1.1)	3 (0.3)	9.20

Table 3: Results

that, despite the noise introduced by the automatic methods of lexical extraction, the precision grammar backbone provided by the Grammar Matrix can still provide high-quality parses.

For example, the BASELINE grammar produces six parses of the string in (1):

(1) din khiptukum
din khipt-u-kV-m
day count-3P-IND.NPST-1/2nsA
'(We) count days.' [ctn] (Bickel et al., 2013b)

Among these six is one which produces the semantic representation in (2). While this grammar does not yet capture any of the agreement morphology that indicates that the subject is first person plural, it does correctly link the 'day' to the semantic ARG2 of 'count'.

$$(2)\quad \left\langle h_1, \left| \begin{array}{l} h_3\text{:\_din\_n\_day}(x_4), \\ h_5\text{:\_exist\_q\_rel}(x_4, h_6, h_7), \\ h_6\text{:\_khipt-u-kv-m\_v\_count}(e_2, x_9, x_4) \end{array} \right| \{ h_6 =_q h_3 \} \right\rangle$$

Finally, we note that the longest items we are able to parse consist of one verb and two NPs, each of which can have only up to two words (a determiner and a noun). Most of the examples that do parse consist of only one or two words, while the full data set ranges from items of length 1 to items of length 25 (average 4.5 words/item in training, 5 words/item in test). The Grammar Matrix already supports some longer sentences in the form of coordination, so one avenue for future work is to explore the automatic detection of coordination strategies. Otherwise, branching out to longer sentences will require additions to the Grammar Matrix allowing the specification of modifiers and a wider range of valence types for verbs.

choices files involved analyses of words for 'yes', 'well', 'what' and the like as verbs. Note that one form of 'yes' is the copula, and such examples were accepted. Another source of incorrect parses for many grammars involves homophony between the focus particle and a verb meaning 'come'.

5 Error Analysis

The opportunity to work closely with one language has allowed us to observe several ways in which the assumptions of the systems we are building on do not match what we find in the data. Here we briefly review some of those mismatches and reflects on what could be done to handle them.

The first observation concerns the non-glossing of zero-marked morphosyntactic features, such as absolutive case in Chintang. From the point of view of a consumer of IGT it is certainly desirable to have as much information as possible made explicit in the glossing. From the point of view of a project creating IGT in the context of on-going fieldwork, however, it is likely often difficult to reliably gloss zero morphemes and thus the decision to leave them systematically unglossed is quite sensible. Both the GRAM method and especially the SAO method for detecting case systems, which we extended to extracting case frames for particular verbs, are not yet fully robust to the possibility that certain case values are unmarked morphologically and thus not glossed in the data.

While we extended them to a certain extent in this work, there is still more to be done on this front.

A second observation concerns the glossing of proper names, as in (3):

(3) pailego ubhiyauti paphuma
paile-ko u-bhiya paphu-ma
first-GEN 3A-marriage a.clan.of.Rai.people-F
'His first marriage was with a Phuphu woman.' [ctn] (Bickel et al., 2013a)

We use statistical alignment between the translation line and the gloss line and between the gloss line and the language line in order to project information from the analysis of the translation line onto the language line. Glosses such as 'a.clan.of.Rai.people' tend to confuse this alignment process, though they are very informative to a human reader of the IGT. Error analysis of sentences for which we were unable to extract subject and object arguments at all suggested that many of the errors were caused by misalignments likely due to the aligner not being able to cope with this kind of glossing. Future work will explore how to train the aligner to function better in such cases.

In addition to properties of the glossing conventions, there are also properties of the language that proved challenging for our system. The first is the intricate nature of the case-marking system as discussed in §3.1. In particular, our system does not model any distinction between 1st and 2nd person pronouns and other nouns, such that when the pronouns appear without a case marker, they are taken to be in the unmarked case (i.e. absolutive), though this is not necessarily so. The second property of the language that our system found difficult is the optionality of arguments. We were able to adapt our case frame extraction strategy to handle dropped subjects, but dropped objects are more confounding: our system is unable so far to distinguish such verbs from intransitives. One possible way forward in this case is to draw more information from the English translation in the IGT: English tends not to drop arguments, and so when we find an object (especially a pronominal object) in the English translation that is not aligned to anything in the language line, we would have evidence that the verb in question may be transitive.

Finally, we looked closely at the items in the test data for which we had complete lexical analysis, but which still failed to parse. We did this both for the fullform and MOM-based lexicons. The goal here was to evaluate whether (a) our assignment of items to lexical categories was correct (and there was some other issue standing in the way of analyzing the item) or (b) we should have parsed a given item, but our system had misidentified the words in question in such a way that no syntactic analysis could be found. For the baseline system, we found that although some items had misidentified categories (specifically, pronouns and adverbs were sometimes misidentified as determiners), the two major obstacles to parsing came from multiverb constructions or sentential fragments. Of the 26 unparsed items with lexical coverage, 10 contained multiple verbs and 12 were NP or interjectory fragments (eg: 'Yes, yes, yes.'). We observed a similar pattern among 23 unparsed items from the MOM-based lexicon. We can take two lessons from this assessment: (1) since much of our data comes from naturally occurring speech, it may be useful to rerun our tests with an NP fragment as a valid root symbol in our grammars; (2) proper identification of auxiliary verbs is an important next step for improving our system.

6 Conclusion

In this paper we have taken the first steps towards creating actual precision grammars by creating Grammar Matrix customization system choices files on the basis of automated analysis of IGT. Measured in terms of coverage over held-out data, the results are hardly impressive and might seem discouraging. However, we see in these initial forays rather a proof-of-concept. Moreover, the process of digging into the details of getting an IGT-to-grammar system working for one particular language has been a very rich source of information on the mismatches between the assumptions of systems built to handle high-level properties and the linguistic facts and glossing conventions of the kind of data they are meant to handle.

7 Acknowledgments

This material is based upon work supported by the National Science Foundation under Grant No. BCS-1160274. Any opinions, findings, and conclusions or recommendations expressed in this material are those of the author(s) and do not necessarily reflect the views of the NSF.

We would like to thank David Wax for his assistance in setting up the MOM system, Olga Zamaraeva for general discussion, and especially the CRLP for providing access to the Chintang data.

References

Peter Adolphs, Stephan Oepen, Ulrich Callmeier, Berthold Crysmann, Dan Flickinger, and Bernd Kiefer. 2008. Some fine points of hybrid natural language parsing. Marrakech, Morocco, May.

Emily M. Bender, Dan Flickinger, and Stephan Oepen. 2002. The grammar matrix: An open-source starter-kit for the rapid development of cross-linguistically consistent broad-coverage precision grammars. In John Carroll, Nelleke Oostdijk, and Richard Sutcliffe, editors, *Proceedings of the Workshop on Grammar Engineering and Evaluation at the 19th International Conference on Computational Linguistics*, pages 8–14, Taipei, Taiwan.

Emily M. Bender, Scott Drellishak, Antske Fokkens, Laurie Poulson, and Safiyyah Saleem. 2010. Grammar customization. *Research on Language & Computation*, pages 1–50. 10.1007/s11168-010-9070-1.

Emily M. Bender, Sumukh Ghodke, Timothy Baldwin, and Rebecca Dridan. 2012a. From database to treebank: Enhancing hypertext grammars with grammar engineering and treebank search. In Sebastian Nordhoff and Karl-Ludwig G. Poggeman, editors, *Electronic Grammaticography*, pages 179–206. University of Hawaii Press, Honolulu.

Emily M. Bender, Robert Schikowski, and Balthasar Bickel. 2012b. Deriving a lexicon for a precision grammar from language documentation resources: A case study of Chintang. In *Proceedings of COLING 2012*, pages 247–262, Mumbai, India, December. The COLING 2012 Organizing Committee.

Emily M. Bender, Michael Wayne Goodman, Joshua Crowgey, and Fei Xia. 2013. Towards creating precision grammars from interlinear glossed text: Inferring large-scale typological properties. In *Proceedings of the 7th Workshop on Language Technology for Cultural Heritage, Social Sciences, and Humanities*, pages 74–83, Sofia, Bulgaria, August. Association for Computational Linguistics.

Balthasar Bickel, Goma Banjade, Martin Gaenszle, Elena Lieven, Netra Paudyal, Ichchha Rai, Manoj Rai, Novel Kishor Rai, and Sabine Stoll. 2007. Free prefix ordering in Chintang. *Language*, 83(1):43–73.

Balthasar Bickel, Bernard Comrie, and Martin Haspelmath. 2008. The Leipzig glossing rules: Conventions for interlinear morpheme-by-morpheme glosses. Max Planck Institute for Evolutionary Anthropology and Department of Linguistics, University of Leipzig.

Balthasar Bickel, Martin Gaenszle, Novel Kishore Rai, Elena Lieven, Goma Banjade, Toya Nath Bhatta, Netra Paudyal, Judith Pettigrew, Ichchha P. Rai, Manoj Rai, Robert Schikowski, and Sabine Stoll. 2009. Audiovisual corpus of the chintang language, including a longitudinal corpus of language acquisition by six children, plus a trilingual dictionary, paradigm sets, grammar sketches, ethnographic descriptions, and photographs. *DOBES Archive*, `http://www.mpi.nl/DOBES`.

Balthasar Bickel, Manoj Rai, Netra P. Paudyal, Goma Banjade, Toya N. Bhatta, Martin Gaenszle, Elena Lieven, Ichchha Purna Rai, Novel Kishore Rai, and Sabine Stoll. 2010. The syntax of three-argument verbs in Chintang and Belhare (Southeastern Kiranti). In *Studies in Ditransitive Constructions: A Comparative Handbook*, pages 382–408. Mouton de Gruyter, Berlin.

Balthasar Bickel, Martin Gaenszle, Novel Kishore Rai, Vishnu Singh Rai, Elena Lieven, Sabine Stoll, G. Banjade, T. N. Bhatta, N Paudyal, J Pettigrew, and M Rai, I. P.and Rai. 2013a. Hatuwa. Accessed: 15 January 2013.

Balthasar Bickel, Martin Gaenszle, Novel Kishore Rai, Vishnu Singh Rai, Elena Lieven, Sabine Stoll, G. Banjade, T. N. Bhatta, N Paudyal, J Pettigrew, and M Rai, I. P.and Rai. 2013b. Khadak's daily life. Accessed: 15 January 2013.

Balthasar Bickel, Martin Gaenszle, Novel Kishore Rai, Vishnu Singh Rai, Elena Lieven, Sabine Stoll, G. Banjade, T. N. Bhatta, N Paudyal, J Pettigrew, and M Rai, I. P.and Rai. 2013c. Tale of a poor guy. Accessed: 15 January 2013.

Balthasar Bickel, Martin Gaenszle, Novel Kishore Rai, Vishnu Singh Rai, Elena Lieven, Sabine Stoll, G. Banjade, T. N. Bhatta, N Paudyal, J Pettigrew, and M Rai, I. P.and Rai. 2013d. Talk of kazi's trip. Accessed: 15 January 2013.

Aoife Cahill, Michael Burke, Ruth O'Donovan, Josef Van Genabith, and Andy Way. 2004. Long-distance dependency resolution in automatically acquired wide-coverage pcfg-based lfg approximations. In *Proceedings of the 42nd Meeting of the Association for Computational Linguistics (ACL'04), Main Volume*, pages 319–326, Barcelona, Spain, July.

Eugene Charniak. 1997. Statistical parsing with a context-free grammar and word statistics. In *Proceedings of AAAI-1997*.

John Chen and K. Vijay-Shanker. 2000. Automated Extraction of TAGs from the Penn Treebank. In *Proc. of the 6th International Workshop on Parsing Technologies (IWPT-2000), Italy*.

Alexander Clark. 2001. Unsupervised induction of stochastic context-free grammars using distributional clustering. In *Proc. of the 5th Conference on Computational Natural Language Learning (CoNLL-2001)*.

Ann Copestake, Dan Flickinger, Carl Pollard, and Ivan A. Sag. 2005. Minimal recursion semantics: An introduction. *Research on Language & Computation*, 3(4):281–332.

Bart Cramer and Yi Zhang. 2009. Construction of a german hpsg grammar from a detailed treebank. In *Proceedings of the 2009 Workshop on Grammar Engineering Across Frameworks (GEAF 2009)*, pages 37–45, Suntec, Singapore.

Scott Drellishak. 2009. *Widespread But Not Universal: Improving the Typological Coverage of the Grammar Matrix*. Ph.D. thesis, University of Washington.

Ryan Georgi, Fei Xia, and William D. Lewis. 2013. Enhanced and portable dependency projection algorithms using interlinear glossed text. In *Proceedings of ACL 2013 (Volume 2: Short Papers)*, pages 306–311, Sofia, Bulgaria, August.

Aria Haghighi and Dan Klein. 2006. Prototype-driven grammar induction. In *Proceedings of the 21st International Conference on Computational Linguistics and 44th Annual Meeting of the Association for Computational Linguistics (COLING/ACL 2006)*, pages 881–888, Sydney, Australia, July. Association for Computational Linguistics.

Julia Hockenmaier and Mark Steedman. 2002. Acquiring compact lexicalized grammars from a cleaner treebank. In *Proc. of LREC-2002*, pages 1974–1981.

Julia Hockenmaier and Mark Steedman. 2007. Ccgbank: A corpus of ccg derivations and dependency structures extracted from the penn treebank. *Computational Linguistics*, 33(3):355–396.

Dan Klein and Christopher Manning. 2002. A general constituent context model for improved grammar induction. In *Proceedings of the 40th Annual Meeting of the Association for Computational Linguistics (ACL-2002)*, Philadelphia, PA.

Dan Klein and Christopher Manning. 2004. Corpus-based induction of syntactic structure: models of dependency and constituency. In *Proceedings of the 42nd Annual Meeting of the Association for Computational Linguistics (ACL-2004)*, Barcelona, Spain.

Alexander Krotov, Mark Hepple, Robert Gaizauskas, and Yorick Wilks. 1998. Compacting the Penn Treebank Grammar. In *Proc. of the 36th Annual Meeting of the Association for Computational Linguistics (ACL-1998)*, Montreal, Quebec, Canada.

William D. Lewis and Fei Xia. 2008. Automatically identifying computationally relevant typological features. In *Proceedings of the Third International Joint Conference on Natural Language Processing*, pages 685–690, Hyderabad, India.

Yusuke Miyao, Takashi Ninomiya, and Junichi Tsujii. 2004. Corpus-oriented grammar development for acquiring a head-driven phrase structure grammar from the penn treebank. In *Proc. of the First International Joint Conference on Natural Language Processing (IJCNLP-2004)*, Hainan, China.

Carl Pollard and Ivan A. Sag. 1994. *Head-Driven Phrase Structure Grammar*. Studies in Contemporary Linguistics. The University of Chicago Press and CSLI Publications, Chicago, IL and Stanford, CA.

Robert Schikowski, Balthasar Bickel, and Netra Paudyal. in press. Flexible valency in Chintang. In B. Comrie and A. Malchukov, editors, *Valency Classes: A Comparative Handbook*. Mouton de Gruyter, Berlin.

Noah A. Smith and Jason Eisner. 2006. Annealing structural bias in multilingual weighted grammar induction. In *Proceedings of the 21st International Conference on Computational Linguistics and 44th Annual Meeting of the Association for Computational Linguistics (ACL/COLING 2006)*, pages 569–576, Sydney, Australia, July. Association for Computational Linguistics.

Benjamin Snyder, Tahira Naseem, and Regina Barzilay. 2009. Unsupervised multilingual grammar induction. In *Proceedings of the Joint Conference of the 47th Annual Meeting of the ACL and the 4th International Joint Conference on Natural Language Processing of the AFNLP*, pages 73–81, August.

Sabine Stoll and Balthasar Bickel. 2012. How to measure frequency? Different ways of counting ergatives in Chintang (Tibeto-Burman, Nepal) and their implications. In Frank Seifart, Geoffrey Haig, Nikolaus P. Himmelmann, Dagmar Jung, Anna Margetts, and Paul Trilsbeek, editors, *Potentials of Language Documentation: Methods, Analyses, and Utilization*, pages 83–89. University of Hawai'i Press, Manoa.

David Wax. 2014. Automated grammar engineering for verbal morphology. Master's thesis, University of Washington.

Fei Xia and William D. Lewis. 2007. Multilingual structural projection across interlinear text. In *Proc. of the Conference on Human Language Technologies (HLT/NAACL 2007)*, pages 452–459, Rochester, New York.

Fei Xia. 1999. Extracting Tree Adjoining Grammars from Bracketed Corpora. In *Proc. of 5th Natural Language Processing Pacific Rim Symposium (NLPRS-1999)*, Beijing, China.

Creating Lexical Resources for Endangered Languages

Khang Nhut Lam, Feras Al Tarouti and Jugal Kalita
Computer Science department
University of Colorado
1420 Austin Bluffs Pkwy, Colorado Springs, CO 80918, USA
{klam2,faltarou,jkalita}@uccs.edu

Abstract

This paper examines approaches to generate lexical resources for endangered languages. Our algorithms construct bilingual dictionaries and multilingual thesauruses using public Wordnets and a machine translator (MT). Since our work relies on only one bilingual dictionary between an endangered language and an "intermediate helper" language, it is applicable to languages that lack many existing resources.

1 Introduction

Languages around the world are becoming extinct at a record rate. The Ethnologue organization[1] reports 424 languages as nearly extinct and 203 languages as dormant, out a total of 7,106 recorded languages. Many other languages are becoming endangered, a state which is likely to lead to their extinction, without determined intervention. According to UNESCO, "a language is endangered when its speakers cease to use it, use it in fewer and fewer domains, use fewer of its registers and speaking styles, and/or stop passing it on to the next generation...". In America, UNESCO reports 134 endangered languages, e.g., Arapaho, Cherokee, Cheyenne, Potawatomi and Ute.

One of the hallmarks of a living and thriving language is the existence and continued production of "printed" (now extended to online presence) resources such as books, magazines and educational materials in addition to oral traditions. There is some effort afoot to document record and archive endangered languages. Documentation may involve creation of dictionaries, thesauruses, text and speech corpora. One possible way to resuscitate these languages is to make them more easily learnable for the younger generation. To learn languages and use them well, tools such as dictionaries and thesauruses are essential. Dictionaries are resources that empower the users and learners of a language. Dictionaries play a more substantial role than usual for endangered languages and are "an instrument of language maintenance" (Gippert et al., 2006). Thesauruses are resources that group words according to similarity (Kilgarriff, 2003). For speakers and students of an endangered language, multilingual thesauruses are also likely to be very helpful.

This study focuses on examining techniques that leverage existing resources for "resource-rich" languages to build lexical resources for low-resource languages, especially endangered languages. The only resource we need is a single available bilingual dictionary translating the given endangered language to English. First, we create a reverse dictionary from the input dictionary using the approach in (Lam and Kalita, 2013). Then, we generate additional bilingual dictionaries translating from the given endangered language to several additional languages. Finally, we discuss the first steps to constructing multilingual thesauruses encompassing endangered and resources-rich languages. To handle the word sense ambiguity problems, we exploit Wordnets in several languages. We experiment with two endangered languages: Cherokee and Cheyenne, and some resource-rich languages such as English, Finnish, French and Japanese[2]. Cherokee is the Iroquoian language spoken by 16,000 Cherokee people in Oklahoma and North Carolina. Cheyenne is a Native American language spoken by 2,100 Cheyenne people in Montana and Oklahoma.

The remainder of this paper is organized as follows. Dictionaries and thesauruses are introduced in Section 2. Section 3 discusses related work. In

[1] http://www.ethnologue.com/

[2] ISO 693-3 codes for Cherokee, Cheyenne, English, Finnish, French and Japanese are *chr*, *chy*, *eng*, *fin*, *fra* and *jpn*, respectively.

Proceedings of the 2014 Workshop on the Use of Computational Methods in the Study of Endangered Languages, pages 54–62,
Baltimore, Maryland, USA, 26 June 2014.

Section 4 and Section 5, we present approaches for creating new bilingual dictionaries and multilingual thesauruses, respectively. Experiments are described in Section 6. Section 7 concludes the paper.

2 Dictionaries vs. Thesauruses

A dictionary or a lexicon is a book (now, in electronic database formats as well) that consists of a list of entries sorted by the lexical unit. A lexical unit is a word or phrase being defined, also called *definiendum*. A dictionary entry or a lexical entry simply contains a lexical unit and a definition (Landau, 1984). Given a lexical unit, the definition associated with it usually contains parts-of-speech (POS), pronunciations, meanings, example sentences showing the use of the source words and possibly additional information. A monolingual dictionary contains only one language such as The Oxford English Dictionary[3] while a bilingual dictionary consists of two languages such as the English-Cheyenne dictionary[4]. A lexical entry in the bilingual dictionary contains a lexical unit in a source language and equivalent words or multiword expressions in the target language along with optional additional information. A bilingual dictionary may be unidirectional or bidirectional.

Thesauruses are specialized dictionaries that store synonyms and antonyms of selected words in a language. Thus, a thesaurus is a resource that groups words according to similarity (Kilgarriff, 2003). However, a thesaurus is different from a dictionary. (Roget, 1911) describes the organizes of words in a thesaurus as "... not in alphabetical order as they are in a dictionary, but according to the ideas which they express.... The idea being given, to find the word, or words, by which that idea may be most fitly and aptly expressed. For this purpose, the words and phrases of the language are here classed, not according to their sound or their orthography, but strictly according to their signification". Particularly, a thesaurus contains a set of descriptors, an indexing language, a classification scheme or a system vocabulary (Soergel, 1974). A thesaurus also consists of relationships among descriptors. Each descriptor is a term, a notation or another string of symbols used to designate the concept. Examples of thesauruses are Roget's international Thesaurus (Roget, 2008), the Open Thesaurus[5] or the one at thesaurus.com.

We believe that the lexical resources we create are likely to help endangered languages in several ways. These can be educational tools for language learning within and outside the community of speakers of the language. The dictionaries and thesauruses we create can be of help in developing parsers for these languages, in addition to assisting machine or human translators to translate rich oral or possibly limited written traditions of these languages into other languages. We may be also able to construct mini pocket dictionaries for travelers and students.

3 Related work

Previous approaches to create new bilingual dictionaries use intermediate dictionaries to find chains of words with the same meaning. Then, several approaches are used to mitigate the effect of ambiguity. These include consulting the dictionary in the reverse direction (Tanaka and Umemura, 1994) and computing ranking scores, variously called a semantic score (Bond and Ogura, 2008), an overlapping constraint score, a similarity score (Paik et al., 2004) and a converse mapping score (Shaw et al., 2013). Other techniques to handle the ambiguity problem are merging results from several approaches: merging candidates from lexical triangulation (Gollins and Sanderson, 2001), creating a link structure among words (Ahn and Frampton, 2006) and building graphs connecting translations of words in several languages (Mausam et al., 2010). Researchers also merge information from several sources such as bilingual dictionaries and corpora (Otero and Campos, 2010) or a Wordnet (István and Shoichi, 2009) and (Lam and Kalita, 2013). Some researchers also extract bilingual dictionaries from corpora (Ljubešić and Fišer, 2011) and (Bouamor et al., 2013). The primary similarity among these methods is that either they work with languages that already possess several lexical resources or these approaches take advantage of related languages (that have some lexical resources) by using such languages as intermediary. The accuracies of bilingual dictionaries created from several available dictionaries and Wordnets are usually high. However, it is expensive to create such original

[3] http://www.oed.com/

[4] http://cdkc.edu/cheyennedictionary/index-english/index.htm

[5] http://www.openthesaurus.de/

lexical resources and they do not always exist for many languages. For instance, we cannot find any Wordnet for *chr* or *chy*. In addition, these existing approaches can only generate one or just a few new bilingual dictionaries from at least two existing bilingual dictionaries.

(Crouch, 1990) clusters documents first using a complete link clustering algorithm and generates thesaurus classes or synonym lists based on user-supplied parameters such as a threshold similarity value, number of documents in a cluster, minimum document frequency and specification of a class formation method. (Curran and Moens, 2002a) and (Curran and Moens, 2002b) evaluate performance and efficiency of thesaurus extraction methods and also propose an approximation method that provides for better time complexity with little loss in performance accuracy. (Ramírez et al., 2013) develop a multilingual Japanese-English-Spanish thesaurus using freely available resources: Wikipedia and Wordnet. They extract translation tuples from Wikipedia from articles in these languages, disambiguate them by mapping to Wordnet senses, and extract a multilingual thesaurus with a total of 25,375 entries.

One thing to note about all these approaches is that they are resource hungry. For example, (Lin, 1998) works with a 64-million word English corpus to produce a high quality thesaurus with about 10,000 entries. (Ramírez et al., 2013) has the entire Wikipedia at their disposal with millions of articles in three languages, although for experiments they use only about 13,000 articles in total. When we work with endangered or low-resource languages, we do not have the luxury of collecting such big corpora or accessing even a few thousand articles from Wikipedia or the entire Web. Many such languages have no or very limited Web presence. As a result, we have to work with whatever limited resources are available.

4 Creating new bilingual dictionaries

A dictionary *Dict(S,T)* between a source language *S* and a target language *T* has a list of entries. Each entry contains a word *s* in the source language *S*, part-of-speech (POS) and one or more translations in the target language *T*. We call such a translation *t*. Thus, a dictionary entry is of the form $<s_i,POS,t_{i1}>$, $<s_i,POS,t_{i2}>$, ...

This section examines approaches to create new bilingual dictionaries for endangered languages from just one dictionary *Dict(S,I)*, where *S* is the endangered source language and *I* is an "intermediate helper" language. We require that the language *I* has an available Wordnet linked to the Princeton Wordnet (PWN) (Fellbaum, 1998). Many endangered languages have a bilingual dictionary, usually to or from a resource-rich language like French or English which is the intermediate helper language in our experiments. We make an assumption that we can find only one unidirectional bilingual dictionary translating from a given endangered language to English.

4.1 Generating a reverse bilingual dictionary

Given a unidirectional dictionary *Dict(S,I)* or *Dict(I,S)*, we reverse the direction of the entries to produce *Dict(I,S)* or *Dict(S,I)*, respectively. We apply an approach called Direct Reversal with Similarity (DRwS), proposed in (Lam and Kalita, 2013) to create a reverse bilingual dictionary from an input dictionary.

The DRwS approach computes the distance between translations of entries by measuring their semantic similarity, the so-called *simValue*. The *simValue* between two phrases is calculated by comparing the similarity of the *ExpansionSet* for every word in one phrase with *ExpansionSet* of every word in the other phrase. An *ExpansionSet* of a phrase is a union of the synset, synonym set, hyponym set, and/or hypernym set of every word in it. The synset, synonym, hyponym and hypernym sets of a word are obtained from PWN. The greater is the *simValue* between two phrases, the more semantically similar are these phrases. According to (Lam and Kalita, 2013), if the *simValue* is equal to or greater than 0.9, the DRwS approach produces the "best" reverse dictionary.

For creating a reverse dictionary, we skip entries with multiword expression in the translation. Based on our experiments, we have found that approach is successful and hence, it may be an effective way to automatically create a new bilingual dictionary from an existing one. Figure 1 presents an example of generating entries for the reverse dictionary.

4.2 Building bilingual dictionaries to/from additional languages

We propose an approach using public Wordnets and MT to create new bilingual dictionaries *Dict(S,T)* from an input dictionary *Dict(S,I)*. As previously mentioned, *I* is English in our exper-

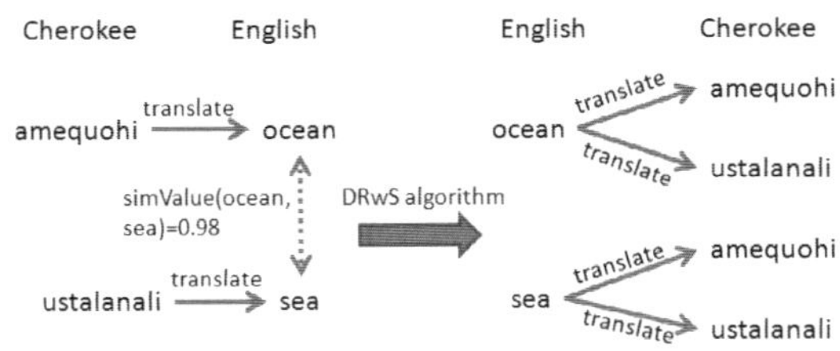

Figure 1: Example of creating entries for a reverse dictionary *Dict(eng,chr)* from *Dict(chr,eng)*. The *simValue* between the words "ocean" and "sea" is 0.98, which is greater than the threshold of 0.90. Therefore, the words "ocean" and "sea" in English are hypothesized to have both meanings "amequohi" and "ustalanali" in Cherokee. We add these entries to *Dict(eng, chr)*.

iments. *Dict(S,T)* translates a word in an endangered language *S* to a word or multiword expression in a target language *T*. In particular, we create bilingual dictionaries for an endangered language *S* from a given dictionary *Dict(S,eng)*. Figure 2 presents the approach to create new bilingual dictionaries.

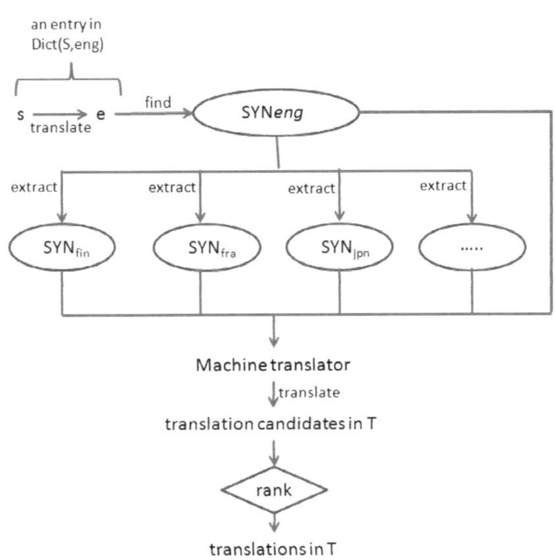

Figure 2: The approach for creating new bilingual dictionaries from intermediate Wordnets and a MT.

For each entry pair *(s,e)* in a given dictionary *Dict(S,eng)*, we find all synonym words of the word *e* to create a list of synonym words in English: SYN_{eng}. SYN_{eng} of the word *eng* is obtained from the PWN. Then, we find all synonyms of words belonging to SYN_{eng} in several non-English languages to generate SYN_L, $L \in \{fin, fra, jpn\}$. SYN_L in the language *L* is extracted from the publicly available Wordnet in language *L* linked to the PWN. Next, translation candidates are generated by translating all words in SYN_L, $L \in \{eng, fin, fra, jpn\}$ to the target language *T* using an MT. A translation candidate is considered a correct translation of the source word in the target language if its rank is greater than a threshold. For each word *s*, we may have many candidates. A translation candidate with a higher rank is more likely to become a correct translation in the target language. The rank of a candidate is computed by dividing its occurrence count by the total number of candidates. Figure 3 shows an example of creating entries for *Dict(chr,vie)*, where *vie* is Vietnamese, from *Dict(chr,eng)*.

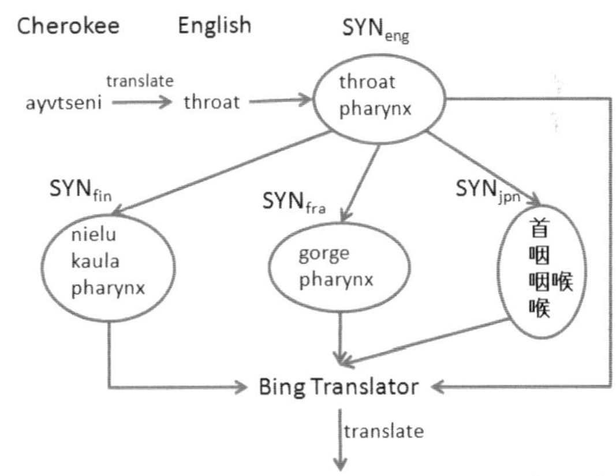

Candidate	Occ.	Rank	Candidate	Occ.	Rank
cổ họng	4	0.36	họng	4	0.36
họng	4	0.36	cổ	2	0.18
họng	4	0.36	đau họng	1	0.09
cổ	2	0.18	cổ họng	4	0.36
họng	4	0.36	cổ họng	4	0.36
cổ họng	4	0.36			

Figure 3: Example of generating new entries for *Dict(chr,vie)* from *Dict(chr,eng)*. The word "ayvtseni" in *chr* is translated to "throat" in *eng*. We find all synonym words for "throat" in English to generate SYN_{eng} and all synonyms in *fin*, *fra* and *jpn* for all words in SYN_{eng}. Then, we translate all words in all SYN_Ls to *vie* and rank them. According to rank calculations, the best translations of "ayvtseni" in *chr* are the words "cổ họng" and "họng" in *vie*.

5 Constructing thesauruses

As previously mentioned, we want to generate a multilingual thesaurus *THS* composed of endangered and resource-rich languages. For example, we build the thesaurus encompassing an endangered language *S* and *eng*, *fin*, *fra* and *jpn*. Our thesaurus contains a list of entries. Every entry has a unique *ID*. Each entry is a 7-tuple: *ID*, SYN_S, SYN_{eng}, SYN_{fin}, SYN_{fra}, SYN_{jpn} and POS. Each SYN_L contains words that have the same sense in language *L*. All SYN_L, $L \in \{S, eng, fin, fra, jpn\}$ with the same ID have the same sense.

This section presents the initial steps in constructing multilingual thesauruses using Wordnets and the bilingual dictionaries we create. The approach to create a multilingual thesaurus encompassing an endangered language and several resource-rich languages is presented in Figure 4 and Algorithm 1.

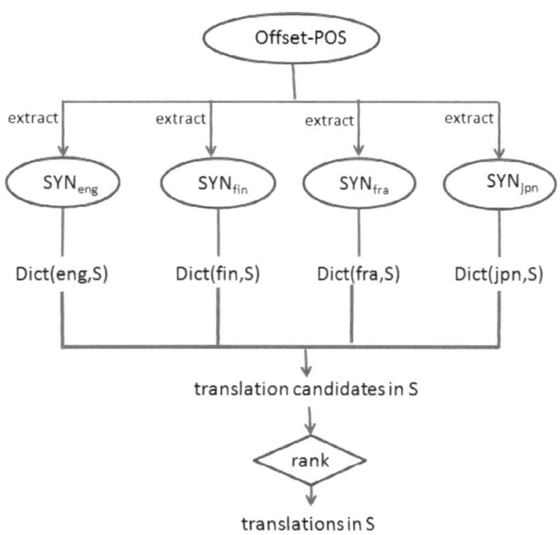

Figure 4: The approach to construct a multilingual thesaurus encompassing an endangered language *S* and resource-rich language.

First, we extract SYN_L in resource-rich languages from Wordnets. To extract SYN_{eng}, SYN_{fin}, SYN_{fra} and SYN_{jpn}, we use PWN and Wordnets linked to the PWN provided by the Open Multilingual Wordnet[6] project (Bond and Foster, 2013): FinnWordnet (FWN) (Lindén, 2010), WOLF (WWN) (Sagot and Fišer, 2008) and JapaneseWordnet (JWN) (Isahara et al., 2008). For each *Offset-POS*, we extract its corresponding synsets from PWN, FWN, WWN and JWN to generate SYN_{eng}, SYN_{fin}, SYN_{fra} and SYN_{jpn} (lines 7-10). The POS of the entry is the POS extracted from the *Offset-POS* (line 5). Since these Wordnets are aligned, a specific *offset-POS* retrieves synsets that are equivalent sense-wise. Then, we translate all SYN_Ls to the given endangered language *S* using bilingual dictionaries we created in the previous section (lines 11-14). Finally, we rank translation candidates and add the correct translations to SYN_S (lines 15-19). The rank of a candidate is computed by dividing its occurrence count by the total number of candidates. If a candidate has a rank value greater than a threshold, we accept it as a correct translation and add it to SYN_S.

Algorithm 1

Input: Endangered language S, PWN, FWN, WWN, JWN, Dict(eng,S), Dict(fin,S), Dict(fra,S) and Dict(jpn,S)
Output: thesaurus *THS*

1: ID:=0
2: **for all** *offset-POS*s in PWN **do**
3:   ID++
4:   candidates := ϕ
5:   POS=extract(offset-POS)
6:   SYN_S:= ϕ
7:   SYN_{eng}=extract(offset-POS, PWN)
8:   SYN_{fin}=extract(offset-POS, FWN)
9:   SYN_{fra}=extract(offset-POS, WWN)
10:   SYN_{jpn}=extract(offset-POS, JWN)
11:   candidates+=translate(SYN_{eng},S)
12:   candidates+=translate(SYN_{fin},S)
13:   candidates+=translate(SYN_{fra},S)
14:   candidates+=translate(SYN_{jpn},S)
15:   **for all** candidate in candidates **do**
16:     **if** rank(candidate) > α **then**
17:       add(candidate,SYN_S)
18:     **end if**
19:   **end for**
20:   add ID, *POS* and all SYN_L into *THS*
21: **end for**

Figure 5 presents an example of creating an entry for the thesaurus. We generate entries for the multilingual thesaurus encompassing of Cherokee, English, Finnish, French and Japanese.

We extract words belonging to *offset-POS* "09426788-n" in PWN, FWN, WWN and JWN and add them into corresponding SYN_L. The POS of this entry is "n", which is a "noun". Next, we use the bilingual dictionaries we cre-

[6] http://compling.hss.ntu.edu.sg/omw/

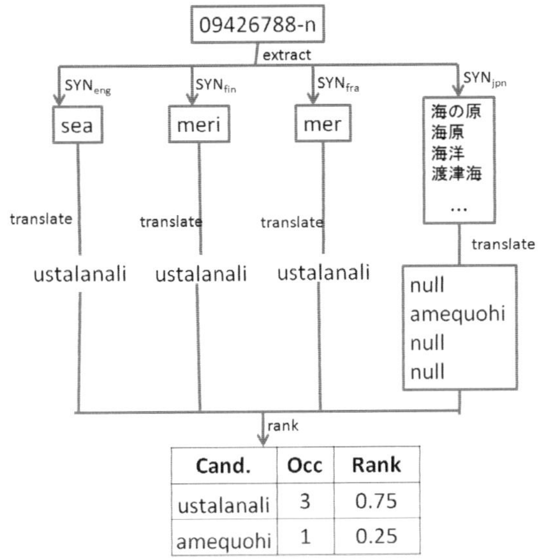

Figure 5: Example of generating an entry in the multilingual thesaurus encompassing Cherokee, English, Finnish, French and Japanese.

ated to translate all words in SYN_{eng}, SYN_{fin}, SYN_{fra}, SYN_{jpn} to the given endangered language, Cherokee, and rank them. According to the rank calculations, the best Cherokee translation is the word "ustalanali". The new entry added to the multilingual thesaurus is presented in Figure 6.

ID	POS	Cherokee	English	Finnish	French	Japanese
...	n	ustalanali	sea	meri	mer	海の原 海原 海洋 渡津海 ...

Figure 6: An entry of the multilingual thesaurus encompassing Cherokee, English, Finnish, French and Japanese.

6 Experimental results

Ideally, evaluation should be performed by volunteers who are fluent in both source and destination languages. However, for evaluating created dictionaries and thesauruses, we could not recruit any individuals who are experts in two corresponding languages. We are in the process of finding volunteers who are fluent in both languages for some selected resources we create.

6.1 Datasets used

We start with two bilingual dictionaries: *Dict(chr,eng)*[7] and *Dict(chy,eng)*[8] that we obtain from Web pages. These are unidirectional bilingual dictionaries. The numbers of entries in *Dict(chr,eng)* and *Dict(chy,eng)* are 3,199 and 28,097, respectively. For entries in these input dictionaries without POS information, our algorithm chooses the best POS of the English word, which may lead to wrong translations. The Microsoft Translator Java API[9] is used as another main resource. We were given free access to this API. We could not obtain free access to the API for the Google Translator.

The synonym lexicons are the synsets of PWN, FWN, JWN and WWN. Table 1 provides some details of the Wordnets used.

Wordnet	Synsets	Core
JWN	57,179	95%
FWN	116,763	100%
PWN	117,659	100%
WWN	59,091	92%

Table 1: The number of synsets in the Wordnets linked to PWN 3.0 are obtained from the Open Multilingual Wordnet, along with the percentage of synsets covered from the semi-automatically compiled list of 5,000 "core" word senses in PWN. Note that synsets which are not linked to the PWN are not taken into account.

6.2 Creating reverse bilingual dictionaries

From *Dict(chr,eng)* and *Dict(chy,eng)*, we create two reverse bilingual dictionaries *Dict(eng,chr)* with 3,538 entries and *Dict(eng,chy)* with 28,072 entries

Next, we reverse the reverse dictionaries we produce to generate new reverse of the reverse (RR) dictionaries, then integrate the RR dictionaries with the input dictionaries to improve the sizes of dictionaries. During the process of generating new reverse dictionaries, we already computed the semantic similarity values among words to find words with the same meanings. We use a simple approach called the Direct Reversal (DR) approach in (Lam and Kalita, 2013) to create

[7] http://www.manataka.org/page122.html

[8] http://www.cdkc.edu/cheyennedictionary/index-english/index.htm

[9] https://datamarket.azure.com/dataset/bing/microsofttranslator

these RR dictionaries. To create a reverse dictionary *Dict(T,S)*, the DR approach takes each entry <*s,POS,t*> in the input dictionary *Dict(S,T)* and simply swaps the positions of *s* and *t*. The new entry <*t,POS,s*> is added into *Dict(T,S)*. Figure 7 presents an example.

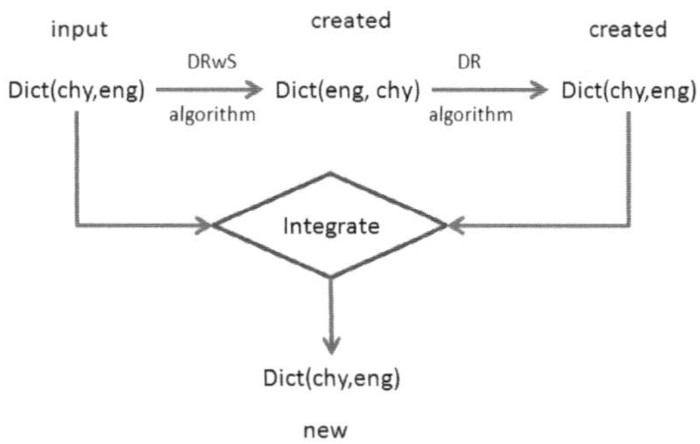

Figure 7: Given a dictionary *Dict(chy,eng)*, we create a new *Dict(eng,chy)* using the DRwS approach of (Lam and Kalita, 2013). Then, we create a new *Dict(chy,eng)* using the DR approach from the created dictionary *Dict(eng,chy)*. Finally, we integrate the generated dictionary *Dict(chy,eng)* with the input dictionary *Dict(chy,eng)* to create a new dictionary *Dict(chy,eng)* with a greater number of entries

The number of entries in the integrated dictionaries *Dict(chr,eng)* and *Dict(chy,eng)* are 3,618 and 47,529, respectively. Thus, the number of entries in the original dictionaries have "magically" increased by 13.1% and 69.21%, respectively.

6.3 Creating additional bilingual dictionaries

We can create dictionaries from *chr* or *chy* to any non-*eng* language supported by the Microsoft Translator, e.g., Arabic (*arb*), Chinese (*cht*), Catalan (*cat*), Danish (*dan*), German (*deu*), Hmong Daw (*mww*), Indonesian (*ind*), Malay (*zlm*), Thai (*tha*), Spanish (*spa*) and *vie*. Table 2 presents the number of entries in the dictionaries we create. These dictionaries contain translations only with the highest ranks for each word.

Although we have not evaluated entries in the particular dictionaries in Table 1, evaluation of dictionaries with non-endangered languages, but using the same approach, we have confidence that these dictionaries are of acceptable, if not very good quality.

Dictionary	Entries	Dictionary	Entries
chr-arb	2,623	chr-cat	2,639
chr-cht	2,607	chr-dan	2,655
chr-deu	2,629	chr-mww	2,694
chr-ind	2,580	chr-zlm	2,633
chr-spa	2,607	chr-tha	2,645
chr-vie	2,618	chy-arb	10,604
chy-cat	10,748	chy-cht	10,538
chy-dan	10,654	chy-deu	10,708
chy-mww	10,790	chy-ind	10,434
chy-zlm	10,690	chy-spa	10,580
chy-tha	10,696	chy-vie	10,848

Table 2: The number of entries in some dictionaries we create.

6.4 Creating multilingual thesauruses

We construct two multilingual thesauruses: THS_1(*chr, eng, fin, fra, jpn*) and THS_2(*chy, eng, fin, fra, jpn*). The number of entries in THS_1 and THS_2 are 5,073 and 10,046, respectively. These thesauruses we construct contain words with rank values above the average. A similar approach used to create Wordnet synsets (Lam et al., 2014) has produced excellent results. We believe that our thesauruses reported in this paper are of acceptable quality.

6.5 How to evaluate

Currently, we are not able to evaluate the dictionaries and thesauruses we create. In the future, we expect to evaluate our work using two methods. First, we will use the standard approach which is human evaluation to evaluate resources as previously mentioned. Second, we will try to find an additional bilingual dictionary translating from an endangered language *S* (viz., *chr* or *chy*) to another "resource-rich" non-English language (viz., *fin* or *fra*), then, create a new dictionary translating from *S* to English using the approaches we have introduced. We plan to evaluate the new dictionary we create, say *Dict(chr,eng)* against the existing dictionary *Dict(chr,eng)*.

7 Conclusion and future work

We examine approaches to create bilingual dictionaries and thesauruses for endangered languages from only one input dictionary, publicly available Wordnets and an MT. Taking advantage of available Wordnets linked to the PWN helps reduce ambiguities in dictionaries we create. We run experiments with two endangered languages: Cherokee and Cheyenne. We have also experimented with two additional endangered languages from Northeast India: Dimasa and Karbi, spoken by about 115,000 and 492,000 people, respectively. We believe that our research has the potential to increase the number of lexical resources for languages which do not have many existing resources to begin with. We are in the process of creating reverse dictionaries from bilingual dictionaries we have already created. We are also in the process of creating a Website where all dictionaries and thesauruses we create will be available, along with a user friendly interface to disseminate these resources to the wider public as well as to obtain feedback on individual entries. We will solicit feedback from communities that use the languages as mother-tongues. Our goal will be to use this feedback to improve the quality of the dictionaries and thesauruses. Some of resources we created can be downloaded from http://cs.uccs.edu/∼linclab/projects.html

References

Adam Kilgarriff. 2003. Thesauruses for natural language processing. In *Proceedings of the Joint Conference on Natural Language Processing and Knowledge Engineering*, pages 5–13, Beijing, China, October.

Benoit Sagot and Darja Fišer. 2008. Building a free French Wordnet from multilingual resources. In *Proceedings of OntoLex*, Marrakech, Morocco.

Carolyn J. Crouch 1990. An approach to the automatic construction of global thesauri, *Information Processing & Management*, 26(5): 629–640.

Christiane Fellbaum. 1998. *Wordnet: An Electronic Lexical Database*. MIT Press, Cambridge, Massachusetts, USA.

Dagobert Soergel. 1974. *Indexing languages and thesauri: construction and maintenance*. Melville Publishing Company, Los Angeles, California.

Dhouha Bouamor, Nasredine Semmar and Pierre Zweigenbaum. 2013 Using Wordnet and Semantic Similarity for Bilingual Terminology Mining from Comparable Corpora. In *Proceedings of the 6th Workshop on Building and Using Comparable Corpora*, pages 16–23, Sofia, Bulgaria, August. Association for Computational Linguistics.

Dekang Lin. 1998. Automatic retrieval and clustering of similar words. In *Proceedings of the 17th International Conference on Computational Linguistics (Volume 2)*, pages 768–774, Montreal, Quebec, Canada.

Francis Bond and Kentaro Ogura. 2008 Combining linguistic resources to create a machine-tractable Japanese-Malay dictionary. *Language Resources and Evaluation*, 42(2): 127–136.

Francis Bond and Ryan Foster. 2013. Linking and extending an open multilingual Wordnet. In *Proceedings of 51st Annual Meeting of the Association for Computational Linguistics (ACL 2013)*, pages 1352–1362, Sofia, Bulgaria, August.

Hitoshi Isahara, Francis Bond, Kiyotaka Uchimoto, Masao Utiyama and Kyoko Kanzaki. 2008. Development of Japanese Wordnet. In *Proceedings of 6th International Conference on Language Resources and Evaluation (LREC 2008)*, pages 2420–2423, Marrakech, Moroco, May.

James R. Curran and Marc Moens. 2002a. Scaling context space. In *Proceedings of the 40th Annual Meeting of Association for Computational Linguistics (ACL 2002)*, pages 231–238, Philadelphia, USA, July.

James R. Curran and Marc Moens. 2002b. Improvements in automatic thesaurus extraction, In *Proceedings of the Workshop on Unsupervised lexical acquisition (Volume 9)*, pages 59–66, Philadelphia, USA, July. Association for Computational Linguistics.

Jessica Ramírez, Masayuki Asahara and Yuji Matsumoto. 2013. Japanese-Spanish thesaurus construction using English as a pivot. *arXiv preprint arXiv*:1303.1232.

Jost Gippert, Nikolaus Himmelmann and Ulrike Mosel, eds. 2006. *Essentials of Lnguage Documentation*. Vol. 178, Walter de Gruyter GmbH & Co. KG, Berlin, Germany.

Khang N. Lam and Jugal Kalita. 2013. Creating reverse bilingual dictionaries. In *Proceedings of the Conference of the North American Chapter of the Association for Computational Linguistics: Human Language Technologies (NAACL-HLT)*, pages 524–528, Atlanta, USA, June.

Khang N. Lam, Feras A. Tarouti and Jugal Kalita. 2014. Automatically constructing Wordnet synsets. To *appear at the 52nd Annual Meeting of the Association for Computational Linguistics (ACL 2014)*, Baltimore, USA, June.

Kisuh Ahn and Matthew Frampton. 2006. Automatic generation of translation dictionaries using intermediary languages. In *Proceedings of the International Workshop on Cross-Language Knowledge Induction*, pages 41–44, Trento, Italy, April. European Chapter of the Association for Computational Linguistics.

Krister Lindén and Lauri Carlson 2010. FinnWordnet - WordNet påfinska via översättning, LexicoNordica. *Nordic Journal of Lexicography (Volume 17)*, pages 119–140.

Kumiko Tanaka and Kyoji Umemura. 1994. Construction of bilingual dictionary intermediated by a third language. In *Proceedings of the 15th Conference on Computational linguistics (COLING 1994), Volume 1*, pages 297–303, Kyoto, Japan, August. Association for Computational Linguistics.

Kyonghee Paik, Satoshi Shirai and Hiromi Nakaiwa. 2004. Automatic construction of a transfer dictionary considering directionality. In *Proceedings of the Workshop on Multilingual Linguistic Resources*, pages 31–38, Geneva, Switzerland, August . Association for Computational Linguistics.

Mausam, Stephen Soderland, Oren Etzioni, Daniel S. Weld, Kobi Reiter, Michael Skinner, Marcus Sammer and Jeff Bilmes 2010. Panlingual lexical translation via probabilistic inference. *Artificial Intelligence*, 174(2010): 619–637.

Nikola Ljubešić and Darja Fišer. 2011. Bootstrapping bilingual lexicons from comparable corpora for closely related languages. In *Proceedings of the 14th International Conference on Text, Speech and Dialogue (TSD 2011)*, pages 91–98. Plzeň, Czech Republic, September.

Pablo G. Otero and José R.P. Campos. 2010. Automatic generation of bilingual dictionaries using intermediate languages and comparable corpora. In *Proceedings of the 11th International Conference on Computational Linguistic and Intelligent Text Processing (CICLing'10)*, pages 473–483, Iaşi, Romania, March.

Peter M. Roget. 1911. *Roget's Thesaurus of English Words and Phrases....* Thomas Y. Crowell Company, New York, USA.

Peter M. Roget. 2008. *Roget's International Thesaurus*, 3rd Edition. Oxford & IBH Publishing Company Pvt, New Delhi, India.

Ryan Shaw, Anindya Datta, Debra VanderMeer and Kaushik Datta. 2013. Building a scalable database - Driven Reverse Dictionary. *IEEE Transactions on Knowledge and Data Engineering*, 25(3): 528–540.

Sidney I. Landau 1984. *Dictionaries: the art and craft of lexicography*. Charles Scribner's Sons, New York, USA.

Tim Gollins and Mark Sanderson. 2001. Improving cross language information retrieval with triangulated translation. In *Proceedings of the 24th Annual International ACM SIGIR Conference on Research and Development in Information Retrieval*, pages 90–95, New Orleans, Louisiana, USA, September.

Varga István and Yokoyama Shoichi. 2009. Bilingual dictionary generation for low-resourced language pairs. In *Proceedings of the 2009 Conference on Empirical Methods in Natural Language Processing (Volume 2)*, pages 862–870, Singapore, August. Association for Computational Linguistics.

Estimating Native Vocabulary Size in an Endangered Language

Timofey Arkhangelskiy
National Research University
Higher School of Economics,
Moscow, Russia
timarkh@gmail.com

Abstract

The vocabularies of endangered languages surrounded by more prestigious languages are gradually shrinking in size due to the influx of borrowed items. It is easy to observe that in such languages, starting from some frequency rank, the lower the frequency of a vocabulary item, the higher the probability of that item being a borrowed one. On the basis of the data from the Beserman dialect of Udmurt, the article provides a model according to which the portion of borrowed items among the items with frequency ranks less than r increases logarithmically in r, starting from some rank r_0, while for more frequent items, it can behave differently. Apart from theoretical interest, the model can be used to roughly predict the total number of native items in the vocabulary based on a limited corpus of texts.

1 Introduction

It is well known that in the situation of language contact the most easily borrowed part of the language is the lexicon (although there are counterexamples, see e.g. (Thomason, 2001:82)). Typically, for an endangered language or dialect L1 whose speakers are bilingual in another language L2 which is more prestigious and/or official in the area, the borrowing process is overwhelmingly unidirectional. Due to the influx of borrowed stems, words, and constructions from L2, as well as frequent code switching in speech, the size of the native vocabulary of L1 (defined as the set of vocabulary items in L1 which were not borrowed from L2 and are still remembered by the language community) is gradually decreasing. The stronger the influence of L2, the less native items remain in the vocabulary of L1, native lexemes being replaced with loanwords or just being lost without any replacement. Eventually the process may lead to a situation whereby L1 is confined to a small range of communicative situations, retaining only that part of native vocabulary which is relevant in these situations, and ultimately to language death (Wolfram, 2002).

It is interesting to study the vocabulary of a language currently undergoing the process of lexical erosion and search for rules that govern the process. Indeed, the process of native vocabulary shrinkage is not chaotic and turns out to conform to certain rules. In this article, I provide a model which shows how the native lexicon of an endangered language is being gradually lost. The model may be used to roughly estimate the native vocabulary size of the language. Apart from theoretical interest, such an estimate could have practical value for a field linguist, since it helps evaluate the coverage of the dictionary she compiled for the language: if the number of items in the dictionary is significantly less than the estimate, chances are there are vocabulary items still not covered by it.

2 The model and the data

The model is based on two observations related to frequency of vocabulary items. The main observation is that in the situation of extensive bilingualism, the probability of an item being a loanword instead of a native one increases with decreasing frequency of that item in L1: the less frequent the item, the more likely it is to turn out to be a borrowing. This synchronic property of the vocabulary is probably a consequence of a diachronic property of the borrowing process

Proceedings of the 2014 Workshop on the Use of Computational Methods in the Study of Endangered Languages, pages 63–67,
Baltimore, Maryland, USA, 26 June 2014.

whereby the less frequent an item in L1, the higher the probability it will be replaced with a non-native item from L2 in a given period of time. The other observation is that such behavior is characteristic of vocabulary items starting with some frequency f_0, while items of higher frequency may be governed by different laws.

The relation between frequency, rank and other properties of lexical (and other linguistic) items has a long history of study, starting at least from Zipf's work (Zipf, 1949). The idea that the most frequent items can have special properties is also well known (see e. g. (Dixon, 1977:20) for syntactic properties or (Bybee, 2010:37–48) for phonetic and morphosyntactic effects of frequency), and it has been widely used in lexicostatistics and glottochronology since Swadesh (Swadesh, 1955) for estimating the degree to which several languages are related to each other and determining the point in time at which they diverged.

Based on these two observations and on the data from an endangered dialect, I propose a model of synchronic distribution of loanword items in the vocabulary of an endangered language. The model highlights the connection between the rank of an item (i. e. its number in the frequency list) and the probability that the item is a borrowed one. By a borrowed item I understand an item that was borrowed from the language L2 whose influence L1 is currently experiencing. This definition might seem a little arbitrary: what if L1 has a number of items left from its previous extensive contact? But since most vocabulary items in most languages were probably borrowed from another language at some point and since it is often impossible to distinguish between native items and old borrowings, one has to draw a line somewhere, and this seems to be the most reasonable way to do so. According to this model, the fact "item of the rank r is a borrowed one" can be viewed as an outcome of a Bernoulli trial in which the probability of success can be approximated quite precisely by a logarithm of the rank of the item in the frequency list, starting from some (not very high) rank r_0, while for any item with smaller rank it can behave differently:

(1) Pr[the item is a borrowed one] $= a \log(r) + b$, if $r > r_0$,

where r is the rank of that item.

The actual language data, however, makes it difficult to prove the hypothesis in the form presented above. The data the model should be tested against is a list of stems with their frequencies in the corpus and labels saying whether a stem was borrowed from L2. Thus, we have a situation of binary choice, as for every frequency rank the stem corresponding to it is either native, or borrowed. Besides, for great many stems it is impossible to determine their rank precisely, since, however large the corpus, there are always many low-frequency stems that have same frequencies in it (there are, for example, more than 1200 hapax legomena in my case). When several stems have the same frequency, we can determine the segment (r_1, r_2) their frequency ranks occupy, but we cannot say which stem has which frequency rank.

To overcome these difficulties, I first will seek an approximation for the function $P(r)$ defined as the portion of borrowed stems among all stems whose rank does not exceed r:

(2) $P(r)$ = (number of borrowed stems among those with rank $< r$) / r

As I will show, P(r) grows logarithmically in r, for r > r0, and this approximation is very precise for our data. In Section 4 I discuss why this fact implies the original claim (1).

The data I used comes from the Beserman dialect of the Udmurt language (Finno-Ugric). All speakers of this dialect are bilingual in Russian (and some in literary Udmurt), the number of speakers is at most 2000 and is decreasing steadily. The dialect, unlike literary Udmurt, is endangered, since most fluent speakers are now in their forties or older, and the children usually communicate in Russian both with each other and in the family. Beserman has a number of older loanwords borrowed from neighboring Turkic languages (which are recognized as native by the speakers and will not be dealt with in this article by definition of a borrowed item) and a vast number of Russian borrowings, either incorporated into the lexicon, or spontaneous. My primary source was a corpus of spoken Beserman totalling about 64,000 tokens that was collected in the village of Shamardan, Yukamensk region, Udmurtia, with my participation.

3 The analysis of the data

The items whose distribution was studied were stems, although similar calculations could be carried out for lexemes. I built a frequency list of all stems, both Beserman and borrowed/Russian, for our corpus of spoken Beserman. Productive derivational affixes were not incorporated into stems, and in Russian stems, aspectual pairs were counted as one stem. The list was manually annotated: each stem was marked as either native or borrowed.

The distribution of native and borrowed stems is plotted at the figures 1 and 2. The only difference between the graphs is that the x axis of the plot on Fig. 1 is logarithmically scaled; all the data points and lines are identical at both plots. For each point, x stands for the rank of a stem in the frequency list, and y denotes the portion of borrowed stems among those with rank less than x.

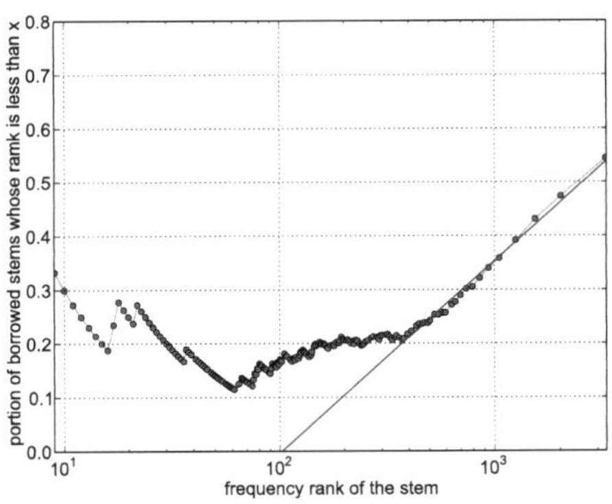

Fig. 1. Portion of borrowed stems with respect to the frequency rank with logarithmic approximation (semi-log plot)

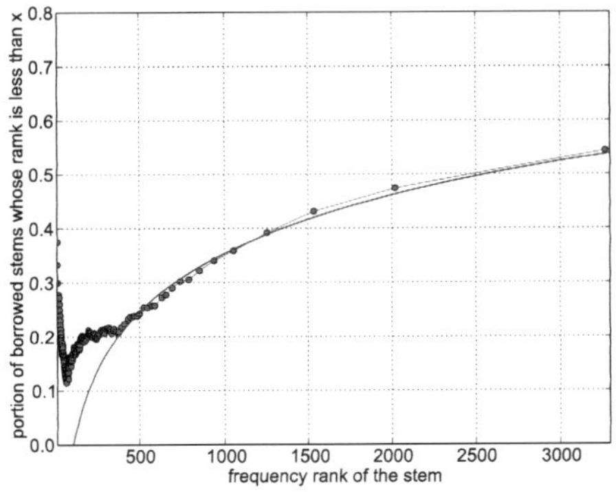

Fig. 2. Portion of borrowed stems with respect to the frequency rank with logarithmic approximation (linear axes)

The data points plotted at the graphs were split in two parts. Starting from r_0 of roughly 350, the data can be approximated nicely by a logarithmic function (a line in the semi-log plot): the blue curves are the approximations of the form $y = a\log(r) + b$ obtained with the least squares method. The peaks and declines in the beginning ot the frequency ranks range, e. g. for $r < 50$, do not provide any real insight into the behavior of the corresponding stems because the denominator in the formula for $P(r)$ is small and every single borrowed stem causes a visible rise of the line. For $50 < r < 350$, it can be seen that the portion of borrowed stems grows with r, but its growth does not conform to the same law which governs the behavior of less frequent items. For $r_0 > 350$, the best fit has the following parameters ($p < 0.001$):

$$a = 0.1550712 \pm 0.000254, \quad (3)$$
$$b = -0.71760178$$

The approximation is quite precise, as can be seen from the picture and the statistics (root-mean-square error 0.0088, coefficient of determination 0.99). One possible point of concern is the fact that the density of data points is much higher on the left part of the plot, so that the result is heavily influenced by the points with low frequency and only slightly influenced by the points with rank greater than 1000. If the items with higher ranks behave slightly differently than those with lower ranks, the difference could go unnoticed and the approximation will be not so precise for items with greater ranks. The only way to overcome this obstacle is testing the model on larger corpora. Another negative effect of such disparity stems from higher variance of the points on the left. However, it seems that for points with $r > 350$, the variance is already small enough for this effect to be significant (note that the y coordinate in such points is an average over at least 350 original observations).

Borrowed stems make up about 0.21 of the first 350 stems, and the behavior of $P(r)$ differs in this segment. The portion of borrowed stems increases slowly until it reaches the level of 0.2 for $r = 150$. For the next 200 frequency ranks or so, $P(r)$ stays at that level until it starts growing again around $r = 350$.

4 Calculating the probability of being borrowed

According to the model I propose, the labels "native" or "borrowed" in the data table can be seen as generated by independent Bernoulli trials: the stem with frequency rank r gets the label "borrowed" with the probability $a \log(r) + b$, for all $r > r_0$. However, the logarithmic approximation that was derived in Section 3, estimates $P(r)$ rather than the probability of rth stem being a borrowed one. Here I will show how a logarithmic approximation for probability can be deduced from the approximation for $P(r)$.

Suppose the label for the rth stem is an outcome of a Bernoulli trial with probability of success (i. e. getting the label "borrowed") equal to $f(r)$, an increasing function whose values do not exceed 0 and 1. We define $z(r)$ as 0 if the rth item is native or 1 otherwise. Then the expectation of $P(r)$ can be estimated as follows:

(4) $E[P(r)] = E[(1/r) \sum z(i)] = (1/r) \sum E[z(i)] = (1/r) \sum f(i)$

The resulting sum may be estimated by the following inequalities:

(5) $$(1/r)\int_1^r f(x-1)\,dx \le (1/r)\sum_1^r f(i) \le (1/r)\int_1^r f(x)\,dx$$

Provided the interval is sufficiently narrow, we can assume that E[P(r)] is approximately equal to the right part of (5). Now, we know that E[P(r)] is well approximated by a logarithmic function $y = c \log(r) + d$ (for points where this logarithmic function is less than 0 or greater than 1, let y equal 0 or 1, respectively). Therefore, the following holds:

(6) $$(1/r)\int_1^r f(x)\,dx = c\log r + d \Rightarrow (1/r)(F(r)-F(1)) = c\log r + d \Rightarrow F(r) = c\,r\log r + d\,r + F(1) \Rightarrow f(r) = F'(r) = c\log r + (c+d),$$

where $F(r)$ stands for the indefinite integral of $f(r)$. Using the constants obtained in the Section 3, we can estimate the probability as follows:

(7) Pr[the item is a borrowed one] = $(0.1550712 \pm 0.000254) \log(r) - (0.534576 \pm 0.000254)$, if $r > 350$.

5 Using the data for assessing dictionary coverage

The logarithmic model predicts that every item which has sufficiently large frequency rank will necessarily be a borrowed one, as the logarithm crosses the line $y = 1$ at some point. Based on this observation, one can estimate the expected total number of native vocabulary items the language retains. To do that, one should sum up the expected values of y for every r from 1 to the rightmost r for which the probability is still less than 1. In doing so, we assume that the events "the item of the rank r is a borrowed one" are independent and random (they happen with probability $(0.1550712 \pm 0.000298) \log(r) - (0.56253058 \pm 0.000298)$ for $r > 350$ and with probability 0.21 for more frequent stems). Calculations reveal that the point at which the probability curve crosses the line $y = 1$ lies in the interval (23770, 24206), and the expected total number of native stems is between 3603 and 3725 (for $a = 0.1550712$, it equals 3664). These bounds should be further widened as the observed value of a random variable is likely to deviate from the expected value within certain limits. Using Hoeffding's inequality for the sum of independently distributed random variables (Hoeffding, 1963) (8), we get that with 0.99 probability, the number of native Beserman stems should lie somewhere between and 3369 and 3962.

(8) $$\Pr[|\sum X_i - E[\sum X_i]| \ge t] \le \exp(-2t^2 / \sum(b_i - a_i)^2), \text{ where } \Pr[a_i \le X_i \le b_i] = 1$$

This estimate is rather imprecise, but nevertheless it provides information on the order of magnitude of the native vocabulary size. At the moment, there are about 2000 native Beserman stems known to us (which yields about 4000 dictionary entries in the dictionary (Kuznetsova et al., 2013)), therefore the model indicates that the list of stems can be significantly expanded and the efforts should be continued.

6 Assumptions and limitations

Apart from the two observations connecting frequency of vocabulary items and the probability of borrowing, there are more subtle assumptions the proposed estimate is based on, which can introduce additional pitfalls to the method.

One of such pitfalls is the assumption of representativeness of the corpus. When speaking of frequencies and frequency ranks of stems or words in the framework of this method, I mean the frequencies of those items in the corpus of texts. In reality, however, an item is less likely to be replaced by a loanword if it is either frequent in speech in general, or frequent in particular communicative situations. As corpus data is the only means to estimate frequencies, we have to substitute the real frequencies with those found in the corpus. Although in the case of corpora of larger languages for which multiple means of communication are available (books, press, broadcasts etc.), the notion of representativeness is quite vague (Leech, 2006), for languages which exist only in spoken form, representativeness is much easier to define: the corpus can be said to be representative if the frequencies of items in the corpus faithfully reproduce the frequencies of the same items in speech. Thus, for the model to yield reliable results, we need a representative corpus. In practice that means that the corpus should contain texts of various genres (interviews, dialogues, folklore etc.), texts should cover a wide range of topics (including topics connected to the traditional culture and way of life as the vocabulary of these areas is especially likely to retain native items), they should be produced by speakers of different age, sex, background, etc. Failure to represent certain genres or topics in the corpus leads to certain items or classes of items being overseen by the researcher. For example, although our corpus covers a wide range of topics and genres, there were no occurrences of the words *ɨ* 'lungs' and *lɨ* 'spine', the only two words in the dialect that retain the phoneme /ɨ/. The reason for that was, of course, not their overall low frequency in speech, but lack of texts recorded in situations where use of those words would be appropriate.

7 Further work

In order to verify the model presented here, it will be necessary to look at the data from other languages with similar status. As there exists a handful of manually annotated corpora for various indigenous languages of Russia which have undergone the same influence for roughly the same period as Beserman, the task of analyzing two or three more languages with comparable data seems realistic. Of course, it would be more productive to analyze larger corpora, but this is more of an obstacle here because such languages usually don't have corpora whose size would significantly exceed one or, at best, several hundred thousand tokens.

Apart from other languages in similar circumstances it would be helpful to see if the model works for languages that are engaged in language contact but not endangered (specifically, languages whose own word-formation mechanisms are still active), e. g. literary Udmurt.

If the data from other comparable language corpora indeed verifies the model, a possible further step would be to come up with a diachronic model that would describe the process whereby the native vocabulary is being gradually replaced with loanwords in a language whose own word-formation system has ceased to function.

References

Joan Bybee. 2010. *Language, usage and cognition.* Cambridge University Press, New York.

Robert M. W. Dixon. 1977. Where have all the adjectives gone? *Studies in Language* 1.1:19–80.

Ariadna I. Kuznetsova et al. 2013. *Slovar' besermjanskogo dialekta udmurtskogo jazyka* [Dictionary of the Beserman dialect of Udmurt]. Tezaurus, Moscow, Russia.

Wassily Hoeffding. 1963. Probability inequalities for sums of bounded random variables. *Journal of the American Statistical Association*, 58 (301):13–30.

Geoffrey Leech. 2006. New resources, or just better old ones? The Holy Grail of representativeness. *Language and Computers*, 59.1:133–149.

Morris Swadesh. 1955. Towards greater accuracy in lexicostatistic dating. *International Journal of American Linguistics*, 21:121–137.

Sarah G. Thomason. 2001. *Language contact.* Edinburgh University Press, Edinburgh, UK.

Walt Wolfram. 2002. Language death and dying. *The handbook of language variation and change*, 764–787. Blackwell Publishing, Oxford, UK.

George K. Zipf. 1949. *Human Behavior and the Principle of Least Effort.* Addison-Wesley, Cambridge, MA.

InterlinguaPlus Machine Translation Approach for Under-Resourced Languages: Ekegusii & Swahili

Edward O. Ombui[1, 2], Peter W. Wagacha[2] and Wanjiku Ng'ang'a[2]
[1] Computer Science Dept. Africa Nazarene University (Kenya)
eombui@anu.ac.ke
[2] School of Computing and Informatics, University of Nairobi (Kenya)
waiganjo@uonbi.ac.ke, wanjiku.nganga@uonbi.ac.ke

Abstract

This paper elucidates the InterlinguaPlus design and its application in bi-directional text translations between Ekegusii and Kiswahili languages unlike the traditional translation pairs, one-by-one. Therefore, any of the languages can be the source or target language. The first section is an overview of the project, which is followed by a brief review of Machine Translation. The next section discusses the implementation of the system using Carabao's open machine translation framework and the results obtained. So far, the translation results have been plausible particularly for the resource-scarce local languages and clearly affirm morphological similarities inherent in Bantu languages.

Keywords: Machine Translation, InterlinguaPlus, Ekegusii

1. Introduction

Development of language applications for local languages in Africa requires innovative approaches since many of these languages are resource scarce. By this we mean that electronic language resources such as digital corpora, electronic dictionaries, spell checkers, annotators, and parsers are hardly available. These languages are also predominately spoken rather than written. Moreover, they are generally used in environments where there are other competing languages like English and French which have been well documented over the years with properly defined grammars, unlike the local languages with poorly defined grammars and dictionaries. This has been a major setback in the development of technologies for African languages. The presence of diacritics in most of these languages has also contributed to the complexity involved in the development of language technology applications. (Ombui & Wagacha, 2007).

Nevertheless, there is pioneering work with the South African languages, which includes the definition of proper language grammars and development of a national language policy framework to encourage the utilization of the indigenous languages as official languages (NLPF, 2003).

In this paper, we consider two Bantu languages in Kenya namely Ekegusii and Swahili. There are approximately two million Ekegusii language speakers (KNBS, 2009). Swahili is widely spoken in East and Central Africa and is one of the official languages of the African Union with lots of printed resources.

For the work that we are reporting, we have adopted the InterlinguaPlus approach using the Carabao open machine translation framework (Berman, 2012). In this approach, all similar meaning words, synonyms, from each language and across the languages existing in the system are stored under the same category and assigned an identical family number. These words are also tagged with numbered lexical information[1]. For example, *Egetabu* (a book) [1=N; 2=SG; 5=No]. Tag1 stands for the part of speech (1-POS), Noun, tag2 for number (2-No.), Singular, and tag5 indicates whether the noun is animate or inanimate etc. An amalgamation of the word's family identification number and tag numbers form a unique ID for the word. In addition, a novel way of only storing the base forms of each word and having a different table containing affixes that inflect the word drastically reduces the lexical database size and development time in general. This approach is implemented through the manual encoding of the sequence rules for the two languages.

Preliminary results are encouraging and clearly reveal similarities in the language structure of Ekegusii and Swahili. The advantage of this approach is that the translation is bidirectional and maintains the semantic approach to translation just as a human translator. In addition, it is suitable for rapid generation of domain specific translations for under-resourced languages.

[1] Grammatical, Stylistic and Semantic tags

Proceedings of the 2014 Workshop on the Use of Computational Methods in the Study of Endangered Languages, pages 68–72,
Baltimore, Maryland, USA, 26 June 2014.

2. Machine Translation

Over the history of MT, several techniques and approaches have continued to be developed despite previous discouraging reports (ALPAC, 1966). The major approaches and methodologies include: Rule-based and Corpus-based, Direct translation and indirect translation (i.e. transfer-based and Interlingua-based) (Hutchins, 1993 & Hutchins, 1994). With the introduction of Artificial Intelligence technology in MT, more recent approaches have been proposed including alignment template approach to Statistical MT (Och & Ney, 2004), Knowledge-based approach (Nirenburg et al., 1992), Human in loop, and Hybrid methods (Groves & Way, 2006).

One of the strengths of the InterlinguaPlus approach (Berman, 2012) is that it preserves semantic information of the lexicon. Therefore, translation is primarily based on semantic equivalents between the lexicons of these languages.

As a result, the traditional language pair-based translation is replaced by bidirectional translations between the languages existing in the system. Any language can be the source or a target language.

Consequently, the lexical database size is drastically reduced and the task of building multiple dictionaries is concentrated in constructing just one Interlingua lexical database. This kind of approach is evidently advantageous when building machine translation applications for under-resourced African languages because it expedites the process of adding a new language with minimal effort especially when adding languages of similar grammatical makeup, which could reuse some of the existing grammar rules.

3. Implementation

Figure 1 below illustrates the translation process in the Ekegusii Machine Translation (EMT) system. The user inputs a sentence, which is parsed into its constituent tokens. These tokens are then matched and mapped to their equivalent target-language tokens using the Family and mapping Identification numbers respectively. In addition, the sequence[2] e.g. Subject+Verb+Object is parsed into elements (lexical units) and authenticated against the elements of the analyzed sentence. If it is valid, the elements are mapped according to the sequence and modified by the corresponding sequence in the target language. Some of the features that can be modified include deleting or adding a new element. E.g. He ate a mango.[eng:SVO]. *A+li+kula Embe* . Note that Swahili and generally the local African languages do not have determiners. Therefore, when translating from Eng-Swa, the English determiner is dropped. However, it is added if the translation is vice-versa. This is made possible by assigning a locally unique identity number, preserved across languages in the database, to each lexical unit of a sequence. The sequence manager in the system uses these identity numbers to appropriately handle lexical holes and the source/target of each transformation.

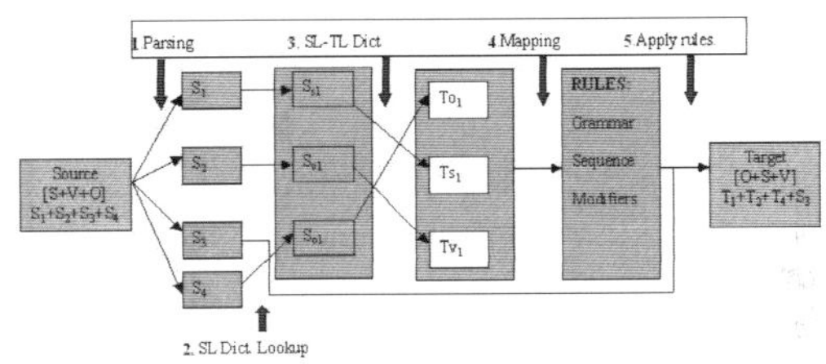

Figure1: EMT's MR-PDF

Subject (S_1); Verb (V_1); Object (O_1); Determinant (det); delimiter (del).

The above process, MR-PDF[3], is an acronym for the five translation stages (explained below) with the last two stages shifted at the beginning so as to give it an easy-to-remember name. We will use example 1, English to Ekegusii SVO phrase to elucidate the process.

Example 1

He ate a mango.

Stage 1: Parsing

The sentence is analyzed syntactically according to its constituent structures i.e. tokens including syntax delimiters like question marks, exclamation marks etc.

He + ate + a + mango.

S_{s1}:[He] S_{v1}:[ate] Det:[a] S_{o1}:[Mango] del:[.]

It is worth noting that at this stage, the parts of speech have not yet been identified.

Stage 2: Source Language Dictionary Lookup

Each token from stage 1 is looked up in the respective source language dictionary to check whether it exists in that language. In case it is not

[2] Set of elements, which refer to tokens that have specified features e.g. grammatical data, style, word-order, etc.

[3] Mapping (M), Rules (R), Parsing (P), Dictionary look-up (D), Family word-match (F).

found, the word is left untagged and passed-on as it is to the next stages up to the output.

Stage 3: Family word-match

Every morpheme is examined considering all possible combination of affixes to it and each configuration stored. These are then aligned with the corresponding target language dictionary entities.

[He]= [*Ere*]

[ate]= [*ariete*] Past form of eat=*karia*

[a]= [a] yields the same token if an equivalent is not found in the target language.

[Mango]= [*Riembe*] Singular, noun.

All other delimiters, e.g. question marks (?), comas (,) are presented as they appeared in the source string. From the above example, all possible modifiers of the verb "to eat" are generated i.e. eat, ate, eaten, eats, eating, and matched with the corresponding verb in Ekegusii dictionary i.e. *Karia, ariete, nkoria,* etc.

The tricky part of it is that one may not always have an equivalent number of modified verbs in the target or source dictionaries. To resolve this ambiguity, the program picks the modified verb with the best match in the target language dictionary i.e. in terms of matching lexical or style information e.g. the type of tense, number, animation, gender etc.

If we refer to the same example above, the following is examined as shown in Table 1and Table 2.

Language	**Morpheme**	**Part Of Speech**	**"Modified Morphemes"**
English	Eat	Verb	Ate; eaten; eating, eats, etc.
Ekegusii	Ria	Verb	Karia, ariete, nkoriare, etc.

Table 1: *Lexical information*

"Modified Morphemes"	**Tense**	**Number**
Ate	Past	Singular or Plural
Eating	Present continuous	Singular or plural
Mbariete	Past	Plural
Ariete	Past	Singular

Table 2: *Style information*

Language: English

Ate [tense-past; number-any]

It is apparent that both dictionaries are used to provide grammatical information, semantic data and potential equivalents in the target language during this stage.

Stage 4: Mapping

At the mapping stage, the Source text is validated against all existing sequences trees in the language. Only the most complete and detailed tree is picked. From example 1 above, the most appropriate sequence tree will be as follows and illustrated in figure 2.

He ate a mango	*Ri-embe a-rie-te*
[PN] + [V] + [Det] + [N]	[N] + [V]

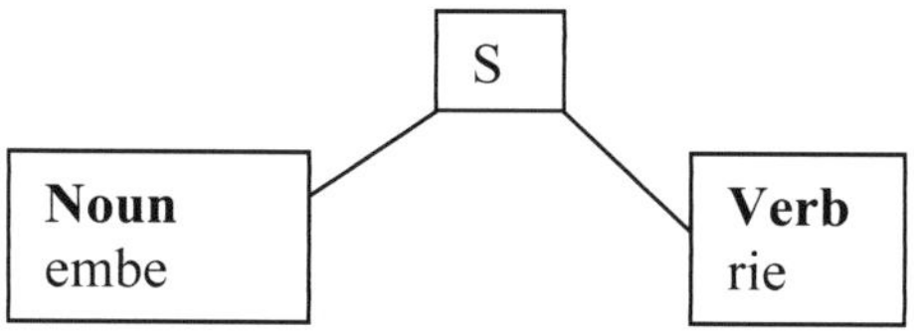

Figure 2: Sequence tree

The elements in the source sequence will map exactly into the [N] + [V] sequence. At this point all the redundant guesses are eliminated and disambiguation occurs. There are more comparisons and checks - like subject and style checks, etc.

Stage 5: Apply Rules.

The elements in the source sequence are modified by the corresponding sequence in the target language. The affixes are attached, or some new elements added or others completely deleted. Each element's unique identity is used to map the source sequence to the equivalent target sequence identities. Remember that Ekegusii does not have determiners and therefore it is dropped.

From the example above, the noun is then modified by adding the singular prefix- *ri*, (noun class 13) while the verb is modified by concatenating the subject- *a* (singular pronoun) to the verb- *rie* and finally adding the suffix- *te* (Past tense). The final sentence then becomes as shown below

Riembe ariete -> ri-embe a-rie-te

In case it is converted to plural, the noun prefix will change to- *ama* (noun class 6) and the pronoun to- *ba* while maintaining the past tense suffix- *te*

Amaembe bariete -> Ama-embe ba-rie-te

Finally, the sentence word order is rearranged according to the best fitting sequence tree in the target language sequence table.

4. Results

The results gotten so far are plausible. The word order is correct as per the programmed sequence rules for each language e.g. English: *This is a book*; Ekegusii. *Eke n'egetabu*; Kiswahili: *Hiki ni kitabu*. In addition, the bidirectional functionality is often more than 50% accurate on the wider domains and about 90% accurate on specific domains, in our case the obituary's domain. This evaluation is based on phrase level. Besides, once a phrase text has been translated, it can also be used as the source text and the translator will yield the exact translation as the initial source text. This therefore makes a strong case for the high intelligibility of the system.

The idea of storing only the word base forms and having a separate table for the affixes has drastically reduced the lexical database size as well as the building time. It was also noted that there is need for careful configuration of the rule units[4] for the affixes and lexicon otherwise the translation will be inaccurate. If we are to use the example above, the canonical[5] form will be as follows: English: FID-144 Book [POS: N; Number: SG; Animation: No]. However, for Ekegusii, there is need for additional rules units to indicate the noun class[6] because the nouns inflection is dependent on the noun class, otherwise the machine translator might concatenate the wrong prefix. Therefore, the English example above will be matched as follows. Ekegusii: FID-144 ***tabu*** [POS: N; Animation: No, EkeNC[7]: 8/9].

Consequently, the translator compares the rule units of the word with the rule units of the modifiers[8] in the affixes table and picks the most matching affix, in this case the prefix *"ege"* [POS: N; Number: SG; Animation: No, EkeNC[9]:8/9], ensuing n accurate translated word "ege***tabu***". On the contrary, if the Ekegusii rule units were not added or wrongly configured, the translation will be bizarre e.g. "Omo***tabu***" which is an invalid Ekegusii name. In fact, the prefix "omo" [EkeNC: 1] is often reserved for singular human[10] nouns.

The results obtained also expound the diversity of Ekegusii language linguistic rules[11] as compared to English. Most Indo-European languages, specifically English, espouse the SVO[12] sentence structure rule. However, in Ekegusii both SVO and VOS rules are valid sentence structure rules. For example, English: Mum ate mangoes [SVO]. Ekegusii: 1.*Omog'ina nariete amaembe [SVO]. 2. Nariete amaembe Omong'ina [VOS]*. Interestingly, the Ekegusii sequence and grammar rules that were copied and pasted to Swahili with minimal alteration resulted in almost precise translations between the two languages. This inevitably affirms the similarity in the language structure of the two languages and the ease in defining, constructing and translating between local languages as compared to/or from English.

The project demonstrations made so far to peers and students have generated a lot of enthusiasm in African languages research and given a good indication of the reception of technology in a familiar language platform.

5. Conclusion

The InterlinguaPlus approach is good particularly for under-resourced languages in terms of generating rapid translations that give a good gist of the meaning in the second language. Although it takes some time to write the grammar rules for a new language at the beginning, it however takes a relatively shorter time when adding languages of similar grammatical makeup. Therefore, the approach is very feasible especially when considering under-resourced languages which may not be afforded the appropriate finances and sufficient political will to have technological resources built for them.

The lexical database building methodology, whereby words and their grammatical data are stored in respective families and assigned a unique identification, provides an excellent way of reducing the chances of ambiguity that may exist in the phonetic disparities inherent in these local languages.

The InterlinguaPlus approach employed in the Carabao Open MT framework forms a good foundation to scale existing language resources

[4] A tag bearing any piece of grammatical data: part of speech, number contrast, gender, conjugation pattern, etc.
[5] Base form of the word before any inflection
[6] There are about 17 Ekegusii noun classes
[7] Ekegusii Noun Class
[8] In this case, Prefixes
[9] Ekegusii Noun Class
[10] Professions, etc.
[11] Sequence and grammar rules
[12] Subject, Verb, Object

to many other under-resourced languages using minimal effort i.e. the number of rules written for a language and consequently the time taken to develop a new language.

6. References

Automatic Language Processing Advisory Committee (ALPAC). 1966. Languages and Machines: Computers in Translation and *Linguistics*. National Academy of Sciences, National Research Council, 1966. (Publication 1416).

Declan Groves, and Andy Way. 2006. Hybrid Data-Driven Model of MT. ttp://citeseerx.ist.psu.edu/showciting?cid=5495125 (Retrieved March 15, 2014)

Declan Groves. Bringing Humans into the Loop: Localization with Machine Translation at Traslán http://citeseerx.ist.psu.edu/viewdoc/versions?doi=10.1.1.210.2867 (Retrieved March 15, 2014)

Edward Ombui, and Peter Wagacha. 2007. Machine Translation for Kenyan Local Languages. In *Proceedings of COSCIT conference*. Nairobi, Kenya.

Franz J. Och, and Hermann Ney. 2004. The Alignment Template Approach to Statistical Machine Translation. http://acl.ldc.upenn.edu/J/J04/J04-4002.pdf (Retrieved January 25, 2014)

John W. Hutchins. 1993. Latest Developments in Machine Translation Technology: Beginning a New Era in MT Research. *MT Summit* (1993), pp. 11-34.

John W. Hutchins. 1994. *Research Methods and System Designs in Machine Translation: A Ten-Year Review, 1984-1994*. http://www.mt-archive.info/BCS-1994-Hutchins.pdf (Retrieved August 1, 2013)

Kenya National Bureau of Statistics (KNBS, 2009). Ethnic Affiliation http://www.knbs.or.ke/censusethnic.php. (Retrieved September 6, 2013)

National Language Policy Framework. 2003. Retrieved from the Department of Arts and Culture website of South Africa. https://www.dac.gov.za/sites/default/files/LPD_Language%20Policy%20Framework_English_0.pdf

Sergei Nirenburg, Jaime Carbonell, Masaru Tomita, and Kenneth Goodman. 1992. Machine Translation: A Knowledge-Based Approach. http://acl.ldc.upenn.edu/J/J93/J93-1013.pdf (Retrieved November 22, 2013)

Vadim Berman. 2012. Inside Carabao: Language Translation Software for XXI Century. Retrieved from the LinguaSys website http://www.linguasys.com/web_production/PDFs/InsideCarabaoWhitePaper.pdf.

Building and Evaluating Somali Language Corpora

Nimaan Abdillahi
Institut des Sciences et des Nouvelles Technologies
Centre d'Etudes et de Recherche de Djibouti
B.P 486 Djibouti
Nimaan.abdillahi@gmail.com

Abstract

In this paper we outline our work to build Somali language Corpora. A read-speech corpus named ***Asaas*** and containing about 10 hours and 26 minutes of good quality signal fully transcribed and well corrected with a well-balanced phonetic distribution is presented. Secondly we outline a Web-based Somali textual corpus named ***Wargeys*** and containing about 3 million of words and more than 120 000 different words. This corpus is formatted and the spelling fluctuation is standardized.

1 Introduction

Transcribed speech corpora and huge text corpora are the core of systems used to construct acoustic and language models (Jelinek, F. 1976). Constructing of large transcribed corpora is time consuming and expensive, even if some researchers (Hughes et al, 2010; Badenhorst et al, 2009; Schlippe et al, 2012; De Pauw et al, 2009) are working on how to create automatically and quickly speech corpora by using different systems including phone applications.

If large transcribed speech corpora, more than 100 hours, exist for European languages like English, French or Spanish, the situation is quite different for African languages. About 2000 languages are spoken in Africa. Large part of them is not yet written and is today threatened of disappearing. Building speech Corpora and speech processing tools are crucial for each African language.

In this paper we present in section 2 the Somali language. Section 3 will focus on the first Somali read-speech corpus called ***Asaas*** (Beginning in Somali) and also the first Web-Based Somali Language Model and text Corpus called ***Wargeys*** (Newspaper in Somali) in Section 4.

2 Somali language

Four languages are spoken in Djibouti. French and Arabic are official languages, Somali and Afar are native and widely spoken. Somali and Afar are Cushitic languages within the Afro- asiatic family. Somali language is spoken in several countries in East of Africa (Djibouti, Ethiopia, Somalia and Kenya) by a population estimated between 11 to 13 million of inhabitants. The different variants are Somali-somali, Somali-maay, Somali-dabarre, Somali-garre, Somali-jiiddu and Somali-tunni. Somali-somali and Somali-maay are the most widely spread variants (80% and 17%). We only process the Somali-somali variant, commonly known as Somali language and spoken in Djibouti. The phonetic structure of this language has 22 consonants and 5 basic vowels which all occur in front and back versions (+ATR or -ATR). These 10 vowels occur in long and short pairs, giving 20 in total (Saeed, J. 1999). There are also 5 diphthongs which occur in front and back, long and short versions. Somali is also a tone accent language with 2 to 3 lexical tones (Hyman, L. 2010; Saeed, J. 1987; Gac, D. 2002). The written system was adopted in 1972, and there are no textual archives before this date. It uses Roman letters and doesn't consider the tonal accent in the current form. Somali words are composed by the concatenation of syllable structures (Bendjaballah, S. 1998. Saeed, J. 1999).

3 Somali Read-Speech corpus

3.1 Prompts Selection

A series of documents was selected from Somali online newspapers that use variant Somali-

Proceedings of the 2014 Workshop on the Use of Computational Methods in the Study of Endangered Languages, pages 73–76,
Baltimore, Maryland, USA, 26 June 2014.

Somali presented in Section 2. These texts are used to prepare the prompts. Particular attention was given to the quality of the selected texts (diversity of topics, phoneme distribution, readability, number of errors, etc.). Table 1 shows the distribution of selected text. It consists of 72,407 words (representing 2,335 sentences) with 12,807 different words.

Component	Amount
Sentences	2 335
Words	72 407
Different Words	12 807

Table 1: Distribution of selected text

3.2 Speakers selection

French and Arabic languages are official languages in Djibouti. The transcription of Somali language in Roman letters facilitates its reading. But it is difficult to find persons who can read it fluently. Fifteen Somali-speaking men living in Djibouti and without any problem of pronunciation were preselected. At last 10 people were selected for recordings according to their reading fluency. Table 2 shows information on their social class, their study level and their age. All recorders were volunteers.

Spakers Initials	Profession	Study Level	Age
Aaa	Technician	secondary	30-40
Abg	Researcher	University	40-50
Ahd	Journalist	secondary	40-50
Hha	Businessman	secondary	30-40
Hhdj	Technician	secondary	20-30
Hnm	Jobless	secondary	30-40
Ind	Technician	secondary	20-30
Ism	Policemen	University	40-50
Mar	Writer	University	50-60
sha	Writer	University	50-60

Table 2: Speakers Characteristics

3.3 Recordings

The recordings took place in the Djibouti Institute of Science and Information Technologies. They were recorded in mono in an office without any environment noise (fan, air-conditioner, phone, etc.) with a standard microphone with a sampling frequency of 16 KHz and a 16-bit encoding.

3.4 Corpus characteristics

The duration of the Somali read-speech corpus is 10 hours and 26 minutes. We named it ***Asaas***, which means "beginning" in the Somali language. Its phonetic distribution is given in Figure 1. We can consider that this distribution is well-balanced because it is quite similar to the one of the huge amount of the Somali text corpus (3 million of words). The phoneme /**a**/ occurs approximately 20 % of all the phonemes. The glottal phoneme /'/ (ʔ in IPA) represents about 0,2%.

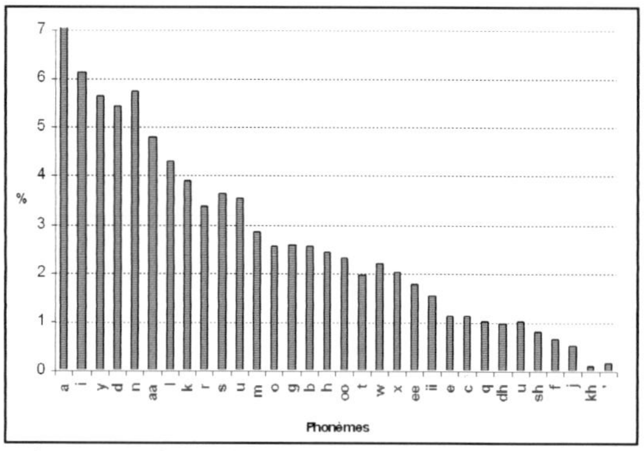

Figure 1: Phonetic distribution of Asaas Corpus

The duration of phonemes varies according to the speakers. However, in general, long vowels and fricatives are the longest ones. The short vowels and plosives have smaller duration. The phoneme which has the longest duration is /***sh***/ (ʃ in IPA). The average duration of all phonemes is given in Figure 2. Plosives phonemes are split into two parts: the burst (*Btt* for the /***t***/ phoneme, *Bkk* for the /***k***/ one and the occlusion *Ott* for the /***t***/ one and *Okk* for the /***k***/).

The average rate of the speech is 1.93 words per second.

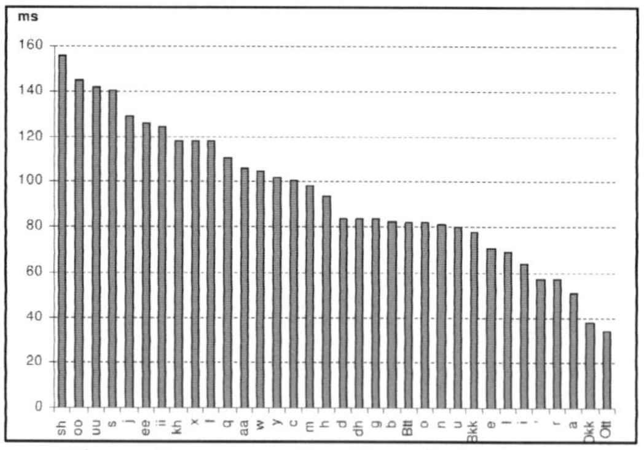

Figure 2: average duration of phonemes

There is a real difference between the duration of short and long vowels. Thus, long /***a***/ (written ***aa*** is Somali) is 2 times longer than the short /a/ (written ***a*** in Somali) and the /***uu***/ is 1.75 times longer than the /***u***/. On average, the ratio of duration between long and short vowels is 1.86. A comparison of the duration of long and short vowels is given in Figure 3. This feature can be used in acoustic modeling by creating two separate models for each vowel (long and short). It is also possible to recognize them with the language model. But both language model and separate acoustic models will probably improve the Word Error Rate.

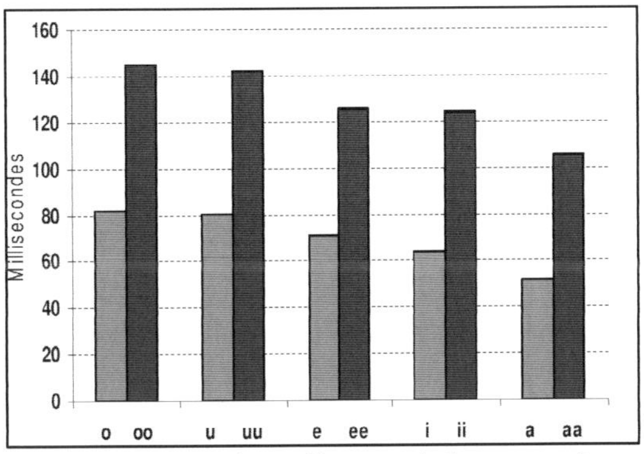

Figure 3: Duration of long and short vowels

4 Somali Text Corpus

Corpus containing millions of words or even billions of words is usually used for language modeling. If these data are mostly available for English and French languages, it is quite different for newly written languages like African languages. The lack of textual data constitutes a real handicap.

Grefenstette (2002) shows that African languages are gaining ground on the Web, even if European languages are largely dominant. Despite this growth their presence on the web is insufficient. This growth is relative, because in large part due to South African websites. Shigeaki (2008) clearly shows the prominence of South African sites on the continent.

Grefenstette and Nioche (2000) propose a formula to estimate the number of words found on the Internet for a given language. For this, we divide the number of times a word has been found by a search engine in cyberspace by the relative frequency of the word in that language. The average result on a predefined list of words provides an estimation of the number of words on the web. Estimation calculated in March 2014 for the Somali language gives about 500 million Somali words on the Web. The frequency of Somali words used was calculated on the textual corpus WARGEYS.

Many researchers are involved on how to create automatically textual corpora from the Internet for under-resourced languages (Ghani et al, 2001. Vaufreydaz et al, 1999). For our purposes we selected and downloaded a set of Somali newspapers on the Internet. As the audio corpus, the selection criteria were the variant of the language, the diversity of topics and the number of errors.

4.1 Formatting

The text downloaded is not directly usable. After removal of HTML tags, we proceeded to some transformations dealing with abbreviations, dates and times, numbers, proper names, foreign words and punctuation.

4.2 Spelling normalization

The Somali language as most of African languages is written after the independence period (1960-1970). So the orthography is not yet stabilized. The same word can be written in different ways according to people. Calvet, L. (1987) shows that the word eight in Mandingo is written *segin* in Mali, *seyin* in Guinea and *seegin* in Burkina Faso. In Somali Language the word President appears like *madaxweyne* or *madaxwayne*. This lack of standardization is common for most of the African languages and disrupts the language models quality as well as the Automatic Speech Recognition systems accuracy.

To resolve this problem, for a given simple word like *madaxweyne* we considered that the most frequent spelling is the good one. If *madaxweyne* appears 17 times in the corpus and *madaxwayne* 9 times, *Madaxweyne* is selected and all the *madaxwayne* were changed to *madaxweyne*.

For the component words like *iskumid* and *isku mid*, we choice the separate orthography like *isku mid*. This choice is made to separate syllable because if *iskumid* (Perhaps Out of Vocabulary Word) is not recognized by a ASR system, *isku* can be recognized or *mid* can be recognized.

4.3 Corpus Characteristics

Somali web-based textual corpus was named WARGEYS (Newspaper in Somali) because this corpus contains News topics and is similar to the French one called BREF (Lamel, L 1991) and gathered from the French newspaper Le Monde. Table 4 shows the characteristics of this corpus. WARGEYS contains 2 820 000 words with 121

000 different words and 84 000 sentences with an average of 33 words per sentence.

Component	Amount
Words	2 820 000
Different words	121 000
Sentences	84 000

Table 1: Distribution WARGEYS corpus

The figure 4 shows that the phonetic distribution of the two corpus **Asaas** and **WARGEYS** are similar.

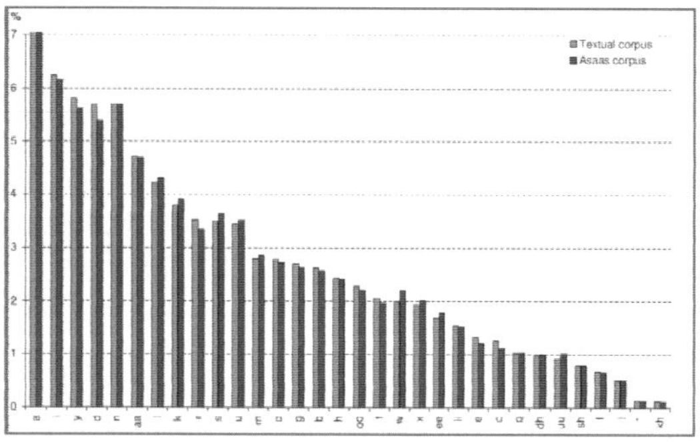

Figure 4: Phonetic distribution of Asaas and WARGEYS corpora

5 Conclusion

Somali read-speech corpus **Asaas,** consists of 10 hours and 26 minutes of good quality signal fully transcribed and well corrected. The phonetic distribution of this corpus is well-balanced. The Web-based Somali textual corpus **WARGEYS** contains 3 million of words and more than 120 000 different words. This corpus is formatted and the spelling fluctuation is standardized.

Reference

Badenhorst, J. Heerden, C. Marelie, D. Barnard. E. 2009. AfLaT '09 Proceedings of the First Workshop on Language Technologies for African Languages. Pages 1-8 ACL, Stroudsburg, PA.

Bendjaballah, S. 1998. La palatalisation en somali. *Linguistique africaine*, 21, 5-52.

Calvet, L. J. 1987. *Guerre des langues*. Payot, Paris.

Gac, D. L. 2002. Tonal alternations and prosodic structure in Somali. In *Speech Prosody 2002, International Conference*.

Ghani, R., Jones, R., & Mladenić, D. 2001. Mining the web to create minority language corpora. In *Proceedings of the Tenth International Conference on Information and Knowledge Management* (pp. 279-286). ACM.

Grefenstette, G., & Nioche, J. 2000. Estimation of English and non-English language use on the WWW. *arXiv preprint cs/0006032*.

Grefenstette, G., & Nioche, J. 2002. The WWW as a Resource for Lexicography. Lexicography and Natural Language Processing. A Festschrift in Honour of BTS Atkins. Göteborg, EURALEX, 199-215.

Hughes, T., Nakajima, K., Ha, L., Vasu, A., Moreno, P. J., & LeBeau, M. 2010. Building transcribed speech corpora quickly and cheaply for many languages. In *INTERSPEECH*, 1914-1917.

Hyman, L. M. 1981. Tonal accent in Somali. *Studies in African linguistics*, 12(2).

Jelinek, F. 1976. Continuous speech recognition by statistical methods. IEEE. 64(4), 532-556

Lamel, L. F., Gauvain, J. L., & Eskénazi, M. 1991. BREF, a Large Vocabulary Spoken Corpus for French1. *Training*, *22*(28), 50.

Mori, R. D. 1998. Spoken Dialogue with computers. Academic Press, London.

Saeed, J. I. 1987. *Somali reference grammar*. Dunwoody Press, Wheaton, MD.

Saeed, J. 1999. *Somali*. John Benjamins Publishing, Amsterdam.

Schlippe, T., Djomgang, E. G. K., Vu, N. T., Ochs, S., & Schultz, T. 2012. Hausa large vocabulary continuous speech recognition. *Proc. of SLTU*.

Shigeaki. K. 2008. Languages on the Asian and African Domains. *Proceedings of the International Symposium on CDG*.

Vaufreydaz, D., Akbar, M., & Rouillard, J. 1999. Internet documents: a rich source for spoken language modeling. In *IEEE Workshop ASRU'99 (Automatic Speech Recognition and Understanding)*.

SeedLing: Building and using a seed corpus for the Human Language Project

Guy Emerson, Liling Tan, Susanne Fertmann, Alexis Palmer, and Michaela Regneri
Universität des Saarlandes
66123 Saarbrücken, Germany
{emerson, liling, susfert, apalmer, regneri}
@coli.uni-saarland.de

Abstract

A broad-coverage corpus such as the Human Language Project envisioned by Abney and Bird (2010) would be a powerful resource for the study of endangered languages. Existing corpora are limited in the range of languages covered, in standardisation, or in machine-readability. In this paper we present SeedLing, a seed corpus for the Human Language Project. We first survey existing efforts to compile cross-linguistic resources, then describe our own approach. To build the foundation text for a Universal Corpus, we crawl and clean texts from several web sources that contain data from a large number of languages, and convert them into a standardised form consistent with the guidelines of Abney and Bird (2011). The resulting corpus is more easily-accessible and machine-readable than any of the underlying data sources, and, with data from 1451 languages covering 105 language families, represents a significant base corpus for researchers to draw on and add to in the future. To demonstrate the utility of SeedLing for cross-lingual computational research, we use our data in the test application of detecting similar languages.

1 Introduction

At the time of writing, 7105 living languages are documented in Ethnologue,[1] but Simons and Lewis (2011) calculated that 37% of extant languages were at various stages of losing transmisson to new generations. Only a fraction of the world's languages are well documented, fewer have machine-readable resources, and fewer again have resources with linguistic annotations (Maxwell and Hughes, 2006) - so the time to work on compiling these resources is now.

Several years ago, Abney and Bird (2010; 2011) posed the challenge of building a Universal Corpus, naming it the Human Language Project. Such a corpus would include data from all the world's languages, in a consistent structure, facilitating large-scale cross-linguistic processing. The challenge was issued to the computational linguistics community, from the perspective that the language processing, machine learning, and data manipulation and management tools well-known in computational linguistics must be brought to bear on the problems of documentary linguistics, if we are to make any serious progress toward building such a resource. The Universal Corpus as envisioned would facilitate broadly cross-lingual natural language processing (NLP), in particular driving innovation in research addressing NLP for low-resource languages, which in turn supports the language documentation process.

We have accepted this challenge and have begun converting existing resources into a format consistent with Abney and Bird's specifications. We aim for a collection of resources that includes data: (a) from as many languages as possible, and (b) in a format both in accordance with best practice archiving recommendations and also readily accessible for computational methods. Of course, there are many relevant efforts toward producing cross-linguistic resources, which we survey in section 2. To the best of our knowledge, though, no existing effort meets these two desiderata to the extent of our corpus, which we name SeedLing: a seed corpus for the Human Language Project.

To produce SeedLing, we have drawn on four web sources, described in section 3.2. To bring the four resources into a common format and data structure (section 3.1), each required different degrees and types of cleaning and standardisation. We describe the steps required in section 4,

[1] http://www.ethnologue.com

Proceedings of the 2014 Workshop on the Use of Computational Methods in the Study of Endangered Languages, pages 77–85,
Baltimore, Maryland, USA, 26 June 2014.

presenting each resource as a separate mini-case study. We hope that the lessons we learned in assembling our seed corpus can guide future resource conversion efforts. To that end, many of the resources described in section 2 are candidates for inclusion in the next stage of building a Universal Corpus.

We believe the resulting corpus, which at present covers 1451 languages from 105 language families, is the first of its kind: large enough and consistent enough to allow broadly multilingual language processing. To test this claim, we use SeedLing in a sample application (section 5): the task of language clustering. With no additional pre-processing, we extract surface-level features (frequencies of character n-grams and words) to estimate the similarity of two languages. Unlike most previous approaches to the task, we make no use of resources curated for linguistic typology (e.g. values of typological features as in WALS (Dryer and Haspelmath, 2013), Swadesh word lists). Despite our approach being highly dependent on orthography, our clustering performance matches the results obtained by Georgi et al. (2010) using typolological features, which demonstrates SeedLing's utility in cross-linguistic research.

2 Related Work

In this section, we review existing efforts to compile multilingual machine-readable resources. Although some commercial resources are available, we restrict attention to freely accessible data.[2]

Traditional archives. Many archives exist to store the wealth of traditional resources produced by the documentary linguistics community. Such documents are increasingly being digitised, or produced in a digital form, and there are a number of archives which now offer free online access.

Some archives aim for a universal scope, such as The Language Archive (maintained by the Max Planck Institute of Psycholinguistics), Collection Pangloss (maintained by LACITO), and The Endangered Languages Archive (maintained by SOAS). Most archives are regional, including AILLA, ANLA, PARADISEC, and many others.

However, there are two main problems common to all of the above data sources. Firstly, the data is not always machine readable. Even where the data is available digitally, these often take the form of scanned images or audio files. While both can provide invaluable information, they are extremely difficult to process with a computer, requiring an impractical level of image or video pre-processing before linguistic analysis can begin. Even textual data, which avoids these issues, may not be available in a machine-readable form, being stored as pdfs or other opaque formats. Secondly, when data is machine readable, the format can vary wildly. This makes automated processing difficult, especially if one is not aware of the details of each project. Even when metadata standards and encodings agree, there can be idiosyncractic markup or non-linguistic information, such as labels for speakers in the transcript of a conversation.

We can see that there is still much work to be done by individual researchers in digitising and standardising linguistic data, and it is outside of the scope of this paper to attempt this for the above archives. Guidelines for producing new materials are available from the E-MELD project (Electronic Metastructure for Endangered Languages Data), which specifically aimed to deal with the expanding number of standards for linguistic data. It gives best practice recommendations, illustrated with eleven case studies, and provides input tools which link to the GOLD ontology language, and the OLAC metadata set. Further recommendations are given by Bird and Simons (2003), who describe seven dimensions along which the portability of linguistic data can vary. Various tools are available from The Language Archive at the Max Planck Institute for Psycholinguistics.

Many archives are part of the Open Language Archive Community (OLAC), a subcommunity of the Open Archives Initiative. OLAC maintains a metadata standard, based on the 15-element Dublin Core, which allows a user to search through all participating archives in a unified fashion. However, centralising access to disparate resources, while of course extremely helpful, does not solve the problem of inconsistent standards. Indeed, it can even be hard to answer simple questions like "how many languages are represented?"

In short, while traditional archives are invaluable for many purposes, for large-scale machine processing, they leave much to be desired.

Generic corpus collections. Some corpus collections exist which do not focus on endangered

[2]All figures given below were correct at the time of writing, but it must be borne in mind that most of these resources are constantly growing.

languages, but which nonetheless cover an increasing number of languages.

MetaShare (Multilingual Europe Technology Alliance) provides data in a little over 100 languages. While language codes are used, they have not been standardised, so that multiple codes are used for the same language. Linguistic Data Consortium (LDC) and the European Language Resources Association (ELRA) both offer data in multiple languages. However, while large in size, they cover only a limited number of languages. Furthermore, the corpora they contain are stored separately, making it difficult to access data according to language.

Parallel corpora. The Machine Translation community has assembled a number of parallel corpora, which are crucial for statistical machine translation. The OPUS corpus (Tiedemann, 2012) subsumes a number of other well-known parallel corpora, such as Europarl, and covers documents from 350 languages, with various language pairs.

Web corpora. There has been increasing interest in deriving corpora from the web, due to the promise of large amounts of data. The majority of web corpora are however aimed at either one or a small number of languages, which is perhaps to be expected, given that the majority of online text is written in a handful of high-resource languages. Nonetheless, there have been a few efforts to apply the same methods to a wider range of languages.

HC Corpora currently provides download of corpora in 68 different language varieties, which vary in size from 2M to 150M words. The corpora are thus of a respectable size, but only 1% of the world's languages are represented. A further difficulty is that languages are named, without the corresponding ISO language codes.

The Leipzig Corpora Collection (LCC)[3] (Biemann et al., 2007) provides download of corpora in 117 languages, and dictionaries in a number of others, bringing the total number of represented languages up to 230. The corpora are large, readily available, in plain-text, and labelled with ISO language codes.

The Crúbadán Project aims to crawl the web for text in low-resource languages, and data is currently available for 1872 languages. This represents a significant portion of the world's languages; unfortunately, due to copyright restrictions, only lists of n-grams and their frequencies are publically available, not the texts themselves. While the breadth of languages covered makes this a useful resource for cross-linguistic research, the lack of actual texts means that only a limited range of applications are possible with this data.

Cross-linguistic projects. Responding to the call to document and preserve the world's languages, highly cross-linguistic projects have sprung up, striving towards the aim of universality. Of particular note are the Endangered Languages Project, and the Rosetta Project. These projects are to be praised for their commitment to universality, but in their current forms it is difficult to use their data to perform large-scale NLP.

3 The Data

3.1 Universal Corpus and Data Structure

Building on their previous paper, Abney and Bird (2011) describe the data structure they envisage for a Universal Corpus in more detail, and we aim to adopt this structure where possible. Two types of text are distinguished:

Aligned texts consist of parallel documents, aligned at the document, sentence, or word level. Note that monolingual documents are viewed as aligned texts only tied to a single language.

Analysed texts, in addition to the raw text, contain more detailed annotations including parts of speech, morphological information, and syntactic relations. This is stored as a table, where rows represent words, and columns represent: document ID, language code, sentence ID, word ID, wordform, lemma, morphological information, part of speech, gloss, head/governor, and relation/role.

Out of our data sources, three can be straightforwardly represented in the aligned text structure. However, ODIN contains richer annotations, which are in fact difficult to fit into Abney and Bird's proposal, and which we discuss in section 3.2 below.

3.2 Data Sources

Although data size matters in general NLP, *universality* is the top priority for a Universal Corpus. We focus on the following data sources, because they include a large number of languages, include several parallel texts, and demonstrate a variety of data types which a linguist might encounter (structured, semi-structured, unstructured): the Online

[3] `http://corpora.uni-leipzig.de`

	Langs.	Families	Tokens	Size
ODIN	1,270	100	351,161	39 MB
Omniglot	129	20	31,318	677 KB
UDHR	352	46	640,588	5.2 MB
Wikipedia	271	21		37 GB
Combined	1,451	105		

Table 1: Corpus Coverage

Database of Interlinear Text (ODIN), the Omniglot website, the Universal Declaration of Human Rights (UHDR), and Wikipedia.

Our resulting corpus runs the full gamut of text types outlined by Abney and Bird, ranging from single-language text (Wikipedia) to parallel text (UDHR and Omniglot) to IGTs (ODIN). Table 1 gives some coverage statistics, and we describe each source in the following subsections. For 332 languages, the corpus contains data from more than one source.

Universal Declaration of Human Rights. The Universal Declaration of Human Rights (UDHR) is a document released by the United Nations in 1948, and represents the first global expression of human rights. It consists of 30 articles, amounting to about four pages of text. This is a useful document for NLP, since it has been translated into a wide variety of languages, providing a highly parallel text.

Wikipedia. Wikipedia is a collaboratively-edited encyclopedia, appealing to use for NLP because of its large size and easy availability. At the time of writing, it contained 30.8 million articles in 286 languages, which provides a sizeable amount of monolingual text in a fairly wide range of languages. Text dumps are made regularly available, and can be downloaded from `http://dumps.wikimedia.org`.

Omniglot. The Omniglot website[4] is an online encyclopedia of writing systems and languages. We extract information from pages on *'Useful foreign phrases'* and the *'Tower of Babel'* story, both of which give us parallel data in a reasonably large number of languages.

ODIN. ODIN (The Online Database of Interlinear Text) is a repository of interlinear glossed texts (IGTs) extracted from scholarly documents (Lewis, 2006; Lewis and Xia, 2010). Compared to other resources, it is notable for the breadth of languages included and the level of linguistic annotation. An IGT canonically consists of three lines: (i) the source, a sentence in a target language, (ii) the gloss, an analysis of each source element, and (iii) the translation, done at the sentence level. The gloss line can additionally include a number of linguistic terms, which means that the gloss is written in metalanguage rather than natural language. In ODIN, translations are into English, and glosses are written in an English-based metalanguage. An accepted set of guidelines are given by the Leipzig Glossing Rules,[5] where morphemes within words are separated by hyphens (or equal signs, for clitics), and the same number of hyphens should appear in each word of the source and gloss.

The data from ODIN poses the first obstacle to straightforwardly adopting Abney and Bird's proposal. The suggested data structure is aligned at the word level, and includes a specific list of relevant features which should be used to annotate words. When we try to adapt IGTs into this format, we run into certain problems. Firstly, there is the problem that the most fundamental unit of analysis according to the Leipzig Glossing Rules is the morpheme, not the word. Ideally, we should encode this information explicitly in a Universal Corpus, assigning a unique identifier to each morpheme (instead of, or in addition to each word). Indeed, Haspelmath (2011) argues that there is no cross-linguistically valid definition of *word*, which undermines the central position of words in the proposed data structure.

Secondly, it is unclear how to represent the gloss. Since the gloss line is not written in a natural language, we cannot treat it as a simple translation. However, it is not straightforward to incorporate it into the proposed structure for analysed texts, either. One possible resolution is to move all elements of the gloss written in capital letters to the MORPH field (as functional elements are usually annotated in this way), and all remaining elements to the GLOSS field. However, this loses information, since we no longer know which morpheme has which meaning. To keep all information encoded in the IGT, we need to modify Abney and Bird (2011)'s proposal.

The simplest solution we can see is to allow morphemes to be a level of structure in the Universal Corpus, just as documents, sentences, and

[4] `http://www.omniglot.com`

[5] `http://www.eva.mpg.de/lingua/resources/glossing-rules.php`

		Total #	Omniglot	Wikipedia	UDHR	ODIN	Combined
0	International	6	100.0%	100.0%	100.0%	100.0%	100.0%
1	National	95	53.7%	73.7%	83.2%	83.2%	91.6%
2	Provincial	70	31.4%	48.6%	57.1%	71.4%	80.0%
3	Wider Comm.	166	3.6%	12.0%	20.5%	38.0%	44.6%
4	Educational	345	3.2%	8.1%	15.1%	33.0%	38.0%
5	Developing	1534	0.5%	2.2%	4.6%	23.2%	26.1%
6a	Vigorous	2502	0.0%	0.2%	0.4%	6.4%	6.7%
6b	Threatened	1025	0.6%	1.7%	2.9%	15.0%	17.1%
7	Shifting	456	0.2%	0.9%	1.8%	14.5%	16.0%
8a	Moribund	286	0.3%	1.0%	1.0%	22.4%	23.1%
8b	Nearly Extinct	432	0.2%	0.2%	0.9%	15.3%	16.0%
9	Dormant	188	0.5%	1.1%	0.0%	10.6%	11.2%

Figure 1: Heatmap of languages in SeedLing according to endangerment status

words already are. The overall architecture remains unchanged. We must then decide how to represent the glosses.

Even though glosses in ODIN are based on English, having been extracted from English-language documents, this is not true of IGTs in general. For example, it is common for documentary linguists working on indigenous languages of the Americas to provide glosses and translations based on Spanish. For this reason, we believe it would be wise to specify the language used to produce the gloss. Since it is not quite the language itself, but a metalanguage, one solution would be to use new language codes that make it clear both that a metalanguage is being used, and also what natural language it is based on. The five-letter code `gloss` cannot be confused with any code in any version of ISO 639 (with codes of length two to four). Following the convention that subvarieties of a language are indicated with suffixes, we can append the code of the natural language. For example, glosses into English and Spanish-based metalanguages would be given the codes `gloss-eng` and `gloss-spa`, respectively.

One benefit of this approach is that glossed texts are treated in exactly the same way as parallel texts. There is a unique identifier for each morpheme, and glosses are stored under this identifier and the corresponding gloss code. Furthermore, to motivate the important place of parallel texts in a Universal Corpus, Abney and Bird view translations into a high-resource reference language as a convenient surrogate of meaning. By the same reasoning, we can use glosses to provide a more detailed surrogate of meaning, only written in a metalanguage instead of a natural one.

3.3 Representation and Universality

According to Ethnologue, there are 7105 living languages, and 147 living language families. Across all our data sources, we manage to cover 1451 languages in 105 families, which represents 19.0% of the world's languages. To get a better idea of the kinds of languages represented, we give a breakdown according to their EGIDS scores (Expanded Graded Intergenerational Disruption Scale) (Lewis and Simons, 2010) in Figure 1. The values in each cell have been colored according to proportion of languages represented, with green indicating good coverage and red poor. It's interesting to note that vigorous languages (6a) are poorly represented across all data sources, and worse than more endangered categories. In terms of language documentation, vigorous languages are less urgent goals than those in categories 6b and up, but this highlights an unexpected gap in linguistic resources.

4 Data Clean-Up, Consistency, and Standardisation

Consistency in data structures and formatting is essential to facilitate use of data in computational linguistics research (Palmer et al., 2010). In the following subsections, we describe the processing required to convert the data into a standardised form. We then discuss standardisation of language codes and file formats.

4.1 Case Studies

UDHR. We used the plain-text UDHR files available from the Unicode website[6] which uses UTF-8 encoding for all languages. The first four lines of each file record metadata, and the rest is the translation of the UDHR. This dataset is extremely clean, and simply required segmentation into sentences.

Wikipedia. One major issue with using the Wikipedia dump is the problem of separating text from abundant source-specific markup. To convert compressed Wikipedia dumps to textfiles, we used the WikiExtractor[7] tool. After conversion into textfiles, we used several regular expressions to delete residual Wikipedia markup and so-called "*magic words*".[8]

Omniglot. The main issue with extracting the Omniglot data is that the pages are designed to be human-readable, not machine-readable. Cleaning this data required parsing the HTML source, and extracting the relevant content, which required different code for the two types of page we considered ('*Useful foreign phrases*' and '*Tower of Babel*'). Even after automatic extraction, some noise in the data remained, such as explanatory notes given in parentheses, which are written in English and not the target language. Even though the total amount of data here is small compared to our other sources, the amount of effort required to process it was not, because of these idiosyncracies. We expect that researchers seeking to convert data from human-readable to machine-readable formats will encounter similar problems, but unfortunately there is unlikely to be a one-size-fits-all solution to this problem.

ODIN. The ODIN data is easily accessible in XML format from the online database[9]. Data for each language is saved in a separate XML file and the IGTs are encoded in tags of the form `<igt><example>...</example></igt>`. For example, the IGT in Figure 2 is represented by the XML snippet in Figure 3.

The primary problem in extracting the data is a lack of consistency in the IGTs. In the above ex-

21 a. o lesu mai
2sg return here
'You return here.'

Figure 2: Fijian IGT from ODIN

```
<igt>
  <example>
    <line>21 a. o lesu mai</line>
    <line>2sg return here</line>
    <line>'You return here.'</line>
  </example>
</igt>
```

Figure 3: Fijian IGT in ODIN's XML format

amples, the sentence is introduced by a letter or number, which needs to be removed; however, the form of such indexing elements varies. In addition, the source line in Figure 4 includes two types of metadata: the language name, and a citation, both of which introduce noise. Finally, extraneous punctuation such as the quotation marks in the translation line need to be removed. We used regular expressions for cleaning lines within the IGTs.

4.2 Language Codes

As Xia et al. (2010) explain, language names do not always suffice to identify languages, since many names are ambiguous. For this reason, sets of language codes exist to more accurately identify languages. We use ISO 639-3[10] as our standard set of codes, since it aims for universal coverage, and has widespread acceptance in the community. The data from ODIN and the UDHR already used this standard.

To facilitate the standardization of language codes, we have written a python API that can be used to query information about a language or a code, fetching up-to-date information from SIL International (which maintains the ISO 639-3 code set), as well as from Ethnologue.

Wikipedia uses its own set of language codes, most of which are in ISO 639-1 or ISO 639-3. The older ISO 639-1 codes are easy to recognise, being two letters long instead of three, and can be straightforwardly converted. However, a small number of Wikipedia codes are not ISO codes at all - we converted these to ISO 639-3, following

[6] http://unicode.org/udhr/d

[7] http://medialab.di.unipi.it/wiki/Wikipedia_Extractor

[8] http://en.wikipedia.org/wiki/Help:Magic_words

[9] http://odin.linguistlist.org/download

[10] http://www-01.sil.org/iso639-3/default.asp

```
<igt>
  <example>
    <line>(69) na-Na-tmi-kwalca-t
    Yimas (Foley 1991)</line>
    <line>3sgA-1sgO-say-rise-PERF
    </line>
    <line>'She woke me up'
    (by verbal action)</line>
  </example>
</igit>
```

Figure 4: Yimas IGT in ODIN's XML format

documentation from the Wikimedia Foundation.[11]

Omniglot does not give codes at all, but only the language name. To resolve this issue, we automatically converted language names to codes using information from the SIL website.

Some languages have more than one orthography. For example, Mandarin Chinese is written with either traditional or simplified characters; Serbian is written with either the Cyrillic or the Roman alphabet. For cross-linguistic NLP, it could be helpful to have standard codes to identify orthographies, but at present none exist.

4.3 File Formats

It is important to make sure that the data we have compiled will be available to future researchers, regardless of how the surrounding infrastructure changes. Bird and Simons (2003) describe a set of best practices for maintaining portability of digital information, outlining seven dimensions along which this can vary. Following this advice, we have ensured that all our data is available as plaintext files, with UTF-8 encoding, labelled with the relevant ISO 639-3 code. Metadata is stored separately. This allows users to easily process the data using the programming language or software of their choice.

To allow access to the data following Abney and Bird's guidelines, as discussed in section 3, we have written an API, which we distribute along with the data. Abney and Bird remain agnostic to the specific file format used, but if an alternative format would be preferred, the data would be straightfoward to convert since it can be accessed according to these guidelines. As examples of functionality, our API allows a user to fetch all sentences in a given language, or all sentences from a given source.

[11] http://meta.wikimedia.org/wiki/Special_language_codes

5 Detecting Similar Languages

To exemplify the use of SeedLing for computational research on low-resource languages, we experiment with automatic detection of similar languages. When working on endangered languages, documentary and computational linguists alike face a lack of resources. It is often helpful to exploit lexical, syntactic or morphological knowledge of related languages. For example, similar high-resource languages can be used in bootstrapping approaches, such as described by Yarowsky and Ngai (2001) or Xia and Lewis (2007).

Language classification can be carried out in various ways. Two common approaches are genealogical classification, mapping languages onto family trees according to their historical relatedness (Swadesh, 1952; Starostin, 2010); and typological classification, grouping languages according to linguistic features (Georgi et al., 2010; Daumé III, 2009). Both of these approaches require linguistic analysis. By contrast, we use surface features (character n-gram and word unigram frequencies) extracted from SeedLing, and apply an off-the-shelf hierarchical clustering algorithm.[12] Specifically, each language is represented as a vector of frequencies of character bigrams, character trigrams, and word unigrams. Each of these three components is normalised to unit length. Data was taken from ODIN, Omniglot, and the UDHR.

Experimental Setup. We first perform hierarchical clustering, which produces a tree structure: each leaf represents a language, and each node a cluster. We use linkage methods, which recursively build the tree starting from the leaves. Initially, each language is in a separate cluster, then we iteratively find the closest two clusters and merge them. Each time we do this, we take the two corresponding subtrees, and introduce a new node to join them.

We define the distance between two clusters by considering all possible pairs of languages, with one from each cluster, and taking the largest distance. We experimented with other ways to define the distance between clusters, but results were poor and we omit results for brevity.

To ease evaluation, we produce a partitional clustering, by stopping when we reach a certain number of clusters, set in advance.

[12] http://www.scipy.org

	Precision	Recall	F-score
SeedLing	0.255	0.205	0.150
Base. 1: random	0.184	0.092	0.068
Base. 2: together	0.061	1.000	0.112
Base. 3: separate	1.000	0.086	0.122

Table 2: Clustering compared with baselines

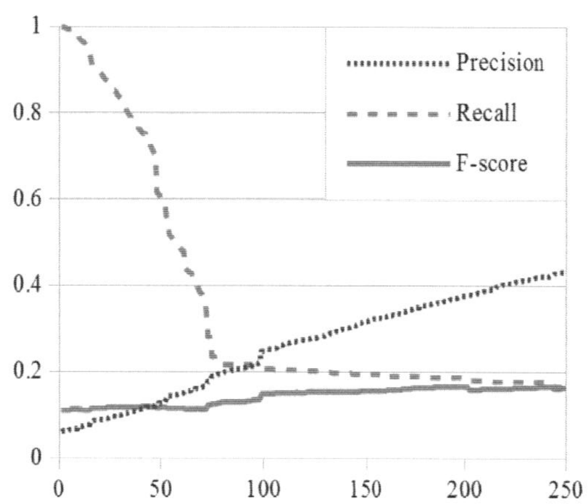

Figure 5: Performance against number of clusters

Evaluation. We compare our clustering to the language families in Ethnologue. However, there are many ways to evaluate clustering quality. Amigó et al. (2009) propose a set of criteria which a clustering evaluation metric should satisfy, and demonstrate that most popular metrics fail to satisfy at least one of these criteria. However, they prove that all criteria are satisfied by the BCubed metric, which we therefore adopt. To calculate the BCubed score, we take the induced cluster and gold standard class for each language, and calculate the F-score of the cluster compared to the class. These F-scores are then averaged across all languages.

In Table 2, we set the number of clusters to be 105, the number of language families in our data, and compare this with three baselines: a random baseline (averaged over 20 runs); putting all languages in a single cluster; and putting each language in a separate cluster. Our clustering outperforms all baselines. It is worth noting that precision is higher than recall, which is perhaps expected, given that related languages using wildly differing orthographies will appear distinct.

To allow a closer comparison with Georgi et al. (2010), we calculate pairwise scores - i.e. considering if pairs of languages are in the same cluster or the same class. For 105 clusters, we achieve a pairwise f-score of 0.147, while Georgi et al. report 0.140. The figures are not quite comparable since we are evaluating over a different set of languages; nonetheless, we only use surface features, while Georgi et al. use typological features from WALS. This suggests the possibility for cross-linguistic research to be conducted based on shallow features.

In Figure 5, we vary the number of clusters. The highest f-score is obtained for 199 clusters. There is a notable jump in performance between 98 and 99, just before the true number of families, 105.

Interpreting the clusters directly is difficult, because they are noisy. However, the distribution of cluster sizes mirrors the true distribution - for 105 clusters, we have 48 clusters of size 1 or 2, with the largest cluster of size 130; while in our gold standard, there are 51 families with only 1 or 2 languages in the data, with the largest of size 150.

6 Conclusion and Outlook

In this paper, we have described the creation of SeedLing, a foundation text for a Universal Corpus, following the guidelines of Abney and Bird (2010; 2011). To do this, we cleaned and standardised data from several multilingual data sources: ODIN, Omniglot, the UDHR, Wikipedia. The resulting corpus is more easily machine-readable than any of the underlying data sources, and has been stored according to the best practices suggested by Bird and Simons (2003). At present, SeedLing has data from 19% of the world's living languages, covering 72% of language families. We believe that a corpus with such diversity of languages, uniformity of format, cleanliness of data, and ease of access provides an excellent seed for a Universal Corpus. It is our hope that taking steps toward creating this resource will spur both further data contributions and interesting computational research with cross-linguistic or typological perspectives; we have here demonstrated SeedLing's utility for such research by using the data to perform language clustering, with promising results.

SeedLing (data, API and documentation) is currently available via a GitHub repository.[13] We have yet to fully address questions of long-term access, and we welcome ideas or collaborations along these lines.

[13] https://github.com/alvations/SeedLing

Acknowledgements

We thank the three anonymous reviewers for their helpful comments. This research was supported in part by the Cluster of Excellence "Multi-modal Computing and Interaction" in the German Excellence Initiative.

References

Steven Abney and Steven Bird. 2010. The Human Language Project: Building a Universal Corpus of the world's languages. In *Proceedings of the 48th Annual Meeting of the Association for Computational Linguistics*, pages 88–97. Association for Computational Linguistics.

Steven Abney and Steven Bird. 2011. Towards a data model for the Universal Corpus. In *Proceedings of the 4th Workshop on Building and Using Comparable Corpora: Comparable Corpora and the Web*, pages 120–127. Association for Computational Linguistics.

Enrique Amigó, Julio Gonzalo, Javier Artiles, and Felisa Verdejo. 2009. A comparison of extrinsic clustering evaluation metrics based on formal constraints. *Information retrieval*, 12(4):461–486.

Chris Biemann, Gerhard Heyer, Uwe Quasthoff, and Matthias Richter. 2007. The Leipzig Corpora Collection-monolingual corpora of standard size. *Proceedings of Corpus Linguistic 2007*.

Steven Bird and Gary Simons. 2003. Seven dimensions of portability for language documentation and description. *Language*, pages 557–582.

Hal Daumé III. 2009. Non-parametric bayesian areal linguistics. In *Proceedings of human language technologies: The 2009 annual conference of the north american chapter of the association for computational linguistics*, pages 593–601. Association for Computational Linguistics.

Matthew S. Dryer and Martin Haspelmath, editors. 2013. *WALS Online*. Max Planck Institute for Evolutionary Anthropology, Leipzig.

Ryan Georgi, Fei Xia, and William Lewis. 2010. Comparing language similarity across genetic and typologically-based groupings. In *Proceedings of the 23rd International Conference on Computational Linguistics*, pages 385–393. Association for Computational Linguistics.

Martin Haspelmath. 2011. The indeterminacy of word segmentation and the nature of morphology and syntax. *Folia Linguistica*, 45(1):31–80.

M Paul Lewis and Gary F Simons. 2010. Assessing endangerment: expanding fishman's GIDS. *Revue roumaine de linguistique*, 2:103–119.

William D Lewis and Fei Xia. 2010. Developing ODIN: A multilingual repository of annotated language data for hundreds of the world's languages. *Literary and Linguistic Computing*, 25(3):303–319.

William D Lewis. 2006. ODIN: A model for adapting and enriching legacy infrastructure. In *e-Science and Grid Computing, 2006. e-Science'06. Second IEEE International Conference on*, pages 137–137. IEEE.

Mike Maxwell and Baden Hughes. 2006. Frontiers in linguistic annotation for lower-density languages. In *Proceedings of the workshop on frontiers in linguistically annotated corpora 2006*, pages 29–37. Association for Computational Linguistics.

Alexis Palmer, Taesun Moon, Jason Baldridge, Katrin Erk, Eric Campbell, and Telma Can. 2010. Computational strategies for reducing annotation effort in language documentation. *Linguistic Issues in Language Technology*, 3.

Gary F Simons and M Paul Lewis. 2011. The world's languages in crisis: A 20-year update. In *26th Linguistic Symposium: Language Death, Endangerment, Documentation, and Revitalization. University of Wisconsin, Milwaukee*, pages 20–22.

George Starostin. 2010. Preliminary lexicostatistics as a basis for language classification: a new approach. *Journal of Language Relationship*, 3:79–117.

Morris Swadesh. 1952. Lexico-statistic dating of prehistoric ethnic contacts: with special reference to north american indians and eskimos. *Proceedings of the American philosophical society*, pages 452–463.

Jörg Tiedemann. 2012. Parallel data, tools and interfaces in OPUS. In *LREC*, pages 2214–2218.

Fei Xia and William D Lewis. 2007. Multilingual structural projection across interlinear text. In *HLT-NAACL*, pages 452–459.

Fei Xia, Carrie Lewis, and William D Lewis. 2010. The problems of language identification within hugely multilingual data sets. In *LREC*.

David Yarowsky and Grace Ngai. 2001. Inducing multilingual pos taggers and np bracketers via robust projection across aligned corpora. In *Proceedings of NAACL-2001*, pages 200–207.

Short-term projects, long-term benefits: Four student NLP projects for low-resource languages

Alexis Palmer and Michaela Regneri
Department of Computational Linguistics
Saarland University
Saarbrücken, Germany
{apalmer,regneri}@coli.uni-saarland.de

Abstract

This paper describes a local effort to bridge the gap between computational and documentary linguistics by teaching students and young researchers in computational linguistics about doing research and developing systems for low-resource languages. We describe four student software projects developed within one semester. The projects range from a front-end for building small-vocabulary speech recognition systems, to a broad-coverage (more than 1000 languages) language identification system, to language-specific systems: a lemmatizer for the Mayan language Uspanteko and named entity recognition systems for both Slovak and Persian. Teaching efforts such as these are an excellent way to develop not only tools for low-resource languages, but also computational linguists well-equipped to work on endangered and low-resource languages.

1 Introduction

There is a strong argument to be made for bringing together computational and documentary linguistics in order to support the documentation and description of endangered languages (Abney and Bird, 2010; Bird, 2009). Documentation, description, and revitalization work for endangered languages, as well as efforts to produce digital and machine-readable resources for languages currently lacking such data, benefit from technological support in many different ways. Here we focus on support via (a) tools facilitating more efficient development of resources, with easy learning curves, and (b) linguistic analysis tools.

Various meetings and workshops in recent years have helped to bring the two fields closer together, but a sizeable gap remains. We've come far enough to, for example, have a relevant workshop at a major computational linguistics conference, but not so far that issues around language endangerment are well-known to even a large subset of the computational linguistics community. One way to get computational linguists thinking about issues related to endangered languages is for them to get their hands dirty – to work directly on related projects. In this paper we describe our own local effort to bridge this gap: a course for Master's and Bachelor's students in computational linguistics in which small teams of students each produced working, non-trivial natural language processing (NLP) tools for low-resource languages (LRLs) over the span of a single semester. The individual projects are described in Section 3.

Such a course benefits the students in a number of ways. They get hands-on experience in system building, they learn about a new subfield within computational linguistics, with a different set of concerns (some of these are discussed in Section 2), and, in some cases, they get the opportunity to develop tools for their own native languages. From the perspective of computational work on endangered languages, the positive outcomes are not only a new set of NLP tools, but also a group of students and young researchers armed with experience working on low-resource languages and better equipped to take on similar projects in the future.

2 Teaching NLP for LRLs

Working on LRLs from a computational perspective requires training beyond the typical computational linguistics curriculum. It is not the case that the most widely-used methods from computational linguistics can be straightforwardly adapted for any arbitrarily-selected language. Thus an important part of our teaching agenda in this context is to familiarize students with the challenges inherent to NLP for LRLs as well as some of the main

Proceedings of the 2014 Workshop on the Use of Computational Methods in the Study of Endangered Languages, pages 86–90,
Baltimore, Maryland, USA, 26 June 2014. ©2014 Association for Computational Linguistics

approaches for addressing these same challenges. This section briefly surveys some of the relevant issues, with pointers to representative studies.

The first and most obvious concern is *data sparsity*. Many of the most successful and widely-taught methods and models in computational linguistics rely on either large amounts of labeled data or massive amounts of unlabeled data. Methods and models explicitly addressing LRLs need to maximize the utility of available data. Approaches for addressing data sparsity range from data collection proposals (Abney and Bird, 2010) to leveraging high-resource languages (Xia and Lewis, 2007) to maximizing annotation effort (Garrette and Baldridge, 2013). A second concern is *model suitability*. Many existing models in computational linguistics implicitly encode or expect characteristics of high-resource languages (Bender, 2011); for example, much work on computational syntax uses models that exploit linear ordering of elements in utterances. Such models are not straightforwardly applicable for languages with free or flexible word order, nor for highly agglutinative languages where, for example, complete utterances are encoded as single words. Approaches to this issues include adaptation of models using linguistic knowledge and/or universals (Boonkwan and Steedman, 2011; Naseem et al., 2010). The third issue to note is the *difficulty of evaluation*. The output of systems or tools performing automated analysis are predictions of analyses for new data; these predictions must be evaluated against a ground truth or human-supplied analysis of the same data. Evaluation is difficult in the low-resource setting, both because of limited availability of expert-labeled data and because, in some cases, the ground truth isn't known, or analyses are shifting as knowledge about the language develops.

We began the course with a discussion of these issues, as well as an introduction to a range of existing tools, projects and resources. We did not explicitly teach programming skills in the course, but we also did not require extensive programming background. Rather, we aimed to balance the teams such that each contained a mix of backgrounds: a bit more than half of the students had previous experience with software development, and the rest had at least taken one introductory programming course. The projects were scoped such that there were clear ways for students without programming experience to contribute. For example, in some cases, students with extensive background in linguistics performed linguistic analysis of the data which informed the design of the system.

Evaluation of students was designed to emphasize three objectives: production of a working system, communication of challenges faced and solutions to those challenges, and personal development of professionally-relevant skills. Students were graded on their weekly progress (more detail in Section 3), one 15-20 minute talk per student, individual written reports detailing specific contributions to the project, and a conference-style end-of-semester poster and demo session. Systems were required to be working and demonstratable both at the midway point of the semester (as a simplified prototype) and at the end of the semester.

3 Four projects in four months

The course described here ("NLP tools for Low-Resource Languages") was offered as part of the regular curriculum for undergraduate and graduate students in the Computational Linguistics department at Saarland University. We started with 10 students and formed four teams (based on preferences for general topics and programming languages). The teams could choose their own project or select from a set of proposed topics.

During the teaching period, we regularly monitored the student's progress by using some methods of agile software development.[1] For each weekly meeting, each team had to set three goals which constituted their homework. Goals could be minor tasks (*fixing a certain bug*), bigger chunks (*choosing and implementing a strategy for data standardization*) or course requirements (*preparing a talk*). Not fulfilling a (project-related) goal was acceptable, but students had to analyze why they missed the goal and to learn from the experience. They were expected over the course of the semester to become better both at setting reachable goals and at estimating how long they would need to meet each goal. Under this obligation to make continuous, weekly progress, each team had a working system within three months. At the end of month four, systems were suitable for demonstration at the poster session.

The projects differ according to their scopes and goals, as well as their immediate practical utility.

[1] http://en.wikipedia.org/wiki/Agile_software_development

One project (3.1) makes previous research accessible to users by developing an easy-to-use frontend; a second project (3.2) aims to extend the number of languages addressed for an existing multilingual classification task; and the remaining two (3.3 and 3.4) implement language-specific solutions for individual language processing tasks. We additionally required that each project be open-source; the public code repositories are linked in the respective sections.

3.1 Small-vocabulary ASR for any language

This project[2] builds on existing research for small-vocabulary (up to roughly 100 distinct words) speech recognition. Such technology is desirable for, among other things, developing speech interfaces to mobile applications (e.g. to deliver medical information or weather reports; see Sherwani (2009)), but dedicated speech recognition engines are available only for a relatively small number of languages. For small-vocabulary applications, though, an existing recognizer for a high-resource language can be used to do recognition in the target language, given a pronunciation lexicon mapping the relevant target language words into sequences of sounds in the high-resource language. This project produces the required lexicon.

Building on the algorithms developed by Qiao et al. (2010) and Chan and Rosenfeld (2012), two students developed an easy-to-use interface that allows a user with no knowledge of speech technologies to build and test a system to recognize words spoken in the target language. In its current implementation, the system uses the English-language recognizer from the freely-available Microsoft Speech Platform;[3] for this reason, the system is available for Windows only. To build a recognizer for a target language, a user needs only to specify a written form and upload one or more audio samples for each word in the vocabulary; generally, the more audio samples per word, the better the performance. The students additionally implemented a built-in recorder; this means a user can spontaneously make recordings for the desired words. Finally, the system includes implementations of two different variants of the algorithm and an evaluation module, thus facilitating use for both research and development purposes.

The main challenges for this project involved managing the interaction between the algorithm and the Microsoft speech recognition platform, as well as getting familiar with development in Windows. The practical utility of this project is immediately evident: any user with a Windows machine can install the necessary components and have a working small-vocabulary recognizer within several hours. Of course, more time and data may be required to improve performance of the recognizer, which currently reaches in the mid-70s with five audio samples per word. These results, as well as further details about the system (including where to download the code, and discussion of substituting other high-resource language recognizers), are described in Vakil et al. (2014).

3.2 Language ID for many languages

This project[4] addresses the task of language identification. Given a string of text in an arbitrary language, can we train a system to recognize what language the text is written in? Excellent classification rates have been achieved in previous work, but for a relatively small number of languages, and the task becomes noticeably more difficult as the number of languages increases (Baldwin and Lui, 2010; Lui and Baldwin, 2012, for example). With few exceptions (Brown, 2013; Xia et al., 2010; Xia et al., 2009), existing systems have only attempted to distinguish between fewer than 200 of the thousands of written languages currently in use. This team of three students aimed to expand coverage of language identification systems as much as possible given existing sources of data.

To do this, they first needed to gather and standardize data from various sources. They targeted three sources of data: the Universal Declaration of Human Rights, Wikipedia,[5] ODIN (Lewis and Xia, 2010), and some portions of the data available from Omniglot.[5] The challenges faced by this group lay primarily in two areas: issues involving data and those involving classification. In the first area, they encountered expected and well-known issues such as clean-up and standardization of data, dealing with encoding issues, and managing large amounts of data. The second set of challenges have to do with the high degree of skew in the data collected. Though their system covers over 1000 languages, the amount of data per language ranges from a single sentence to hundreds of thousands of words. Along the way, the students realized that this collection of data in a stan-

[2] https://github.com/lex4all/lex4all

[3] http://msdn.microsoft.com/en-us/library/hh361572

[4] https://github.com/alvations/SeedLing

[5] http://www.wikipedia.com, http://www.omniglot.com

dard, machine-readable form is useful for many other purposes. The corpus and how to access it are described in Emerson et al. (2014). A second paper presenting the language identification results (including those for low-resource languages) is planned for later this year.

3.3 A lemmatizer for Uspanteko

The third project[6] involved implementing a lemmatizer for the Mayan language Uspanteko. Using data that had been cleaned, standardized (as described in Palmer et al. (2010)), and made available through the Archive of Indigenous Languages of Latin America,[7] these three students implemented a tool to identify the citation form for inflected word forms in texts. The lemmatization algorithm is based on longest common substring matching: the closest match for an inflected form is returned as the lemma. Additionally, a table for irregular verb inflections was generated using the annotated source corpus (roughly 50,000 words) and an Uspanteko-Spanish dictionary (Can Pixabaj et al., 2007), to map inflected forms translated with the same Spanish morpheme.

This group more than any other faced the challenge of evaluation. Not all lemmas covered in the texts appear in the dictionary, and the Uspanteko texts, though fully analyzed with morphological segmentation and glossing, part of speech tags, and translation into Spanish, do not include citation forms. Manual evaluation of 100 sentences, for which a linguist on the team with knowledge of Spanish determined citation forms, showed accuracy of 59% for the lemmatization algorithm.

3.4 NER for Slovak & Persian

Finally, the fourth project[8] (two students) chose to tackle the task of named entity recognition (NER): identifying instances of named entities (*NEs*, e.g. people, locations, geopolitical entities) in texts and associating them with appropriate labels. The students developed a single platform to do NER in both Slovak and Persian, their native languages. The approach is primarily based on using gazetteers (for person names and locations), as well as regular expressions (for temporal expressions). The students collected the gazeteers for the two languages as part of the project. Their system builds on a modular design; one can swap out gazetteers and a few language-specific heuristic components to perform NER in a new language.

In this project, resource acquisition and evaluation were the main challenges. The students used some existing resources for both languages, but also devoted quite some time to producing new gazetteers. For Slovak, additional challenges were presented by the language's large number of inflectional cases and resulting variability in form. For example, some inflected forms used to refer to people from a given location are string-identical to the names of the locations with a different case inflection. In Persian, the main challenges were detection of word boundaries (many names are multi-word expressions) and frequent NE/proper noun ambiguities. For evaluation, the students hand-labeled over 35,000 words of Slovak (with 545 NE instances) and about 600 paragraphs of Persian data (306 NE instances). Performace varies across named entity category: temporal expression matching is most reliable (f-score 0.96 for Slovak, 0.89 for Persion), followed by locations (0.78 Slovak, 0.92 Persian) and person names (0.63 Slovak, 0.87 Persian). Note that for Persian, only NEs with correctly matched boundaries are counted (which are 50% for persons).

4 Conclusion

In this paper we have presented four student software projects, each one addressing a different NLP task relevant for one or more low-resource languages. The successful outcomes of the four projects show that much progress can be made even with limited time and limited prior experience developing such systems. Local teaching efforts such as these can be highly successful in building a group of young researchers who are both familiar with issues surrounding low-resource and endangered languages and prepared to do research and development in this area in the future. We think of this as planting seeds for an early harvest: with one semester's combined effort between instructors and students, we reap the rewards of both new tools and new researchers who can continue to work on closing the gap between computational and documentary linguistics.

Course materials are publicly available from the course homepage,[9] and from the project repositories linked from the descriptions in Section 3.

[6] https://code.google.com/p/mayan-lemmatizer/

[7] http://www.ailla.utexas.org

[8] https://code.google.com/p/named\-entity\-tagger/

[9] http://www.coli.uni-saarland.de/courses/cl4lrl-swp/

Acknowledgements

First of all, we want to thank the students who participated in our course and put so much effort and passion in their projects. They are (in alphabetical order): Christine Bocionek, Guy Emerson, Susanne Fertmann, Liesa Heuschkel, Omid Moradiannasab, Michal Petko, Maximilian Paulus, Aleksandra Piwowarek, Liling Tan and Anjana Vakil. Further, we want to thank the anonymous reviewers for their helpful comments. The second author was funded by the Cluster of Excellence "Multimodal Computing and Interaction" in the German Excellence Initiative.

References

Steven Abney and Steven Bird. 2010. The Human Language Project: Building a universal corpus of the world's languages. In *Proceedings of the 48th Annual Meeting of the Association for Computational Linguistics*, pages 88–97. Association for Computational Linguistics.

Timothy Baldwin and Marco Lui. 2010. Language identification: The long and the short of the matter. In *Human Language Technologies: The 2010 Annual Conference of the North American Chapter of the Association for Computational Linguistics*, HLT '10, pages 229–237, Stroudsburg, PA, USA. Association for Computational Linguistics.

Emily M Bender. 2011. On achieving and evaluating language-independence in NLP. *Linguistic Issues in Language Technology*, 6(3):1–26.

Steven Bird. 2009. Natural language processing and linguistic fieldwork. *Computational Linguistics*, 35(3):469–474.

Prachya Boonkwan and Mark Steedman. 2011. Grammar induction from text using small syntactic prototypes. In *IJCNLP*, pages 438–446.

Ralf D Brown. 2013. Selecting and weighting n-grams to identify 1100 languages. In *Text, Speech, and Dialogue*, pages 475–483. Springer.

Telma Angelina Can Pixabaj, Oxlajuuj Keej Maya' Ajtz'iib' (Group) Staff, and Centro Educativo y Cultural Maya Staff. 2007. *Jkemiix yalaj li uspanteko*. Cholsamaj Fundacion, Guatemala.

Hao Yee Chan and Roni Rosenfeld. 2012. Discriminative pronunciation learning for speech recognition for resource scarce languages. In *Proceedings of the 2nd ACM Symposium on Computing for Development*, page 12. ACM.

Guy Emerson, Liling Tan, Susanne Fertmann, Alexis Palmer, and Michaela Regneri. 2014. SeedLing: Building and using a seed corpus for the Human Language Project. In *Proceedings of ACL Workshop on the use of computational methods in the study of endangered languages (ComputEL)*.

Dan Garrette and Jason Baldridge. 2013. Learning a part-of-speech tagger from two hours of annotation. In *Proceedings of NAACL-HLT*, pages 138–147.

William D Lewis and Fei Xia. 2010. Developing ODIN: A multilingual repository of annotated language data for hundreds of the world's languages. *Literary and Linguistic Computing*, 25(3):303–319.

Marco Lui and Timothy Baldwin. 2012. Langid.py: An off-the-shelf language identification tool. In *Proceedings of the ACL 2012 System Demonstrations*, ACL '12, pages 25–30, Stroudsburg, PA, USA. Association for Computational Linguistics.

Tahira Naseem, Harr Chen, Regina Barzilay, and Mark Johnson. 2010. Using universal linguistic knowledge to guide grammar induction. In *Proceedings of the 2010 Conference on Empirical Methods in Natural Language Processing*, pages 1234–1244. Association for Computational Linguistics.

Alexis Palmer, Taesun Moon, Jason Baldridge, Katrin Erk, Eric Campbell, and Telma Can. 2010. Computational strategies for reducing annotation effort in language documentation. *Linguistic Issues in Language Technology*, 3.

Fang Qiao, Jahanzeb Sherwani, and Roni Rosenfeld. 2010. Small-vocabulary speech recognition for resource-scarce languages. In *Proceedings of the First ACM Symposium on Computing for Development*, page 3. ACM.

Jahanzeb Sherwani. 2009. *Speech interfaces for information access by low literate users*. Ph.D. thesis, SRI International.

Anjana Vakil, Max Paulus, Alexis Palmer, and Michaela Regneri. 2014. lex4all: A language-independent tool for building and evaluating pronunciation lexicons for small-vocabulary speech recognition. In *Proceedings of ACL2014 Demo Session*.

Fei Xia and William Lewis. 2007. Multilingual structural projection across interlinear text. In *Proceedings of HLT/NAACL 2007*, Rochester, NY.

Fei Xia, William D Lewis, and Hoifung Poon. 2009. Language ID in the context of harvesting language data off the web. In *Proceedings of the 12th Conference of the European Chapter of the Association for Computational Linguistics*, pages 870–878. Association for Computational Linguistics.

Fei Xia, Carrie Lewis, and William D Lewis. 2010. The problems of language identification within hugely multilingual data sets. In *LREC*.

Data Warehouse, Bronze, Gold, STEC, Software

Doug Cooper
Center for Research in Computational Linguistics
doug.cooper.thailand@gmail.com

Abstract

We are building an analytical *data warehouse* for linguistic data – primarily lexicons and phonological data – for languages in the Asia-Pacific region. This paper briefly outlines the project, making the point that the need for improved technology for endangered and low-density language data extends well beyond completion of fieldwork. We suggest that *shared task evaluation challenges* (STECs) are an appropriate model to follow for creating this technology, and that stocking data warehouses with clean *bronze-standard* data and baseline tools – no mean task – is an effective way to elicit the broad collaboration from linguists and computer scientists needed to create the *gold-standard* data that STECs require.

1 Introduction

The call for this workshop mentions the first step of the language documentation process, pointing out that the promise of new technology in documenting endangered languages remains unfulfilled, particularly in the context of modern recording technologies.

But lack of tools extends far beyond this first step. It encompasses the accessibility of data long since gathered and (usually, but not always) published, as well as applications *for* the data by its most voracious consumer: the study of comparative and historical linguistics.

We encounter these problems daily in preliminary development of data and software resources for a planned *Asia-Pacific Linguistic Data Warehouse*. Briefly, our initial focus is on five phyla (~2,000 languages): Austroasiatic, Austronesian, Hmong-Mien, Kra-Dai, and Sino-Tibetan, which form a Southeast Asian convergence area, and individually extend well into China, India, the Himalayas, and the Pacific. Data for languages of Australia and New Guinea will follow.

Not all of these languages are endangered, but many are; not all are low-density, but most are.

Our data are preferentially drawn from the sort of lexicography gathered for comparative purposes (ideally 2,500 items per language), and the phonological, semantic, and phylogenetic data that can be found for, or inferred from, them. These are the only kind of data for which we are likely to find near-complete language representation. We include smaller lexicons when necessary, and intra-language dialect surveys when available. All available metadata are incorporated, including typological and phonotactic features, (phylogenetic) character sets, geo-physical and demographic data, details of lexicon coverage, extent, or quality, and bibliographic or source data.

Such data are not always easily found. Their delivery packages – primarily books and journals – may be discoverable via bibliographic metadata, but details of the datasets themselves are not. As a result, traditional bibliographic documentation, accessed via portals like OLAC (Simons and Bird, 2000) and Glottolog (Nordhoff and Hammarström, 2011), tends to have low recall and precision in regard to data resource discovery.

Our experience in acquiring and performing methodical *data audits* of large quantities of published and unpublished materials reveals sets of lexical, grammatical, phonological, corpus, and other materials that are regular enough in form, and extensive enough in content, to comprise aggregable *linguistic data supersets* for the Asia-Pacific region.

These ongoing data audits take a three-tiered approach, separately documenting texts (to enable source recovery), their abstract data content (to enable high-recall *resource discovery*), and any concrete, transcribed data instances (to enable high-precision *data aggregation*).

Discovery and aggregation only open the door. Many datasets are hand-crafted for a researcher's specific needs and interests, even if they fall into larger research categories. Yet far from having reliable algorithms for central concerns (such as proto-language reconstruction, or subgrouping of linguistic phyla in family trees or networks) the field has not yet had to grapple with basic problems – such as normalizing phonological transcription or gloss semantics, or accurately assembling large-scale cognate sets – that will be

Proceedings of the 2014 Workshop on the Use of Computational Methods in the Study of Endangered Languages, pages 91–99,
Baltimore, Maryland, USA, 26 June 2014. ©2014 Association for Computational Linguistics

presented by datasets that include millions of data items for thousands of languages, and many more thousands of dialectal variants.

The central issue we face is the gap between:

- the results of published and unpublished fieldwork, and
- their usability in downstream research and reference applications.

In some cases this gap is painfully obvious – as in the backlog of carefully elicited wordlists still awaiting phonetic transcription. In others, the gap becomes evident when we begin to assemble large comparable datasets from published data; deceptively difficult, and never accomplished for collections broader than a single language family, or larger than about 200 words per language. Such tasks are still basically hand work; often requiring the specialized knowledge of the field researcher.

1.1 Data life cycle: anticipate or participate

We see the need for tools as part of a new sort of *data life cycle management* that extends the concerns of content, format, discovery, access, citation, preservation, and rights as usually articulated, notably in Bird and Simons (2003).

Simply put, producing publishable or "correct" results is not sufficient to guarantee the downstream usability of data. Rather, data must undergo a series of transformations as it travels from one research specialty to the next. We hope there will be an increasing expectation that the data producer either anticipate or participate in this process.

At one end of the cycle, this often requires small, specialized datasets of the sort needed to support software development for tasks like automated transcription or phonemic analysis – still open problems in the context of under-resourced languages.

At the other, building massive datasets that are suitable for improving and extending quantitative comparative linguistic applications – or discovering the scales at which different methods might be most useful – has not been a priority for the linguistics community: if a few representative items demonstrate a relationship or support a reconstruction convincingly, then exhaustive coverage does not make the argument stronger.

We face a classic resource deadlock. High-quality "last-user" datasets are not constructed because traditional methods are too expensive and time-consuming. However, tools for refining "first-producer" data on an industrial scale are not built because the high-quality datasets needed to validate them do not exist. Development of computational methods for problems like subgrouping tends to focus on a small number of available datasets, while their results are criticized for precisely this.

2 STECs and gold-standard data

Log jams in natural language processing are nothing new. A *shared task evaluation challenge* (STEC) presents an open challenge to the field in the context of evaluating performance on a specific task. Originally developed in the context of the TIPSTER Text Program (which initiated the long-running MUC and TREC conference series) as discussed in Belz and Kilgarriff (2006), see also Hirschmann (1998) "*Over the past twenty years, virtually every field of research in human language technology (HLT) has introduced STECS.*"

The STEC is the culmination of a series of efforts intended to focus and advance progress by asking such questions as:

- what problems need to be solved in order to advance the field? Where are we trying to go, and what is standing in our way?
- what kinds of necessary data are not generally available? What kinds of datasets are too difficult for individual researchers to create?
- what kind of functional decomposition into simpler goals will help demonstrates and measure progress in quantitative and qualitative terms?

Both data, and evaluation metrics, are made available well before the STEC, which is often held in conjunction with a major conference. The task is typically initiated by the release of a dataset; results are submitted by some deadline, and the results of evaluation are announced before or at the conference.

The terms *gold-standard* and more recently, *silver-standard* (for machine-generated sets) are used to describe datasets created for use in STECs and NLP applications. These can be thought of as being "correct answers" for quantitative evaluation (Kilgarriff 1998).

Gold-standard datasets are built to enable comparable evaluation of alternative algorithms or implementations. Frequently, part of the set will be publicly released in advance to serve as training data, while part of it is held back to provide test data (and is released at a later date).

Gold-standard datasets reflect the state of the art in an area, such as the specification of word senses, delineation of word boundaries, or evaluation of message sentiment, for which there may not be any purely objective ground truth. We can reasonably expect to allow alternative formulations of gold-standard sets in areas in which the state of the art may be uncertain, even in the eyes of experts. And we can anticipate increased critical scrutiny of previously accepted judgments as more base data and better investigative tools become available; see e.g. Round (2013, 2014).

2.1 STECs for low-density languages

In our opinion, all of the reasons for which STECs are devised and gold-standard datasets defined apply equally to the low-density language problems we touched on in Section 1. These include:

- normalization and syllabification of transcribed data,
- phonetic transcription of audio and orthographic data,
- morphemic analysis of transcribed data,
- extraction of a phonemic analysis from phonetic data,
- identification of internal cognates and/or derivationally related forms, as well as loan-word identification and stratification,
- automated reglossing / translation (to a standardized gloss set) of glosses and/or definitions.
- automated inference of phylogenetic subgrouping.
- automated generation of proto-forms,

All are characterized by the same requirement for human judgment in processing, and lack of absolute certainty as to outcomes.

The critical difference is that (as far as we know) STECs in NLP invariably focus on high-density languages for which both data and expertise are readily available. In contrast, low-density languages – which presumably includes the entire range of endangered languages – are by their nature specialty realms, for which expertise, even within a single phylum, is often widely dispersed.

Thus, the problem we face in creating successful STECs for documentary linguistics is not simply a matter of thinking up tasks, and relying on in-house expertise to develop gold-standard datasets. Rather, advancing development of computational tools requires participation from a large community of independently working linguists as well.

3 Cast bronze to net gold

Our approach to achieving this begins by laying the groundwork for collaboration between:

- computer scientists who recognize the need for better data, and will join the challenge of solving practical problems in building massive, comparable datasets, and
- linguists willing to help create and validate the gold-standard reference sets and training data needed to establish quality metrics for improving software tools.

We think this collaboration is best motivated in the old-fashioned way: reduce participants'

vapor	no data could be located (useful when documenting data availability by ISO code)
water	untranscribed audio recording only
paper	print/image/PDF data are in hand, but not transcribed or extracted
tin	raw e-orthography and definitions (as in typical documentary dictionaries)
copper	raw e-forms and glosses (as in purpose-collected comparative lexicons; e.g. Holle lists)
bronze	clean electronic data and metadata, ready for hand or machine processing, naive normalization of forms and glosses, cognate sets partially specified, capable of demonstrating preliminary data warehouse functionality (**Software**: baseline vanilla algorithms)
silver	machine-normalized or grouped data, not yet verified by humans (**Software:** better than baseline)
gold	human-verified/accepted, machine-usable comparable datasets (**Software:** (best) able to produce gold-standard results)

Table 1. Data quality standards re lexicons, cognate sets, reconstructions, and subgrouping, with parallels to software tools. **Silver-** and **gold-standard** are the only terms commonly used in this context.

startup costs, flatten their learning curves, highlight expected outcomes that will advance collaborators' self-interests, and help provide the data, tools, and/or metrics that collaborators will need to seek funding themselves.

This in itself as a long-term effort – easily 5–8 years for our region, with optimal funding – whose thrust can be summarized as **cast bronze to net gold** (see **Table 1**).

Locating data, and bringing it to the minimal state required for computer applications requires a massive amount of work. Consider just the discovery aspect, for which the data audit mentioned earlier entails an ongoing, two-pronged effort.

On one hand, we identify potential data content by acquiring as much published and unpublished print material as possible, including complete journal runs, monograph series, informally published "gray literature," extensive sets of unpublished field notes, and regular publication backlists (notably, a half-century of works from *Pacific Linguistics*, which will be added to our on-line repository later this year).[1]

On the other, we systematically work through the complete ISO 639-3 inventory (as a proxy for the on-the ground truth, and as a means of helping to perfect the standard, as well as identifying documentary shortfalls that might be short-listed for fieldwork) of our region, attempting to find at least lexical content for every language.

Overall, our summary project development plan has four steps, which relate to content and scale, and determined our choice of a regional focus – for which we could take responsibility – rather than either working at greater depth on a single phylum, or attempting to build a global framework, and then relying primarily on outside contributors.

First, define an area that is broad enough to be of wide linguistic interest, and able to supply a range of control and alternative test conditions for both traditional and computational methods. Even allowing for typological variation that may be found in individual phyla, we think this usually requires a regional perspective.

[1] For New Guinea, this required a special sub-project dubbed *INGA*, dedicated to tracking down "invisible" New Guinea archives held in libraries and file cabinets around the world! As implied, when possible we negotiate rights to scan and make all materials freely available in an on-line repository, and will begin to register DOI names (when appropriate) for texts and data this year.

Second, locate and prepare raw data of sufficient breadth and depth. We think that aiming for blanket rather than selective coverage is appropriate – it enables the broadest range of research agendas by reflecting the natural state of human migration and constant language contact.

Third, establish research goals that capture the interest of both fields – documentary / comparative / historical linguistics and computer science. This extends the argument for complete regional coverage, especially in convergence areas. But it also argues for *limiting* scope to an area in which it is realistically possible to actively recruit involvement, conference by conference.

Finally, we need to lower barriers to participation We think we can do this by providing a framework that allows data owners to take advantage of existing software tools, and which provides software developers with easily customized data test beds – the analytical *data warehouse*.

4 The data warehouse

A *data warehouse* is an integrated collection of databases that incorporates tools for sampling, analyzing, and visualizing query results. Unlike repository databases intended for storage and retrieval of prepared values (perhaps for off-line processing), data warehouses assume that data filtering, transformation, and analysis are essential to satisfying every query. In the context of comparative lexicons, such tasks are well beyond the scope of existing *virtual research environments* such as WebLicht (Hinrichs et al 2010) and TextGrid (Neuroth et al 2011), which focus primarily on text corpora.

Because sampling filters allow selection of homogeneous or representative subsamples, we can be as inclusive as possible in regard to data acquisition. We are not talking about data quality; rather (working within our overall criterion of comparative lexical data) we want to avoid excluding sets because of concerns about dataset size or content disparity, or over-representation of dialect survey data.

Many operations we wish to perform on or with data involve open research questions. Although users may perceive the warehouse as providing access to tools, we intend to present it to tool developers as a tunable test bed of data that does not require them to deal with data management, as well as a means of using, and encouraging development of, open-source toolkits such as the pioneering work of Kleiweg (2009) and List and Moran (2013). We return to the idea of plug-and-play operations on lexicons in Section 6.

The warehouse also helps provide added value to potential data contributors. Even if software is freely available, preparing data or setting up tools can impose substantial, even insurmountable, burdens on data creators, particularly in regions in which cooperation between linguists and computer scientists is less common than in the US or Europe.

4.1 Data warehouse query-flow

In our test warehouse implementation, functionality is divided as follows:

- *filter*: define a *search universe* based on phylogenetic or phonotactic properties, geophysical or proximal location, lexicon characteristics, or other data or metadata features.
- *frame*: specify data and/or metadata to be returned, e.g. specific aspects of the form and/or gloss, or metadata details that might be useful for correlation testing.
- *analyze*: extract phone inventories, calculate functional load, investigate lexical neighborhoods, cluster data by phonological similarity, etc.
- *visualize*: provide alternatives to tables as appropriate, e.g. tree/graph/map layouts.
- *recycle*: search within returned data, use faceting to extend searches, or let the visualization serve as a chooser for a new search.

For brevity we discuss just one feature: filtering. This lets the search universe be defined in as much detail as possible, and is partly common sense: our overall data universe is decidedly lumpy due to the decision to include small samples (some <100 items) when necessary, and dialect surveys (perhaps with only minor differences between doculects) when possible.

It is also intended to take advantage of the large quantities of available metadata, whether it is *explicit / external* – that is, related to the language or doculect, or *implicit / internal*, i.e. can be derived from individual datasets or samples.

Such metadata includes proposed phylogenetic relations, typological features, geophysical and demographic data, characteristics of lexicon composition, extent, or quality, bibliographic or source data, and phonological properties of the doculect itself. Some of this metadata may be returned with individual items as part of the *data frame*.

Filter targets may be specified if appropriate. For example, a filter might limit a search to languages that contain sesquisyllables, or instead require that returned *items* be sesquisyllabic.

4.2 An example query and result

Figure 1 shows the result of a relatively simple warehouse query (using our unreleased exploratory implementation): a *geo-constrained phylogenetic tree* for Trans-New Guinea languages. Tree topology follows Ethnologue 16 (Lewis, 2009) as provided by the MultiTree project (Aristar and Ratliff, 2005); other analyses are

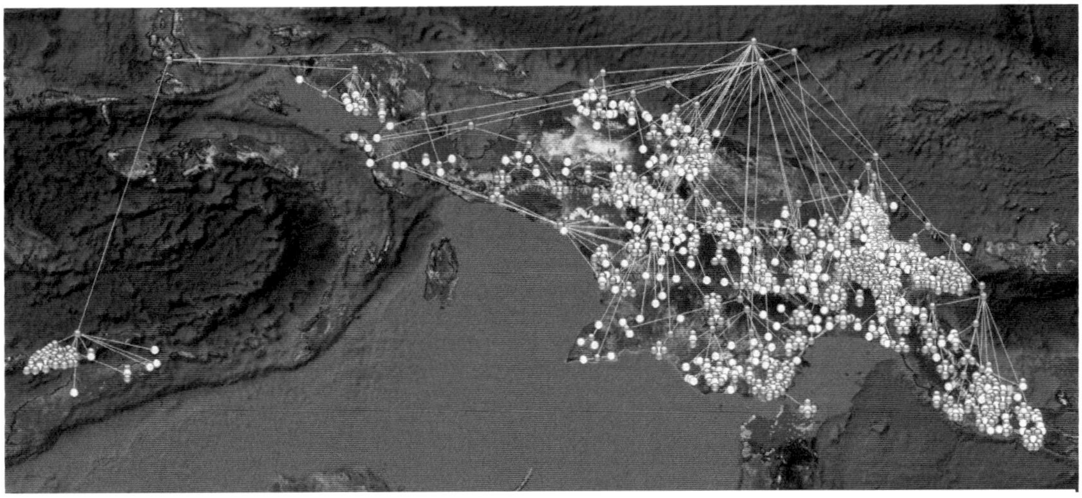

Figure 1 A geo-constrained phylogenetic tree (analysis by Ethnologue via MultiTree). This *cluster tree* keeps low-level group nodes near their daughters, but raises the root nodes. Dialects are green, languages yellow, and groups blue

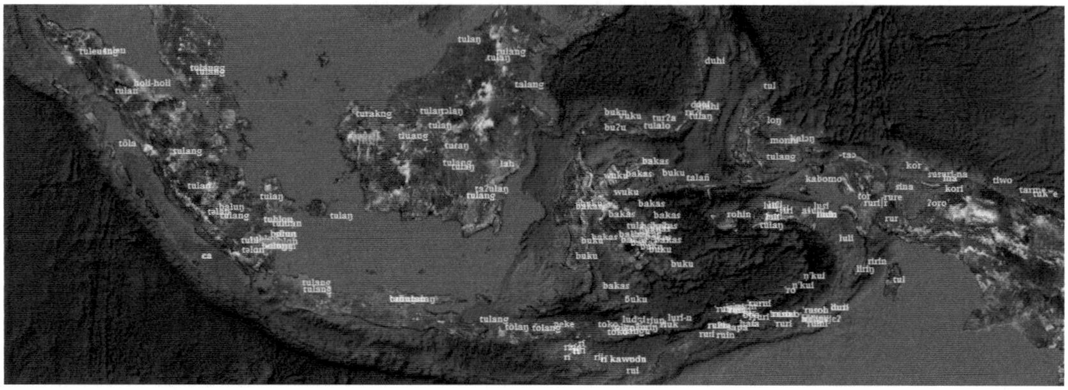

Figure 2 A search for "bone" in ABVD Austronesian data (again, relations by Ethnologue via MultiTree), constrained to locations in Indonesia, and projected onto a map

readily specified. In this example dialects (from the same sources) are arranged in a circular pattern around the ISO 639-3 hub language (and, again, other analyses could be used instead). The same filtering and visualization routines are used in a different manner in **Figure 2**, which shows words for "bone" in Austronesian languages as provided by ABVD (Greenhill et al, 2008).

5 Data comparability and reusability

We will finish the discussion of data warehouses with a quick look at data comparability and reuse. Comparability or equivalence of datasets can be looked at in two ways

- at the *content* level, e.g. to ensure that the same systems of transcription and glossing are used for all datasets, and
- at the *structural* level, in identifying datasets of comparable complexity, structure, or available detail.

At the content level, normalization of forms and glosses is the critical transformation in the journey to gold-standard quality. We will briefly describe our systems for normalization, ***Metagloss*** and ***Metaphon***, because they are ripe for computational assistance. The discussion ends with a quick introduction to ***Etyset***, the framework we intend to use to describe and distribute structured datasets, such as those that incorporate subgroup and cognate detail.

5.1 Gloss, Metagloss, Etygloss

In most of our applications, a *gloss* is semantic annotation provided by the wordlist author in order to index phonological forms. Unfortunately, these may be elicitation terms rather than glosses (*green*? "grue." *blue*? "grue"), or local vernacular rather than common or scientific terms for flora and fauna. Phrasing varies wildly, and proper reading may depend on having the list context available (*short/tall, short/long*). Translation may be lossy (*strew* or *scatter* as nouns) due to differences in grammaticalization or lexification. All of these undermine comparability.

We have begun to define an intermediate, standardized ***metagloss*** layer to express the author's intent (if discernable). A third layer, the ***etygloss***, will help account for semantic shift in labeling cognate groups; i.e. glossing empty placeholders for proto-language reconstructions. In the simple case all three layers are identical.

Metagloss provides a controlled vocabulary for re-annotating or translating existing lexicon glosses; it foregrounds the critical design link between glossing and searching. We map this to *WordNet* senses, creating a low-overhead tool for word-sense disambiguation and facet generation.

The Metagloss controlled vocabulary can be extended; it uses attributes to specify predictable relationships (*sheep:male:castrated* for *wether*) and solve lexicalization problems that arise in gloss translation (e.g. *n@strew* is the noun form of *strew*). Additionally, it allows definition of *lightweight ontologies*; relations between Metaglosses that clarify semantic relations and improve search fallback performance.

5.2 Phon, Metaphon, Etyphon

Phonological forms present similarly difficult search problems; these go beyond easily fixed notational convention. For example, absence of marked syllable boundaries can make phonological searches difficult when we are interested in the phoneme's *role* (such as pre-nasalization) rather than its *sign* (/n/, /m/ etc.).

The same holds true for other context-sensitive symbols (e.g. "h" as /h/, /ʰ/, or as a prepended indicator of unvoiced phonemes). A greater problem arises from parsimonious notations that rely on commentary to clarify unwritten content, e.g. predictable vowel insertion – these must be made explicit.

We define an intermediate layer of standardized notation called ***metaphon***: a conventional notation that allows consistent search, while clearly documenting (and minimizing, in comparison to wild-card searches) the scope of any unavoidable approximation. A third layer, the ***etyphon***, allows temporary specification of a (possibly sub-lexical) phonemic rendition prior to any formal reconstruction.

Metaphon, like metagloss, is intimately tied to search functionality. Normalized transcription enables consistent extraction of phonological and phonotactic data. It lets the search universe be restricted to languages (or items) that have particular phonemes or features. This dynamic, data-driven process lets us weigh relative significance – frequency, salience, functional load – of features in sets that are themselves results drawn from a restricted search universe; e.g. to consider the functional load of tones in sesquisyllables.

5.3 Structural comparability: EtySet

The discussion thus far has focused on the form and quality of data *items*. We are equally concerned with what might be called structural comparability of data *sets*, because this determine the approach we take to systematic description, dissemination, and re-use of cognate sets, phylogenetic trees, or sets of proto-form reconstructions.

This has nothing to do with tagging or interchange standards, which can be handled with borrowed schemes designed for similar purposes, e.g. Newick notation (Felsenstein, 1986) or successors (Nakhleh, 2003). Rather, we require nomenclature that might be used to describe their contents, or to enable identification of sets of comparable complexity, structure, or detail.

We think such comparison is crucial to help research in quantitative historical linguistics move beyond its current state, which many linguists view as interesting but nevertheless ad hoc experimentation. In other words, we would like to see computational approaches to cognate identification, subgrouping, and proto-language reconstruction be developed and tested in environments for which the controlled variable is *linguistic typology*, with as many other factors as possible held equal.

Similarly, we would like to be able to vary starting conditions. For example Bouchard-Côté et al (2013) report on a computational approach to reconstruction given (assumed) prior knowledge of subgrouping in Austronesian. However, any one or two variables from amongst cognate grouping, reconstruction, and phylogenetic subgrouping may be used to test approaches to inferring or generating the third.

We refer to cognate sets, phylogenetic trees, and reconstructed proto-forms as *etysets*. The key terms of our working descriptive nomenclature are outlined in **Table 2**.

Etysets may be *bare* (links only), or *supported* by reconstructed forms or semantics; note that the phylogenetic analyses provided by Ethnologue, Glottolog, or MultiTree may be represent with bare etysets. An internal cognate etyset has depth (number of internal sets) and size (number of forms in each set). A regular cognate etyset has depth (the number of sets / implicit number of root proto-forms) and breadth (the number of lects represented in each cognate set).

For example a *bare cognate etyset* of *Bahnaric, breadth Eth:80% / depth MSEA:90% depth* includes data from 32 (of 40. according to the Ethnologue analysis) Bahnaric languages, and at least 450 of the 500-odd terms in the MSEA (SIL 2002) elicitation list. Cognate groupings are provided, but not reconstructions or etyglosses.

breadth	number of nodes or leaves at any level of a phylogenetic tree.
depth	number of branch levels supplied.
degree	branchy-ness – the number of branches / degree of diversity at a given node.
density	a joint measure of breadth, depth, and degree.
size	# of cited or reconstructed forms associated with a leaf or branch node.
coverage	describes the extent of an etyset in terms of a fixed reference inventory.
phylogenetic etyset	described in term of breadth, depth, degree, and size.
documented node	includes metadata for approximate time depth and geographic location.
cognate etyset	may be *internal* or *regular*, and contains *internal* or *regular cognate sets*.

Table 2. Outline of the *EtySet* descriptive vocabulary.

6 Operations on lexicons

We end with a brief note about computational tasks for and by a data warehouse that is:

- stocked primarily with lexical, phonological, and phylogenetic data and relevant metadata,
- intended to support research in comparative and historical linguistics.

These fall under the general heading of *operations on lexicons*. We do not draw a strict dividing line between software employed to prepare data for use *in* a warehouse, and software used *by* the warehouse. We do exclude operations whose implementation is likely to be closely tied to a particular database implementation.

All would benefit from being implemented as plug-and-play functions, requiring some, but not excessive, programmer effort. This:

- allows head-to-head comparison of alternative algorithms, implementations, or interpretations of how measurements or actions should be carried out,
- allows encapsulation and offloading of computationally expensive algorithms; this is an important issue for some quantitative or statistical comparative methods, and
- encourages re-use of code in building new, alternative platforms for linguistic research.

We assume that all of these can be specified in terms of functionality, required data inputs, and expected data outputs, sticking to a Unix-like model in which data can be minimally formatted plain-text streams which, with the assistance of tabs, parentheses, and newlines, can be interpreted as bags, lists, vectors, matrices, trees, and the like. Higher-level streams (JSON, XML, RDF, HTML) are also reasonable outputs.

For brevity's sake, we limit examples to operations on phonological forms. We could easily list similar sets of operations – some straightforward, some not – on morphology, semantics, alternatives for visualization, cognate identification, phylogenetic subgrouping, proto-form generation, and the like.

Operations on phonological strings / lists

Conversion and markup of transcription

- between standardized and/or special-purpose notations,
- to novel notations, e.g. gestural scores,
- unambiguous conversion of notation from historical (e.g. Americanist) to IPA,
- potentially ambiguous normalization (e.g. interpretation of /h/),
- phonetic to phonemic conversion,
- marking of syllable boundaries,
- marking of syllable-internal features (e.g. onset, nucleus, coda),
- marking of morpheme boundaries.

Extraction / recognition of phonological features

- sonority sequence tagging.
- extraction/recognition of phones, phonation, co-articulatory, suprasegmental features,
- count/extraction of phone/feature n-grams,
- extraction or identification of arbitrary collocational features (e.g. sesquisyllable+tone),

Calculation of distance/similarity measures between strings, lists, and vectors

- weighted and unweighted edit distances,
- substring matching measures,
- vector cosine distance,
- phonologically based distance/similarity,
- language-internal distance/similarity,
- information content distance/similarity.

Clustering

- subgrouping list contents,
- "sounds like..." search (for very large sets).

Neighborhood measures

- generation of phonological neighborhoods,
- identification of neighbors,
- calculation of neighborhood size, density, clustering coefficients.

Load measures

- calculation of functional load of phonemes, features, collocations,
- calculation of salience of phonemes, features, collocations,
- use in pseudo-word generation.

7 Conclusion

The call for this workshop foregrounds development of software to aid in initial documentation of endangered languages, seeks models for collection and management of endangered-language data, and means of encouraging productive interaction between documentary linguists and computer scientists.

We suggest that these same needs exist all down the line, encompassing low-resource languages in general, documentation long-since completed, and analytical applications far removed from fieldwork settings. We propose that addressing them in downstream environments, such as data warehouses and STECs, may be an effective way to meet our common "preeminent grand challenge:" integration of linguistic theories and analyses, relying on massive scaling up of datasets and new computational methods, as articulated by Bender and Good (2010).

References

Anthony Aristar and Martha Ratliff. 2005. *MultiTree: A digital library of language relationships*. Institute for Language Information and Technology: Ypsilanti, MI. http://multitree.org.

Anja Belz and Adam Kilgarriff. 2006. *Shared-task evaluations in HLT: Lessons for NLG*. In Proceedings of INLG-2006.

Emily Bender and Jeff Good. 2010. *A Grand Challenge for Linguistics: Scaling Up and Integrating Models*. White paper contributed to NSF SBE 2020 initiative. http://www.nsf.gov/sbe/sbe_2020/-2020_pdfs/Bender_Emily_81.pdf

Steven Bird and Gary Simons. 2003. *Seven Dimensions of Portability for Language Documentation and Description*. Language 79:2003, 557-5822.

Alexandre Bouchard-Côté, David Hall, Thomas L. Griffiths and Dan Klein. 2013. *Automated reconstruction of ancient languages using probabilistic models of sound change.* Proceedings of the National Academy of Sciences. http://-www.pnas.org/content/110/11/4224

Joseph Felsenstein. 1986. *The newick tree format.* http://evolution.genetics.washington.edu/phylip/ne wicktree.html

Simon Greenhill, Robert Blust, and Russell D.. Gray. 2008. *The Austronesian Basic Vocabulary Database: From Bioinformatics to Lexomics.* Evolutionary Bioinformatics, 4:271-283. http://-language.psy.auckland.ac.nz/austronesian

Erhard W. Hinrichs, Marie Hinrichs and Thomas Zastrow. 2010. WebLicht: Web-Based LRT Services for German. In: *Proceedings of the ACL 2010 System Demonstrations*. pages 25–29.

Lynette Hirschman. 1998. *The evolution of evaluation: Lessons from the Message Understanding Conferences*. Computer Speech and Language, 12:283–285.

Adam Kilgarriff. 1998. *Gold Standard Datasets for Evaluating Word Sense Disambiguation Programs*. Computer Speech and Language, 12 (3) Special Issue on Evaluation of Speech and Language Technology, edited by Robert Gaizauskas. 453-472. http://www.kilgarriff.co.uk/Publications/1998-K-CompSL.pdf For TREC see http://trec.nist.gov. The TIPSTER site has been preserved here: http://www.nist.gov/itl/div894/894.02/related_proj ects/tipster/

Peter Kleiweg. 2006. *RuG/L[04] Software for dialectometrics and cartography*. Rijksuniversiteit Groningen. Faculteit der Letteren. http://www.let.rug.nl-/kleiweg/L04/

M. Paul Lewis. 2009. *Ethnologue: Languages of the World, Sixteenth Edition*. SIL International, Dallas, Texas.

Johann-Mattis List and Steven Moran. 2013. *An Open-Source Toolkit for Quantitative Historical Linguistics*. Proceedings of the 51st Annual Meeting of the Association for Computational Linguistics, 13–18, Sofia, Bulgaria. *http://-* www.zora.uzh.ch/84667/1/P13-4003.pdf

Luay Nakhleh, Daniel Miranker, and Francois Barbancon. 2003. *Requirements of Phylogenetic Databases*. In Third IEEE Symposium on BioInformatics and BioEngineering (BIBE'03). 141-148. IEEE Press. http://www.cs.rice.edu/~nakhleh/Papers/-bibe03_final.pdf

Heike Neuroth, Felix Lohmeier, Kathleen Marie Smith: *TextGrid. Virtual Research Environment for the Humanities*. In: *The International Journal of Digital Curation*. 6, Nr. 2, 2011, S. 222–231.

Sebastian Nordhoff and Harald Hammarström. 2011. *Glottolog/Langdoc: Defining dialects, languages, and language families as collections of resources*. 783 CEUR Workshop, Proceedings of the First International Workshop on Linked Science 2011 http://iswc2011.semanticweb.org/fileadmin/iswc/-Papers/Workshops/LISC/nordhoff.pdf

Erich R. Round. 2013. *'Big data' typology and linguistic phylogenetics: Design principles for valid datasets*. Presented 25 May 2013 at 21st Manchester Phonology Meeting. Accessible via https://uq.academia.edu/ErichRound.

Erich R. Round. 2014. *The performance of STRUCTURE* on linguistic datasets & 'researcher degrees of freedom'. Presented 15 Jan 2014 at TaSil, Aarhus, Denmark. Accessible via https://uq.academia.edu/ErichRound

SIL Mainland Southeast Asia Group. 2002. *Southeast Asia 436 Word List* revised November 2002. http://msea-ling.info/digidata/495/b11824.pdf

Gary Simons and Steven Bird. 2000. *The seven pillars of open language archiving:A vision statement.* http://www.language-archives.org/docs/vision.-html.

Time to change the "D" in "DEL"

Stephen Beale
Linguist's Assistant
Baltimore, MD
stephenbeale42@gmail.com

Abstract

The "D" in "DEL" stands for "documenting" – a code word for linguists that means the collection of linguistic data in audio and written form. The DEL (Documenting Endangered Languages) program run by the NSF and NEH is thus centered around building and archiving data resources for endangered languages. This paper is an argument for extending the 'D' to include "describing" languages in terms of lexical, semantic, morphological and grammatical knowledge. We present an overview of descriptive computational tools aimed at endangered languages along with a longer summary of two particular computer programs: Linguist's Assistant and Boas. These two programs, respectively, represent research in the areas of: A) computational systems capable of representing lexical, morphological and grammatical structures and using the resulting computational models for translation in a minority language context, and B) tools for efficiently and accurately acquiring linguistic knowledge. A hoped-for side effect of this paper is to promote cooperation between these areas of research in order to provide a total solution to describing endangered languages.

1 Introduction

The "D" in "DEL" stands for "documenting" – a code word for linguists that means the collection of linguistic data in audio and written form. The DEL (Documenting Endangered Languages) program run by the NSF and NEH is thus centered around building and archiving data resources for endangered languages. Furthermore, the recent change in the program to include computational tools hasn't changed the central focus on documentation, with one notable exception: the research headed by Emily Bender (Bender, et al. 2013) to automatically extract grammatical information from interlinear text. This paper is an argument for extending the 'D' to include "describing" languages in terms of lexical, semantic, morphological and grammatical knowledge. We present an overview of descriptive computational tools aimed at endangered languages along with a longer summary of two particular computer programs: Linguist's Assistant and Boas. These two programs, respectively, represent research in the areas of A) computational systems capable of representing and translating minority languages, and B) tools for efficiently and accurately acquiring linguistic knowledge. A hoped-for side effect of this paper is to promote cooperation between these areas of research in order to provide a total solution to describing endangered languages.

2 Documenting versus Describing

The code word "documenting" implies data. The DEL program is primarily interested in procuring data about languages that are disappearing. The rationale behind this is obvious: we need to quickly gather data from languages before they become extinct. Data in the form of transcribed audio recordings and texts is certainly invaluable. However, consider the impact of such data in two areas: 1) future analysis by linguists, and 2) revitalization and language promotion today.

Think ahead 50 or 100 years. By all accounts, a majority of the world's languages will be extinct. What resources will be available to the 22nd century linguist? The DEL program seeks to archive audio and textual data for use in the future. While this data is certainly valuable, how useful will it be? Without a living speaker of the language, extracting a useful, accurate and broad-coverage description of the language from archived data will be extremely time consuming

Proceedings of the 2014 Workshop on the Use of Computational Methods in the Study of Endangered Languages, pages 100–107, Baltimore, Maryland, USA, 26 June 2014.

and probably impossible in most cases.[1] Although such data could be used for other purposes, Gippert et al. (2006) agree with the general premise that "without theoretical grounding language documentation is in danger of producing 'data graveyards', i.e. large heaps of data with little or no use to anyone." This is a shame, and quite possibly a non-optimal use of our current linguistic talent pool. On the other hand, if a linguist working today with a living informant and using appropriate computational tools and programs could efficiently and accurately describe these languages at a lexical, semantic, morphological and grammatical level, then the usefulness of such research 100 years from now would be considerably greater.

That is looking ahead. What about now? What kind of work could help revitalize endangered languages so that they will not become extinct in the first place? My experience in language projects in the South Pacific leads me to the conclusion that descriptive work - and the resulting computational and non-computational projects that are enabled by it - have a much greater impact on current language populations than documentary efforts. The community I worked with for three years were the recipients of dictionaries and story books that documented linguistic research. These efforts bore fruit: there was initially quite a bit of interest about them. However, this kind of work quickly lost appeal. On the other hand, descriptive work quickly led to the production of educational materials and interest in translation. Automatic and manual translations followed, especially of songs, religious and health-related materials. A knowledge of how the language works leads to an empowerment with the language.

3 Research in Describing Endangered Languages: knowledge acquisition methodologies

In this section we present an overview of current and past descriptive computational tools aimed at endangered languages. In general, the field can be divided into two parts: A) computational systems capable of representing and translating minority languages, and B) tools for efficiently and accurately acquiring linguistic knowledge. Up until recently, research has focused on the latter.

The most widespread line of computational research in category B can be categorized as grammatical typology questionnaires. These follow in the path of traditional, non-computational linguistic fieldwork methods characterized by Longacre (1964) and Comrie and Smith (1977). Boas (McShane, et al. 2002), the LinGO Grammar Matrix (Bender, et al. 2010) and PAWS (Black & Black 2009) all fit into this paradigm. All these systems extract salient properties of a language through typological questionnaires and then produce computational resources of varying utility. This work must be applauded, and we argue that it is indispensable for a complete solution for describing endangered languages. However, the typology questionnaire approach is limited to creating approximate grammars. Bender et al. (2010) describe the LinGO Grammar Matrix as a 'rapid prototyping' tool. Such a tool is useful, but more is needed to thoroughly describe a language and enable machine translation capabilities. Linguist's Assistant (LA, described below) promotes such a thorough description; however, it comes at a cost. LA is able to represent the kinds of knowledge that is typically extracted by the grammatical typology questionnaire approach, such as rules to represent phrase structure word ordering and phenomena such as case, agreement, nominal declensions and the like. But it is more flexible and able to describe additional linguistic phenomena that are not as easily described using a typological approach (see below for details). But the rules in LA currently must be entered manually by a computational linguist. Thus, the tradeoff: quick descriptions (using well thought-out typologies) that fall short of broad and deep coverage vs. adequate depth and breadth of coverage at a higher cost.

It is perfectly clear that some linguistic phenomena can be most efficiently described using the techniques of the typology questionnaire paradigm. However, the computational grammar and lexicon produced in an LA-type language description project are meant to be comprehensive and complete insofar as they will be able to be used in a text generator to produce accurate translations. It is exactly this completeness and the resulting usefulness of the description (especially in language revitalization) that might be a prime factor in securing research funding from organizations that are interested in endangered languages. Therefore, we argue for: 1) continued research in typology questionnaire methods for

[1] Our experience backs up this claim. We have attempted to use Linguist's Assistant to describe languages using only transcribed texts without a human informant; these experiments failed miserably.

efficiently acquiring the linguistic knowledge appropriate to that paradigm, 2) further development of complete description paradigms like LA, 3) a greater cooperation between the two paradigms, and 4) the resurrection of machine learning, example-based techniques to minimize and semi-automate the comprehensive grammatical and semantic description process needed by systems like LA.

A prime example of this latter point was the Avenue Project at Carnegie Mellon University (Probst, et al. 2003). The Avenue project was a machine translation system oriented towards low-density languages. It consisted of two central parts: 1) the pre-run-time module that handles the elicitation of data and the subsequent automatic creation of transfer rules, and 2) the actual translation engine. We are especially interested in the former:

> "The purpose of the elicitation system is to collect a high-quality, word-aligned parallel corpus. Because a human linguist may not be available to supervise the elicitation, a user interface presents sentences to the informants. The informants must be bilingual and fluent in the language of elicitation and the language being elicited, but do not need to have training in linguistics or computational linguistics. They translate phrases and sentences from the elicitation language into their language and specify word alignments graphically.
>
> The rule-learning system takes the elicited, word-aligned data as input. Based on this information, it infers syntactic transfer rules.... The system also learns the composition of simpler rules into more complicated rules, thus reducing their complexity and capturing the compositional makeup of a language (e.g., NP rules can be plugged into sentence-level rules). The output of the rule-learning system is a set of transfer rules that then serve as a transfer grammar in the run-time system." (Probst, et al. 2003:247–248)

At a high level, this is exactly the approach that LA advocates. However, LA differs from Avenue in several important features, most notably the underlying semantic representation in LA as opposed to Avenue's transfer (source surface language to target surface language) approach. LA attains a greater practicality than Avenue primarily because of this difference, because interlingual-based language description and text generation is an order of magnitude simpler and less prone to error than transfer-based approaches. But again, this benefit comes at a cost: the grammar description modules and all subsequent texts to be translated must be encoded in the semantic representation (as opposed to a natural language like English for transfer-based approaches). See the next section on Document Authoring for more details for how this limitation can be minimized.

Bender et al. (2013) also provide a machine-learning component for their LinGO Grammar Matrix (Bender, et al. 2013). That is the project that is the exception to the "D" word problem. And that exceptional nature (it was funded!) should be instructional for all of us.

The missing ingredient in LA (besides the inclusion of grammar typology techniques such as LinGO and BOAS) is the sort of machine learning capability seen in the Avenue project and Bender's project. The latter system learns LinGO rules from interlinear text. Obviously, that is exciting work and has the added benefit of being able to be used directly in the DEL's data-centric context. However, it has limitations. We argue for a similar type of interlinear machine learning system, but one that is grounded in semantics and works over carefully prepared texts that will maximize the learning capabilities and allow for broad coverage of semantic phenomena. For example, assume we have the following sentences semantically represented:

John hit the tree.
John began to hit the tree.
John finished hitting the tree.
etc...

After a native speaker translates these sentences, a machine learning system could be employed to learn a grammar of inceptives, completives, etc., by comparing the semantic representations of the sentences in the module to find the differences (i.e. the addition of a "inceptive" property on the event) and then mapping those differences to the differences found in the translated texts (for example, added words, affixes or changes in word order). Example elicitation modules have been prepared (including their semantic representations) for a large variety of semantically-based phenomena. Similar techniques are also used to probe different semantic case frame realizations. Such a semantically-based "grammar discovery procedure" is the means currently employed in LA. This grammar discovery procedure can be used to quickly describe how a particular language encodes a wide range of meaning-based communication. The resulting computational description can then be used in the embedded text generation system to enable automatic translation. A grammar discovery procedure guided by semantics will obviously not yield a complete description of a language. It will not document *everything* that can be said in the language; however, we argue that it produces a practical description that will enable future generations to answer the question, "How do you say … in this language?" The approach is also very efficient in terms of the number of man-hours of linguistic work required. Our experience is that (under the right circumstances) a field linguist will require less than a month to complete the process. We expect this timeframe to decrease further as additional techniques such as those used in BOAS and LinGO are added to LA.[2] This type of grammar discovery is also very suitable for a workshop situation where many languages within a single language family could work together.

One valid argument against such an approach comes from linguistic circles. The current trend in linguistic research discourages elicitation, relying instead on the analysis of naturally occurring texts and dialogues. For example, a respected linguist involved in and relatively supportive of LA commented that "I am, in general, a bit reluctant to use ready-made questionnaires, for all sorts of reasons - some of which you mention yourself. It so happens that my personal interest has always been on naturalistic speech... I have always paid a lot of attention to what actually shows up in everyday spoken speech…" (Alex François, personal communication). We understand and accept this inclination towards naturally occurring texts over elicited texts, and in a "normal" situation we would completely agree. However, with the extinction of thousands of languages imminent, more radical techniques are needed. Elicitation techniques are also supported in the linguistic literature, for example, Ameka et al. (2006) state that 'limiting what the grammar should account for to a corpus [of naturally occurring texts] also overlooks the fact that speakers may have quite clear and revealing judgements' and 'the view...that grammars should be answerable just to a published corpus seems an extreme position in practical terms.' And again, Gippert et al. (2006) add their warning that 'without theoretical grounding language documentation is in the danger of producing 'data graveyards', i.e. large heaps of data with little or no use to anyone.' We believe that the semantic-based grammar discovery methodology adds this theoretical grounding.

We also add the argument that "the proof is in the pudding." Allman, et al. (2012) documents that a grammar discovery procedure such as described above combined with a capable knowledge acquisition and text generation environment such as found in LA can produce translations that are as accurate and readable to native speakers as manual translations and that these results indicate that the underlying language description is accurate, natural and broad-coverage.

4 Document authoring: a bridge to practical MT (and language description) in endangered languages

We have already argued that a semantically-based language description environment is superior to a transfer-based system. We will try to bolster that argument here. In terms of machine translation, the analysis of a source text will always be the bottleneck in terms of translation quality. On the other hand, an interlingual text generation process is relatively simple and accurate - assuming the presence of an accurate semantic description of the input text. Furthermore, a semantic description "language" is much simpler than natural languages since it has no ambiguity, fewer atoms (concepts vs. words), and fewer "syntactic" combinations. This leads to an economy when trying to describe how a particular language encodes it (as opposed to trying to describe how a language would encode arbitrary free text from a source language). And finally, as described above, a semantic-based description provides the framework for efficient and potentially machine learnable acquisition of grammar via an organized grammar discovery procedures.

The glue that holds this together is the concept of "document authoring." Authoring a semantic description of a text (or of the elicitation modules) can be accomplished through a semi-automatic authoring interface. Such an interface typically accepts a standardized (or "controlled") subset of a natural language as its input. The input is run through an analyzer and the results are visually presented to the user, who checks and/or assigns semantic concepts and relationships. The

[2] The discovery process itself as well as the underlying semantic representation language need to be refined and validated by our colleagues; we expect such refinements to also improve efficiency.

steps in preparing a semantic analysis of a text or set of elicitation sentences is thus: 1) manually "translate" the text into the controlled language, 2) run this through the automatic analyzer, and 3) manually check and correct the resulting semantic analysis. Although unlimited free text cannot be translated in an LA language project, a wide variety of texts can be semantically authored. This process only needs to be done once and the results can then be used for any language. See (Beale, et al. 2005) for more information on document authoring in the context of endangered languages.

We believe that a semantically-based description of a language is the key to the practical description of endangered languages. It provides an inherently efficient framework for language description in the field. The resulting description not only provides invaluable data for future linguists, but also enables present-day translation capabilities that can aid in language revitalization. A document authoring system provides the means for overcoming one of the main drawbacks to a semantically-based system in that it allows for a relatively quick, once-for-all preparation of semantic representations that can be used in a grammar discovery procedure and in machine translation of texts.

We now present longer summaries of Linguist's Assistant and BOAS.

5 Linguist's Assistant

The Linguist's Assistant (LA) is a practical computational paradigm for describing languages. LA is built on a comprehensive semantic foundation. We combine a conceptual, ontological framework with detailed semantic features that cover (or is a beginning towards the goal of covering) the range of human communication. An elicitation procedure has been built up around this central, semantic core that systematically guides the linguist through the language description process, during which the linguist builds a grammar and lexicon that 'describes' how to generate target language text from the semantic representations of the elicitation corpus. The result is a meaning-based 'how to' guide for the language: how does one encode given semantic representations in the language?

Underlying this approach to knowledge acquisition in LA is a visual, semi-automatic interface for recording grammatical rules and lexical information. Figure 1 shows an example of one kind of visual interface used for "theta-grid adjustment rules." The figure shows an English rule used to adjust the "theta grid" or "case frame" of an English verb. Grammatical rules typically describe how a given semantic structure is realized in the language. The whole gamut of linguistic phenomena is covered, from morphological alternations (Figure 2) to case frame specifications to phrase structure ordering (Figure 3) to lexical collocations – and many others. These grammatical rules interplay with a rich lexical description interface that allows for assignment of word-level features and the description of lexical forms associated with individual roots (Figure 4). As stated above, the user is currently responsible for the creation of rules, albeit with a natural, visual interface that often is able to set up the requisite input semantic structures automatically. As mentioned, we also seek to collaborate with researchers to enable semi-automatic generation of rules similar to what can be found in the Boas (McShane, et al., 2002), LinGO (Bender, et al., 2010), PAWS (Black and Black, 2009) and Avenue (Probst, et al., 2003) projects. Such extensions will make LA accessible to a larger pool of linguists and will shorten the time needed for documenting languages.

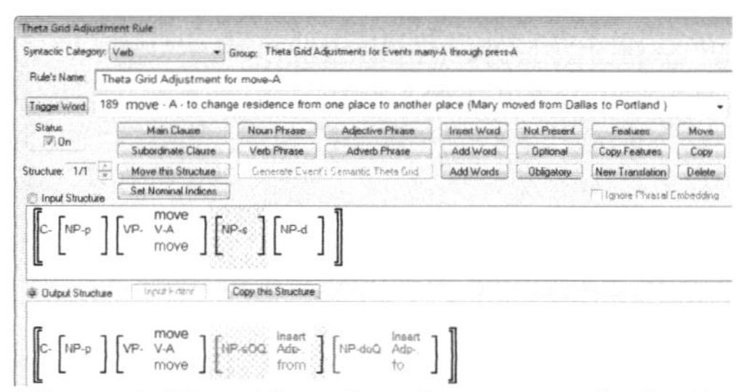

Figure 1. Visual interface for grammatical rules

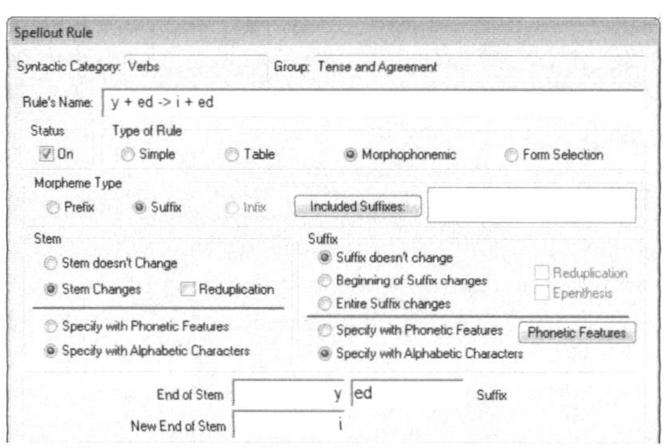

Figure 2. Morphological alternation rule

Integrated with these elicitation and description tools is a text generator that allows for immediate confirmation of the validity of grammatical rules and lexical information. We also provide an interface for tracking the scope and examples of grammatical rules. This minimizes the possibility of conflicting or duplicate rules while providing the linguist a convenient index into the work already accomplished. And finally, we provide a utility for producing a written description of the language - after all, a computational description of a language is of no practical use (outside of translation applications) unless it can be conveniently referenced. Refer to Beale (2012) for a comprehensive description of Linguist's Assistant.

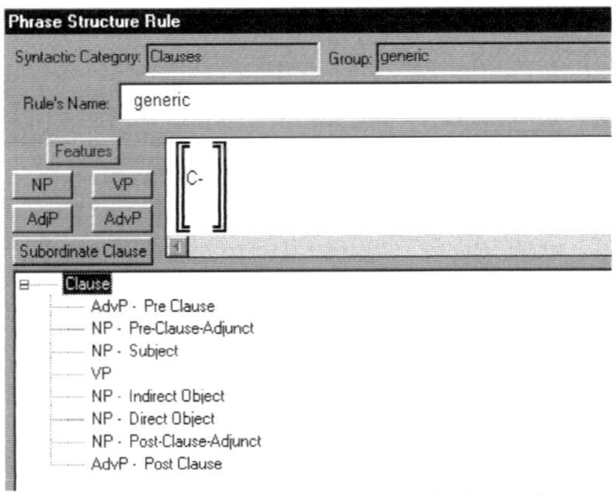

Figure 3. Phrase structure ordering rule

	Stems	Glosses	infinitive	present indic 1st sing
1	aprend	learn	aprender	aprendo
2	habl	speak	hablar	hablo
3	ten	have	tener	tengo
4	viv	live	vivir	vivo

present indic 2nd sing	present indic 3rd sing	present indic 1st pl	present indic 3rd pl
aprendes	aprende	aprendemos	aprenden
hablas	habla	hablamos	hablan
tienes	tiene	tenemos	tienen
vives	vive	vivimos	viven

Figure 4. Lexical forms for Spanish

LA has been used to produce extensive grammars and lexicons for Jula (a Niger-Congo language), Kewa (Papua New Guinea), North Tanna (Vanuatu), Korean and English. Work continues in two languages of Vanuatu (and a new avenue of research has recently opened as a result of a partnership with De La Salle University in the Philippines). The resulting computational language descriptions have been used in LA's embedded text generation system to produce a significant amount of high-quality translations. Figures 5 and 6 present translations of a section of a medical text on AIDS into English and Korean. Please reference Beale et al. (2005) and Allman and Beale (2004; 2006) and Allman et al. (2012) for more information on using LA in translation projects and for documentation on the evaluations of the translations produced. We argue that the high quality achieved in translation projects demonstrate the quality and coverage of the underlying language description that LA produces.

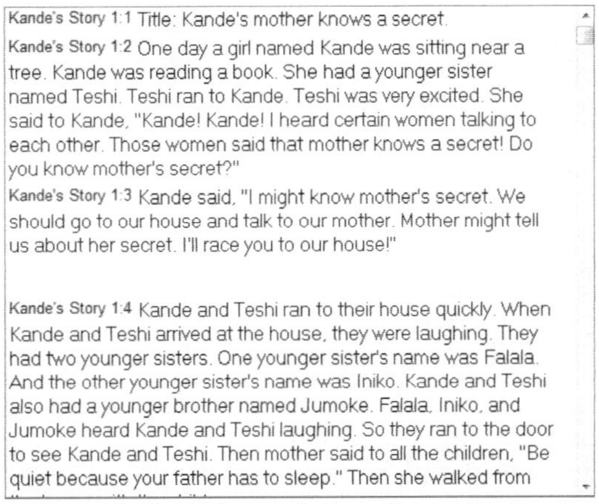

Figure 5. English translation of a medical text

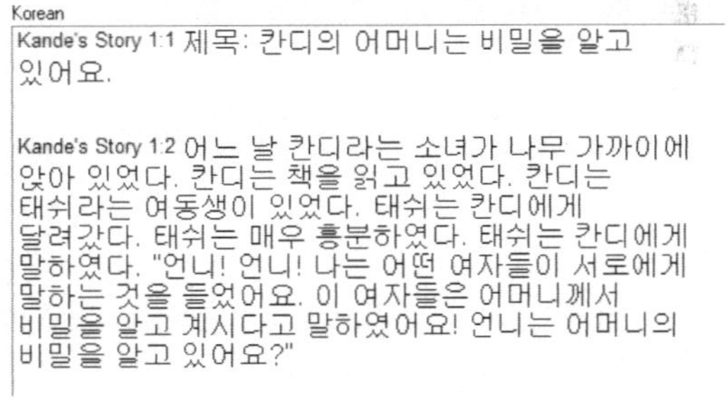

Figure 6. Korean translation of a medical text

6 BOAS

Boas (McShane et al. 2002) is an example of a typology-based questionnaire approach that can be useful for quickly eliciting certain properties of a language. This section is meant as an overview that is representative of this class of programs. The author has no direct connection with the Boas system; permission was given to use the following description.

Boas is used to extract knowledge about a language, L, from an informant with no knowledge engineer present. Boas itself leads the informant through the process of supplying the necessary information in a directly usable way. In order to do this, the system must be supplied with metaknowledge about language – not L, but language in general – which is organized into a typologically and cross-linguistically motivated inventory of parameters, their potential value sets, and modes of realizing the latter. The inventory takes into account phenomena observed in a large number of languages. Particular languages would typically feature only a subset of parameters, values and means of realization. The parameter values employed by a particular language, and the means of realizing them, differentiate one language from another and can, in effect, act as the formal "signature" for the language. Examples of parameters, values and their realizations that play a role in the Boas knowledge-elicitation process are shown in Table 1. The first block illustrates inflection, the second, closed-class meanings, the third, ecology and the fourth, syntax.

In the elicitation process, the parameters (left column) represent categories of phenomena that need to be covered in the description of L, the values (middle column) represent choices that orient what might be included in the description of that phenomenon for L, and the realization options (right column) suggest the kinds of questions that must be asked to gather the relevant information.

Parameter	Values	Means of Realization
Case Relations	Nominative, Accusative, Dative, Instrumental, Abessive, etc.	flective morphology, agglutinating morphology, isolating morphology, prepositions, postpositions, etc.
Number	Singular, Plural, Dual, Trial, Paucal	flective morphology, agglutinating morphology, isolating morphology, particles, etc.
Tense	Present, Past, Future, Timeless	flective morphology, agglutinating morphology, isolating morphology, etc.
Possession	+/-	case-marking, closed-class affix, word or phrase, word order, etc.
Spatial Relations	above, below, through, etc.	word, phrase, preposition or postposition, case-marking
Expression of Numbers	integers, decimals, percentages, fractions, etc.	numerals in L, digits, punctuation marks (commas, periods, percent signs, etc.) or a lack thereof in various places
Sentence Boundary	declarative, interrogative, imperative, etc.	period, question mark(s), exclamation point(s), ellipsis, etc.
Grammatical Role	subjectness, direct-objecness, indirect-objectness, etc.	case-marking, word order, particles, etc.
Agreement (for pairs of elements)	+/- person, +/-number, +/- case, etc.	flective, agglutinating or isolating inflectional markers

Table 1: Sample parameters, values and means of their realization

The selection of parameters and values in Boas is made similar to a multiple choice test which, with the necessary pedagogical support, can be carried out even by an informant not trained in linguistics. This turns out to be a crucial aspect of knowledge elicitation for rare languages, since one must prepare for the case when available informants lack formal linguistic training. Boas also allows a maximum of flexibility and economy of effort. Certain decisions on the part of the user cause the system to reorganize the process of acquisition by removing some interface pages and/or reordering those that remain. This means that the system is more flexible than static acquisition interfaces that require the user to walk through the same set of pages irrespective of context and prior decisions.

The five major modules of the Boas system are:

Ecology:

- inventory of characters
- inventory and use of punctuation marks
- proper name conventions
- transliteration
- dates and numbers
- list of common abbreviations, geographical entities, famous people, etc. (which can be expanded indefinitely)

Morphology:

- selecting language type: flective, agglutinating, mixed
- paradigmatic inflectional morphology, if needed
- non-paradigmatic inflectional morphology, if needed
- derivational morphology

Syntax:

- structure of the noun phrases: NP components, word order, etc.
- grammatical functions: subject, direct object, etc.
- realization of sentence types: declarative, interrogative, etc.
- special syntactic structures: topic fronting, affix hopping, etc.

Closed-Class Lexical Acquisition:

Provide L translations of some 150 closed-class meanings, which can be realized as words, phrases, affixes or features (e.g., Instrumental Case used to realize instrumental 'with', as in hit with a stick). Inflecting forms of any of the first three realizations must be provided as well, as applicable.

Open-Class Lexical Acquisition:

Build a L-to-English lexicon by a) translating entries from an English seed lexicon, b) importing then supplementing an on-line bilingual lexicon, c) composing lists of words in L and translating them into English, or d) any combination of the above. Grammatically important inherent features and irregular inflectional forms must be provided.

Associated with each of these tasks are knowledge elicitation "threads"—i.e., series of pages that combine questions with background information and instruction. If, for example, a user indicates that nouns in L inflect for number, the page shown in Figure 7 will be accessed. Explanatory support for decision-making is provided in help links at the bottom of the page.

Boas offers a good example of an advanced elicitation system by combining extensive and parameterized descriptive material about language, a rich set of expressive means in the user interface, and extensive pedagogical resources.

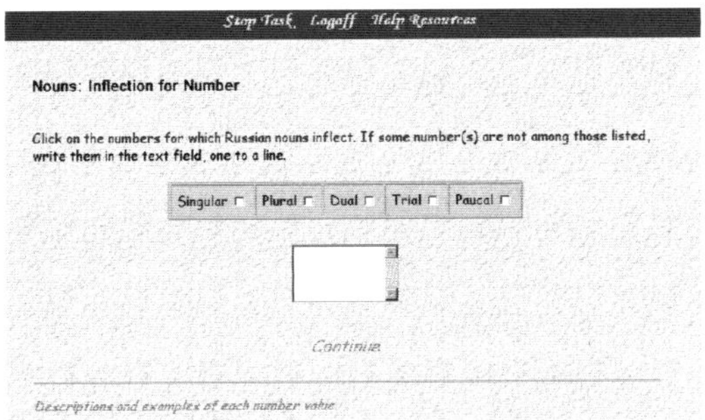

Figure 7: Selecting the values for number for which nouns inflect

7 Conclusion

A quick perusal of the grants awarded by NSF/NEH in the DEL program over the last five years confirms the underlying assumption of this paper: the DEL program funds projects that produce or aid audio and textual documentation (i.e. data) on endangered languages. We argued that descriptive work might return a higher payback as regards to potential linguistic utilization in the future. We also argued that the value of descriptive work in revitalizing languages today exceeds that of purely documentary work. Furthermore, we described several lines of research that would allow such descriptive work to proceed, along with a rationale for continued research to improve the computational tools employed in such work. Linguist's Assistant and Boas represent two sides of the same coin for descriptive work in minority languages. Cooperation between the various research programs that represent each side of that coin is critical to attaining a total solution to describing endangered languages.

References

Tod Allman, Stephen Beale and Richard Denton. 2012. Linguist's Assistant: A Multi-Lingual Natural Language Generator based on Linguistic Universals, Typologies, and Primitives. In Proceedings of 7th International Natural Language Generation Conference (INLG-12), Utica, IL.

Tod Allman and Stephen Beale. 2006. A natural language generator for minority languages. In Proceedings of SALTMIL, Genoa, Italy.

Tod Allman and Stephen Beale. 2004. An environment for quick ramp-up multi-lingual authoring. *International Journal of Translation* 16(1).

Felix Ameka, Alan Dench & Nicholas Evans. 2006. Catching language: the standard challenge of grammar writing. Berlin: Mouton de Gruyter.

Stephen Beale. 2012. Documenting endangered languages with Linguist's Assistant. *Language Documentation and Conservation* 6(1), pp. 104-134.

Stephen Beale, S. Nirenburg, M. McShane, and Tod Allman. 2005. Document authoring the Bible for minority language translation. In Proceedings of MT-Summit, Phuket, Thailand.

Emily Bender, Michael Wayne Goodman, Joshua Crowgey and Fei Xia. 2013. Towards creating precision grammars from interlinear glossed text: inferring large-scale typological properties. In Proceedings of the ACL 2013 workshop on Language Technology for Cultural Heritage, Social Sciences and Humanities.

Emily Bender, S. Drellishak, A. Fokkens, M. Goodman, D. Mills, L. Poulson, and S. Saleem. 2010. Grammar prototyping and testing with the LinGO grammar matrix customization system. In Proceedings of the ACL 2010 System Demonstrations.

Sheryl Black and Andrew Black. 2009. PAWS: parser and writer for syntax: drafting syntactic grammars in the third wave. http://www.sil.org/silepubs/PUBS/51432/SILForum2009-002.pdf.

B. Comrie and N. Smith. 1977. Lingua descriptive questionnaire. *Lingua* 42.

Jost Gippert, Nikolaus Himmelmann & Ulrike Mosel. 2006. *Essentials of language documentation.* Berlin: Mouton de Gruyter.

R.E. Longacre. 1964. *Grammar Discovery Procedures.* Mouton: The Hague.

Marjorie McShane, Sergei Nirenburg, Jim Cowie, and Ron Zacharski. 2002. Embedding knowledge elicitation and MT systems within a single architecture. *Machine Translation* 17(4), pp. 271-305.

Katharina Probst, Lori Levin, Erik Petersen, Alon Lavie and Jaime Carbonell. 2003. MT for minority languages using elicitation-based learning of syntactic transfer rules. *Machine Translation* 17(4), pp. 245-270.

Author Index

Association for Computational Linguistics
209 N. Eighth Street
Stroudsburg, Pennsylvania 18360

CURRAN ASSOCIATES INC
proceedings.com